GOODNIGHT, SWEET

A CAREGIVER'S LONG GOODBYE

LEAH STANLEY

innovo
PUBLISHING

Published by Innovo Publishing, LLC
www.innovopublishing.com
1-888-546-2111

Providing Full-Service Publishing Services for Christian Authors, Artists & Ministries:
Books, eBooks, Audiobooks, Music, Film & Courses

GOODNIGHT, SWEET
A Caregiver's Long Goodbye

Library of Congress Control Number: 2018956215
ISBN: 978-1-61314-444-2

Cover Design & Interior Layout: Innovo Publishing, LLC

Printed in the United States of America
U.S. Printing History
First Edition: 2019

DEDICATION

For Drew and Faith

In these pages, be introduced to your great-grandparents; they are part of you, and you are their heritage. And in these pages, see from my experience that Jesus is eminently worthy of your trust. He will not fail.

ENDORSEMENTS

"What a wonderful, articulate account of the realities of being an Alzheimer's/dementia caregiver. The author beautifully expresses the difficult emotions and physical and spiritual challenges 'caring' for loved ones presents. As a previous professional caregiver with ten years of experience, I was touched not only by her relationship with her grandparents but also her relationship with the Lord and how this influenced the way she cared for her grandparents, showed grace to ruthless relatives, and grieved and found joy throughout the journey. I highly recommend this book for those anywhere on the path of caring for aged loved ones, as it honestly depicts the multifaceted experience of Alzheimer's/dementia caregiving."

—Julie Todd, MSSW, Former Professional Caregiver

"*Goodnight, Sweet* is a beautiful recounting of a young woman's struggle to provide care for her ailing grandparents. It is a message of hope in the midst of despair as Alzheimer's disease and dementia steal her beloved grandparents away, and it shows her struggle to come to terms with the heartbreaking circumstances she now finds herself in. Nevertheless, she relies on her faith in God to carry her through. It is a truly inspiring read and a great help for those who are going through the heartbreak of caring for loved ones who are slipping away."

—Julie Garner, Former Caregiver

"I thank you for the honor of allowing me to walk with you (so to speak) through your journey. [*Goodnight, Sweet*] was moving, heart-warming, and it even made my eyes tear up on occasion. I must say, also, that at times, I felt like an intruder—an interloper—and wanted to back away so as not to eavesdrop on your conversations, actions, and decisions. I had to really concentrate on staying 'technical' in my [review]. Bottom line: It's a wonderful, powerful story and journey and one that many of us could not have accomplished with the determination, success, and reward that you received. You've been a good and faithful servant to your grandparents and the Lord—and blessed beyond measure. *Well done!*"

—Roy Cash, Retired US Navy Captain and Navy Fighter Pilot

"There are certain things that, short of personal experience, simply cannot be adequately described. The responsibility of full-time care for those no longer able to care for themselves is one of those things. In *Goodnight, Sweet*, my dear friend Leah Stanley has taken on an all-consuming chapter in her personal journey and breathed life into it, allowing you to share her experience and come away a better person for it. She has also given testimony to how reliance on Christ *is* what ultimately makes being a caregiver such a blessing; it's a God-given opportunity to express love that few experience. *Goodnight, Sweet* will make you laugh, cry, and marvel at what God can do in *the* most difficult of circumstances. What it will *not* do is leave you the same person you were before reading it."

—Bobby Roseberry, Former Caregiver

"Your journey to a 'new normal' required unwavering strength, faith, and love as caregiver in the loving relationship you shared with your grandparents and other family members. God wanted this story told as part of His story for the good of the whole kingdom. The greater story will resonate with many and uplift them when they struggle through the dark days of caregiving. I am honored to have read the pre-release manuscript and eagerly await your book-signing event."

—Susan Rook, Physical Therapist

ACKNOWLEDGMENTS

Deepest appreciation and gratitude go to Billie Cash for taking time to mentor a new author. Let's sit down again soon over a blueberry muffin, a lemon cookie, and coffee while discussing all things literary. Blessings to you for your time, encouragement, and your prayer cover!

I thank you, Roy Cash, for your time and encouraging words as you performed the initial review of the manuscript for *Goodnight, Sweet*. Your technical knowledge and insight were outstanding guideposts as I endeavored to communicate a difficult and painful experience. Thank you for your service—both to me personally and to our country.

I am deeply grateful to Chris Lott, an outstanding photographer. Your pictures are wonderful, and the time you took shooting them for my author photo and getting them ready is greatly appreciated.

For your encouragement, as well as the challenge you issued to all your students, I thank you, Dr. Cynthia Hopson, my former journalism professor and advisor at the University of Memphis. I never forgot that when you took me to lunch for my graduation, you were "investing" in me; getting to take you to dinner was an absolute delight.

CONTENTS

FOREWORD

"Love seeks one thing only: the good of the one loved. . . . Love, therefore is its own reward."
—*Thomas Merton*

In this poignant memoir, author Leah Stanley invites us to travel down country roads to an Arkansas farm where hard work, peace, and beauty flourish. We are compelled to enter the lives of her dear grandparents whose love for her was the constant embrace of belonging. Love was always waiting.

From childhood through college, Leah anticipated with joy her visits to the farm. Her grandparents anxiously yearned and watched for her coming down that road to home. Eagerly, Leah jumped into the ongoing rituals of cooking, gardening, sowing, reaping, and feeding cows. Her beloved grandparents were always dreaming and planning the next season. The big faces of blue hydrangeas nestled beside rain lilies and pink trumpets welcomed her as she and her grandmother would walk the property. Her grandfather would cast his gaze across the pasture land and say, "If nothin' happens this spring, 'gonna sow all that area with new grass seed." They were farmers who also planted faith in God within the heart of this loving granddaughter. With endearing affection, they addressed her not as "Leah" but as "Sweet." Their love reached down into her tender soul and rooted her future with hope. She and her mother were truly beloved. The farm was home.

The story of Leah returning her grandparents' love in seasons to come would involve making decisions for their lives. Alzheimer's and dementia would claim them in different stages. The journey was arduous, detailed, and heartbreaking; but she assumed her role with determination, loyalty, and devotion. Leah never wavered. Amazing grace surrounded her life.

Her writing is captivating and transparent. This memoir is a legacy tribute. Filled with moments of insight, clarity, and intuition, you will be constantly engaged. After every chapter, you will rush to the next, for she creates expectancy—and yet surprises you. A challenge also awaits. Will you have a role in the life of some family member who will need care? I did. Therefore, I journeyed down her rocky road of love, loss, and lingering grief, remembering the faithfulness of God. He is our strength in the midst of caregiving, and He remains our assurance in the release of home going.

Indeed, we are called to care for our own. God's Word admonishes us, "Anyone who neglects to care for family members in need repudiates the faith" (1 Timothy 5:8 The Message).

She cared.

Will you?

Goodnight, Sweet carries the reader to compassion and courage. Her story will resonate with all families, because this reality will come.

I loved the book.

—**Billie Cash**
International Retreat and Conference Speaker, Author of six books:
Windows of Assurance, Light Breaking Through, Autumn Rain,
PRAYERSURGE, A Pillow on the Highway and *The Shelter,*
Collierville, TN

HOME IN THE HILLS

By Chris Meadows

In my home among the mountains,
Where I still do long to dwell,
Where the robins gently call,
I hear the whip-poor-will.

With my work and worry over,
My rest at last I've found
In my little cabin yonder
On the happy hunting ground.

I'll be here until tomorrow
In the mountains wild and free,
Just a cabin in the Ozarks
Where I'll always want to be.

Where the birds are building nests
In the cedar on the glade,
In my cabin I'm at rest
Neath the elm tree's lovely shade.

So my last years I am spending
In my cabin on the hill,
For I'm not so old as yet
But what I love them still.*

*Taken from *Short Stories and Poems of The Ozark Hills* by Chris Meadows (Caseville, MO: Litho Printers, 1971), 72. Copyright by Chris C. Meadows. All Rights Reserved. Used with permission.

CHAPTER 1

THE MESSAGE

The business day was over, and the blessed ritual of going home for the night was in full swing. I got my favorite parking spot and started up the stairs, fumbling for my apartment key. It was cold, typical of a January night in Memphis. I unlocked the outside door and immediately began wondering what I'd cook for dinner. Maybe we'd have soup, or something with beef? Or maybe we'd just order a pizza—again. It was all so normal. I unlocked the door to number eight and followed my usual routine. My purse and keys landed on the desk, and I breezed by the answering machine, casually glancing down to see if we had received any calls. There was one new message. Chris and I had been married for almost eight months, so I was certain that a Wednesday night call either meant that some of our friends wanted to make weekend plans or one of the in-laws was checking in. But that Wednesday night call was altogether different. I pushed *Play* and the machine began to recite its message.

"Leah, this is Mack Proctor, your grandparents' neighbor," it began. I remember feeling myself go numb, trying to comprehend that it was Mack and not my grandmother who had called. "You need to get up here," Mack said urgently. "Your grandparents are in real bad shape. . . ."

I listened to Mack's lengthy message which ended with his phone number. In an effort to stay calm, I started mumbling, "OK . . . OK," but at the same time I nearly went crazy looking for a pen. My thoughts became jumbled and confused as random questions began to develop. For the hundredth time, I found myself wondering why my grandparents had moved to a place that was nearly three hours away from me, but what really made my heart sink was the fact that I'd been trying unsuccessfully for several days to reach them by phone. I had chalked it up to their inability to hear the phone in spite of the enhanced ringer I'd given them. Or maybe they had gone out—maybe to the grocery store. I had convinced myself the lack of response could have been any number of things, the least likely of which was that something dire had happened. Then I painfully remembered the last conversation I had had with Grandma on Christmas Day only a few weeks earlier. The phone had rung several times before that sweet voice had answered.

"Hello?"

"Hi, Grandma, it's Leah."

"Who?" She sounded confused.

"It's Leah," I said, raising my voice.

"Oh, well hello, Sweet."

"How are you doing?"

"Well, we're fine." She had paused, then she said, "Sweet, how did you get this number?"

Her question had stunned me because the number I'd dialed had been her phone number since 1981.

"Grandma, you gave me this number; this is your telephone number. . . ."

The entire call had been just like that. To top it all off, she had not even known it was Christmas.

"There hasn't been anything on TV about it," she'd said.

Clearly something was wrong, but I hadn't known what to do about it. Each time I talked with her she seemed to be a little worse than the time before, and I would come away feeling utterly helpless.

With all these things on my mind, I played Mack's message a second time so I could write down his number. I dialed urgently, and he answered almost immediately. The tale he told was very disturbing.

Apparently on Saturday, January 11, 1997, my grandparents had set out from their home near Imboden, Arkansas, for some unknown destination. Chris later theorized they must have been trying to come to Memphis, perhaps to see me or maybe Grandma's sister. On Tuesday, January 14, they were found sitting in their car on the side of the road with a flat tire near Forrest City, Arkansas. Their activities between Saturday and Tuesday remain completely unknown. The car, though still drivable, had formidable dents and scratches all along the passenger side. My grandparents didn't appear to be hurt from any kind of car accident, but the temperature had been below freezing for several days.

As the story went, there was a man who had stopped to help them change their tire. He had called the sheriff because he realized these two elderly people just weren't right. The sheriff arranged for my grandparents to be driven to Walnut Ridge, Arkansas, which was about a half hour from their home. The sheriff also made arrangements with a local wrecker service to pick up their car and keep it in Forrest City. They spent the night in a motel in Walnut Ridge, and the next day, Wednesday, a man whose identity is unknown to me drove them back to their home and asked Mack Proctor to keep an eye on them. Apparently the driver had been in a great hurry to get back to Walnut Ridge because a predicted snowstorm was bearing down across northern Arkansas. He kept repeating to Mack that he didn't want to be snowed-in way out in the country.

Mack had known I was the person to call, but he didn't know how to reach me. He happened across a letter that I'd written Grandma only a few weeks earlier, and, using my address, he was able to get my phone number. By Wednesday evening, things had settled down enough for Mack to call me.

"They're really in bad shape," Mack told me again. "They don't seem to know they're at home."

"Should I come tonight?" I asked.

"I wouldn't try it tonight. My wife has already gotten them to bed, and these gravel roads are frozen over. I don't think you could get in here tonight."

I told him my husband and I would be on our way to Imboden first thing Thursday morning.

And so began that incredible journey for me as well as for my grandparents, Edward and Clara Meade. It's one of life's little ironies I guess; when I was born, I was their grandchild, a baby unable to speak or act for myself. Somewhere along the way, we had eclipsed, and I suddenly became for them what they had once been for me. I found that my new role called for me to be their protector and voice; through their legal documents they had entrusted me to guard them and to handle *all* their business.

I know it's true that there is nothing new under the sun, but when dementia struck my grandparents it was totally new to me. Every decision seemed monumental, and I was overwhelmed by the knowledge that the choices I made would directly impact two other lives—not my own. It was agonizing because I loved them so deeply; we were warmly and wonderfully bonded together by the love we shared. I would have given my own life if it would have made them right again, but at the height of their dementia nightmare, I remember hearing Jesus' loving and gentle voice say to me, *You don't have to give your life to restore them; I've already given Mine.* Death finally separated us, but I praise God that I will see them again in eternity where even now they are more fully alive than they ever were on earth.

Overnight, I became what is known in our society as "the caregiver," and I can say without reservation it's one of the toughest things I've ever done. It was like a nighttime walk in a minefield because, in my quiet moments, I would second-guess myself. In the early days, I racked my brain to remember the conversations I'd had with Grandma about how she and my grandfather had wanted their business handled. On an emotional level, it was wrenching to watch them go down mentally. I was being forced to recognize that they were, little by little, slipping away from me. Grief is a peculiar phenomenon; it's expected that one will grieve to some extent following the death of a loved one, but it's quite something else when, as a caregiver, you realize that you're grieving over someone whom your eyes can still see, your hands can still touch, and whose voice you can still hear. You're grieving because they are no longer who you had known them to be.

In recounting this experience, I must give glory to the Lord Jesus Christ because there was never any crisis so great nor pit of despair so deep that He wasn't with me, constantly showing me what the next step was and providing for me as only He can. I write these words now, not as a scientist reporting the latest development in the fight against dementia, nor as a psychologist explaining the behavior patterns of a caregiver, but as an ordinary woman who had an extraordinary experience. I do not look at caregivers and dictate that they should do exactly what I did; that would be impossible because every set of circumstances is different. Instead, it is my sincere hope that my experience as a caregiver can be used by God as a source of encouragement, offering hope to those who are presently providing any level of care for a loved one—whether the cause is dementia or any one of the plethora of other mental or physical maladies. If my story can help others find their way through the maze of decisions and emotional draining that are the caregiver's lot, then I can rest assured that what Satan had designed to be a destructive tool has instead been used for God's glory.

I urge caregivers to understand they are not alone and they do have rights—among them, the right of self-preservation; take care of yourself—physically, mentally, emotionally, and spiritually. In the caregiver wilderness, the notion of looking after your own needs can vanish amid the turbulence of decision-making and crushing heartbreak. As a caregiver, you will run the emotional gamut, experiencing everything from guilt and depression to utter hopelessness. Through it all, you must remember that the only way for you to provide quality care to someone else is to be at your own personal best.

Take time to pray; seek out people who can pray with you as well as for you. Ask God to give you the physical strength, the mental clarity, the emotional control, and the spiritual direction that only He can give. And in those moments when you don't think you can take it anymore, ask God to wrap you up in the blanket of His grace. He alone fully understands that only through His grace will a caregiver be able to face the road that lies ahead.

CHAPTER 2

THE HISTORY

F amily closets will inevitably contain skeletons; ours is no exception. In my case, explaining exactly how I came to be chosen by my grandparents to serve as their legal power of attorney and executrix will require exposing our skeletons and shining the light on the source of this family's shame and heartbreak. While one person dug his heels in to live exactly as it suited him, everyone else was left to pick up the pieces and ponder the meaning of *forgiveness*. Flipping the dusty pages of time back to 1932 will reveal the foundation of a precious love—as well as the pain of a very deep sorrow.

A family friend named "Skinny" Pruitt had stopped by the Archer home one evening, and he brought along a friend of his, a Mr. Edward Meade. Miss Clara Archer took one look at him and knew that if there was a man for her, Edward was the one. He was a striking man, tall and lean with clear blue eyes. Clara had never really seen herself as a person who would get married. She always thought she would wind up doing some kind of mission work. But after a courtship which lasted only a few months, Edward proposed to his lady. Clara couldn't quite bring herself to say she'd marry him. She was, in her own words, "Momma's right arm," and she wasn't sure how a marriage between her and anybody would set with her family. As Clara deliberated, Edward brought things to a head by saying, "You're not going to disappointment me now, are you?" And so they were married on December 25th of that same year.

Clara was the second of Joseph and Mattie Archer's five children. She was born in Decatur, Alabama, in 1908. Joseph Archer worked for the railroad and eventually brought his family to Memphis, Tennessee. As a child, Clara was quiet and never liked being in a crowd. I remember she told me a story about when a close friend of her momma's got married. Mattie had to stay out in the hall trying to soothe her baby girl throughout the ceremony. Repeated attempts to keep Clara quiet inside the packed sanctuary resulted in the embarrassing wails only a baby can produce. Momma learned her lesson.

Early childhood taught Clara that a thrill wasn't worth the risk necessary to achieve it, and she lived by that motto all her life. At the age of six she contracted spinal meningitis following a playtime accident. It seems there was a large tree which grew on the banks of a swampy pond near the Archer home, and tied to one of the tree's branches was a long section of rope. The kids were using it to swing out over the water and then swing back to the tree trunk. Everyone was having a wonderful time, so little Clara decided to take a turn. She swung out over the water, and at that precise moment, the rope broke, and she plunged into the murky reeds below. She was pulled from the pond thoroughly soaked and scared half to death. Within a matter of days, her back was so tender she couldn't lay on it, and the family doctor advised Joseph and Mattie of their daughter's life-threatening illness. It took weeks of round-the-clock nursing, but she finally started to get better.

Many times throughout her life, Clara referred back to this near-death experience, and she wondered why God had let her live through it. The answer, of course, lay in the vastness of God's plan, a part of which was to allow her life and my life to overlap. Today I know Jesus Christ as my Savior and Lord because Clara shared her faith with me, and for her witness I believe she now has a crown in glory.

Clara completed her education through the eighth grade, at which time she, like her older sister Ruth, had to quit school and go to work to help support their family. She and Ruth took jobs working for the telephone company as operators. During her off hours, Clara enjoyed doing a variety of handwork, including crochet, embroidery, and sewing. She made her own clothes and loved dressing up plain pillowcases with fantastically intricate needlework. Throughout her lifetime she made hundreds of table runners and doilies as well as a variety of quilts in every size, color, and pattern imaginable. In her later years, she developed a passion for collecting dolls. She sewed and crocheted a variety of doll dresses, each of which was unique and beautiful. Looking at her neat, delicate stitches, one could easily see the woman behind it all—the work, the persona, the lady—all of which was succinctly summed up in one word: *Grandma*.

Born four years after Clara in Water Valley, Mississippi, Edward Meade was among the older of Arthur and Josephine Meade's twelve children. When he was very small, Edward was routinely mounted on horseback by his father and sent off to the store with a grocery list in one hand and money in the other. The horse knew the way, and the grocer, knowing the drill, filled the order, gave Edward the correct change, and promptly sent the horse and its little passenger back home. When he was a little older, Edward's siblings and some of the neighborhood kids invited him to go with them to pick berries. They took him to a remote spot and told him to "wait here with the bag." They'd go pick the berries and bring them to Edward so he could take them home. He waited and waited and waited some more. Of course, those who had plotted against him, having returned home as soon as they left him, greeted Edward with the laughing of pranksters. While he wasn't overjoyed at the joke that had been played on him, they couldn't have picked a more even-tempered victim. Many years later, while sitting under his carport swatting flies and watching cars go by, he smiled about it, finding humor in his own naiveté.

Edward left home relatively early and did a variety of jobs—everything from highway construction to sheet metal fabrication for airplanes during World War II. His attention to detail and ability to focus had allowed him to settle into a career as an auto mechanic. He was eventually promoted to manager of the wheel alignment and axle straightening department in a local car dealership. He was considered among the best in his field by his peers and was even consulted well into his retirement.

After they had married, Clara wanted to fill her home with little Meades; her doctor, however, told her that it was quite likely she would never have any. But in 1940, to her delight and amazement, she gave birth to her only child, Anthony Raymond Meade. Albeit a son for Edward, Ray would turn out to be a source of great pain to his entire family.

Edward and Clara were very loving parents who provided a stable, though some might argue a trifle overprotective, environment for their son. Ray's growing up years were by all accounts happy ones. He completed his education through high school and then joined the army, a decision which was the first in a series of crushing blows to his mother because Clara's youngest brother, Ralph, while serving in the Air Corps, had been shot down over Japan during World War II. Ralph, who was posthumously promoted to captain, had been like a son to Clara. His loss had been devastating to the Archer family, and Clara feared that military service might claim Ray as well. At the time, she couldn't possibly have known that losing her son would have absolutely nothing to do with "service."

Once his tour of duty was complete, Ray returned to Memphis, and during the summer of 1962, he began dating a girl named Judy Lucas. They were married in November, and for five years they lived what can best be described as an unsettled life. Throughout their marriage, Ray was passionate about only one thing—and that was driving his eighteen-wheeler. His reaction to Judy's announcement that she was pregnant was vague and indifferent.

When I was born in August 1967, Ray was conspicuously absent—but not Clara! After being phoned the night before with the news that Judy was in labor, Clara got in the car and drove herself downtown—indeed a rarity as she hated to drive even in the daytime. Clara, along with Judy's mother and younger brother, waited overnight together to hear the news that a baby girl had been born at 5:25 a.m. Edward had decided he would stay home and get his rest because, after all, Tuesday was a work day. But when the shop closed down at 5 p.m., nothing could keep him away from that hospital maternity ward where he first peered through the glass at his little Leah.

The first few weeks following my birth did nothing to alter the "gone-more-than-he-was-home" schedule that had been Ray's habit, but by the early fall of 1967, our "family" picture was undergoing changes from which we would never recover. In October, Ray got in his truck, drove away, and just disappeared, leaving my mother with a baby, an apartment, and a variety of unpaid bills and hostile creditors' telephone calls. For nearly six months, his whereabouts were a complete mystery; he had vanished without a trace.

Then, during the spring of 1968, word reached my mother that Ray was living in a small Mississippi town—working for the father of his *expectant "wife."* For Judy, the legal wife he'd left in Memphis, the irresponsibility of Ray's abandonment and bigamy was devastating. She used to tell me that she could have better handled hearing that he'd died rather than finding out he'd left her for another woman. Her shock gave way to bitterness and scathing anger as divorce proceedings were instituted. Ray continued to live with his "wife" in Mississippi while his divorce from my mother was working its way through the courts. Once it was finalized, he made the very pregnant "other woman" the second Mrs. Meade. My half-brother, Anthony Raymond Jr., was born in June 1968. Our ages are separated by a mere ten months.

As for my infancy, time took it away, and I never knew the sound of Ray's voice or the feel of his embrace. The truth was Ray never asked for custody; he never even asked for the right to visit me. For reasons that were his own, it seemed that I simply didn't exist. It was not until many years later, well into my adulthood, that I learned Ray had circulated the story that I really wasn't his daughter at all and that my mother was the one who had been unfaithful to him. If there was no other proof than my own physical appearance, that alone would be enough evidence to identify Ray as my biological father. We share eye color and shape, hair color, skin tone, chin, teeth—the list goes on and on. In addition, there is my mother's own word regarding her fidelity. It has been said by many of those who knew Ray that he was one of the world's smoothest liars, and he would lie about something when the truth would make more sense. Ironically, the genetic code which Ray himself passed on to me exposed his lie, and the truth remains on my face to this day.

For all of Ray's failings, his parents came out of their fiery trial like gold. Edward and Clara were embarrassed and bewildered over their son's behavior and endeavored, as much as possible, to pick up all the pieces left in Ray's wake. Much to my mother's surprise, alimony and child support checks were on time every time—because Clara paid them out of her own checking account. My grandma and grandpa longed for a relationship with me, their new granddaughter. When my mother had to go to work and couldn't afford daycare, Grandma was more than willing to take care of me. Grandpa used to tell me that he'd go to my mother's apartment very early in the morning to pick me up. He told me how he would carefully lay me down in the seat beside him (I'm a dinosaur, predating the advent of the car seat), then he'd drive back home and drop me off with Grandma before heading to work himself. My earliest memories are settled in that first house which my grandpa had built. There was no shortage of love in that house, and it was there that Grandma first began to teach me about Jesus.

She would read God's Word to me as I played at her feet, and I remember one day she pulled out her concordance and looked up every single verse where the name "Leah" appeared. Sometimes out of the clear blue, she would ask me a question like, "Do you know what the shortest verse in the Bible is?" I would look up at her with curiosity, and she would tell me the answer: "'Jesus wept.'" She gave me the first Bible I ever had, a gift I have always treasured. It had a white cover with my name embossed at the bottom. She always told me how important is was for her to put a copy of God's Word in my hands.

"That way," she said, "you can read what God said for yourself!"

While I was growing from infant to toddler, my mother's life was a mundane blur of earning a paycheck as well as the wearisome tasks of early motherhood, which included the daily washing of cloth diapers and the soothing of baby's midnight cries. Her friend Sandra, whom she had known since high school, encouraged Judy to get out and date again. Bitterness to one side, Sandra emphasized that socializing was the cure for everything Judy had endured. Sandra and her husband had a friend whom they wanted my mother to meet. Their first date was not exactly romantic poems and pledges of undying love, but for some reason, Larry Sutton wanted a second date. At the time, neither Judy nor Larry made any pretense of being Christian people, but God had a plan for their lives and for mine; He was building a new family, one that would stand the test of time.

During my early years, Larry stayed in relationship with my mother, contrary to her expectations, and thereby proved himself to be conscientious and reliable. They were finally married on July 16, 1971, and when I was five years old, Larry legally adopted me, changing my name from Meade to Sutton. Ray gave his consent to my name being changed after asking his mother what he should do. Grandma told me that he struggled with the decision, and all she could tell him was that it wasn't up to her and that he had to do what he thought was best. He made his decision and apparently never looked back. Ray didn't have a daughter anymore, but that daughter finally had a dad.

My childhood was a happy one in spite of its shaky beginning, because Larry, whom I very affectionately refer to as "Dad," provided my mother and me with stability and a self-sacrificing love we never would have known with Ray. The challenge Dad accepted when he married my mother after what she'd been through, as well as the commitment to parent a child who wasn't biologically his, speaks volumes about his outstanding character. Grandma and Grandpa got on well with my Dad from the beginning, which was even greater evidence of God's grace pouring out on our new family.

My Dad's profession involved, among other things, the drawing of blueprints, so when Grandma and Grandpa wanted to draw up plans for the house in which they intended to retire, they sought my Dad's help. In 1973 Grandma and Grandpa purchased eighty acres of trees and underbrush in the foothills of the Ozarks not far from Hardy, Arkansas. Every Friday afternoon they would make what was, at that time, a three-hour drive from Memphis over to what they generically referred to as "the place." They would work all weekend, and over time they cleared the first forty acres of their land. Grandpa eventually built a one-room cabin with a screened-in porch so they could actually sleep on their green acres instead of having to stay in the motel in town.

In October 1977, Grandpa became an officially retired auto mechanic and construction of their permanent home in Arkansas got underway in earnest. They purchased an additional forty acres on the west end of their property, extending their holdings to a total of one hundred twenty acres. Grandpa began clearing away the underbrush and sowing the land with grass in preparation for the cows he'd dreamed of for so long. By 1980 they had moved into the little cabin, living there for a full year until their house was complete. Once the long-awaited house became a home, they purchased a few cows for Grandpa to tend and then went out and got a mixed-breed puppy who had four white paws and a beautiful golden coat. Lovingly named "Boots," he grew into a sixty-pound lap dog who loved his people almost as much as I did.

When I was a kid, I'd go visit them every chance I got, spending my spring break, two weeks out of the summer, and a week at Christmas, including every New Year's Eve, with Grandma and Grandpa. When I couldn't be over there, Grandma and I wrote long letters to each other, detailing what we were doing. As I grew into adulthood, I began to make monthly trips as my school and work schedules permitted. I would spend two to three days at a time with them. I would also squeeze in trips where I left for their house early in the morning and returned home the same day. My Pontiac Sunbird zipping up and down that awful gravel road came to be a familiar sight to the Meade neighbors.

As for my grandparents' son, Ray proved himself unable to stay anywhere for more than a few years at a time. In 1985 he pulled the same abrupt disappearing act on his second wife. Just as he had done before, he simply got in his truck and drove away, but this time it was forever. It had seemed unthinkable that he would do this even once in a lifetime, let alone twice. Early on, the expectation was high that he would eventually turn up somewhere. What had been so shocking to Grandma and Grandpa the first time proved to be painful and humiliating the second time around. Weeks went into months, and months became years, but there was never any word for my precious, grieving Grandma about her wandering son. I also remember walking with Grandpa out in his woods one day and saying to him, "I know Ray has just broken Grandma's heart." His reply was brief but revealing. "Not just your Grandma's heart," he said.

Undoubtedly over the course of a lifetime there are a myriad of events which can cause anguish in the human heart. It turned out that Ray was but one source of grief in Grandma's life. Joseph Archer, Grandma's one-hundred-and-two-year-old father, had been suffering for some time with an undiagnosed form of dementia. He had been living with Grandma's sister, Ruth, until her health had broken down in 1983. Grandma and Grandpa then brought "Daddy" to their Arkansas home. I recall watching her deal with him, and I remember vividly the toll it took on her. Sitting at her kitchen table one night after he had gone to bed, she and I were talking about it. I was seventeen years old, too young to fully appreciate the predicament Grandma was in.

"What are you going to do with him?" I asked.

"Keep him here," she said wearily. "I promised. . . ."

"You promised? What did you promise?"

"When Momma died, we stood over her grave, and he made me promise I'd never put him in a nursing home. And I promised him I wouldn't."

For the last year of his life, "Daddy" lived comfortably with his daughter and son-in-law because of that promise. And that promise almost broke my grandma to pieces.

Being designated to serve as someone's caregiver can be a testimony to a wonderful and loving relationship; nevertheless, it requires a very serious commitment. In choosing someone to ultimately be a caregiver, one must have access to a person who is both willing and able to make that commitment.

Because of Ray's willful disappearance, my grandparents had no child of their own in whom they could place their trust regarding any care decisions that might have to be made for them as they aged. In 1992, just four days before Christmas, they drew up what turned out to be their final legal documents in which I was appointed to serve as their legal power of attorney and executrix of their last will and testament.

When I received Mack Proctor's phone call, I pulled out copies of those documents that had been supplied to me by Grandma and Grandpa through their lawyer, and I read over them carefully. The document which gave me durable power of attorney specified that I had "full and complete control over [their] care and treatment including any necessary choice and placement with a retirement or nursing home. . . ."

"She never made me promise . . ." I remember telling Chris.

The realization had dawned on me slowly as I read and reread the phrase. Grandma and Grandpa had understood that the difference in our ages would likely land me caring for them while I was still a young woman. They also understood that I probably wouldn't be able to take them in the way Grandma had taken her father in because it was possible I might have a husband and maybe even small children, so she had never bound me with a promise that I wouldn't put her or Grandpa in a nursing home. By the time I began to understand her incredible gift of freedom from the same promise that had almost destroyed her, Alzheimer's disease was too deeply rooted in her, and I was facing their long-term care decisions without their cognizant presence.

As I folded their legal documents and put them back in the envelope, the tears began to fall. I said to Chris, "It's time."

CHAPTER 3

OUR ARRIVAL

Thursday, January 16, 1997, dawned bright and clear but cold. Not having any idea how long we'd need to be gone, we packed enough clothes to last for several days. Chris and I each had to call our respective offices to briefly summarize as much as we knew of what had happened, explaining that we'd need to use personal and vacation days until we could get the emergency resolved.

From the way Mack had talked, my mother figured we'd need help in handling whatever was waiting for us, so she and her little Duchess, a 16-pound Lhasa Apso who thought very highly of herself, joined us as we prepared to leave home. It was one of the smartest things my Mom could have done; affectionately nicknamed Duchy, that precious canine proved to be an uplifting little comforter during those first dark days in Arkansas. My dad decided it would be best if he stayed in Memphis, functioning as our "point person" to provide any help we might need on this end.

Just before we got on the road, I made a phone call to Bruce Hollis, my grandparents' attorney in Walnut Ridge. I spoke with his secretary, Phyllis, hitting the high points of Mack's call, letting her know that we would be leaving for their house within the hour. She was very supportive and understood the gravity of our situation. She made an appointment for me to meet with Bruce on Friday morning to discuss the legal aspects of providing care for Grandma and Grandpa.

By 1997, Highway 63 had undergone major changes from the early days when Grandma and Grandpa had first bought their property. The trip that had once taken a solid three hours had been reduced to only two and a half, but I think the drive we made on that cold January day must have been the longest two-and-a-half hours I'd ever spent behind the wheel. Chris, my mom, Duchy, and I had piled into my Pontiac Sunbird, crossed over the mighty Mississippi, and headed for that house on the ridge in the foothills of the Ozarks. In an effort to relieve some of the tension surrounding the trip, we were making silly jokes and laughing about the stupidest things, but in spite of the humor, I had the uneasy feeling that I was plunging head-first into dark and uncharted waters.

The farther north we went the more snow we saw on the ground, but the highway itself was clear, and we reached Imboden without incident. Sleepy little Imboden greeted me as it had always done, with all the usual landmarks in their proper places. There was the insurance office on the edge of town and the little motel on the west side of the highway, not so very different from the days when Grandma and Grandpa had stayed there before the cabin was finished. The local bank was doing business as usual, and the old country funeral home served as my eternal marker to turn off of Highway 63 onto 115. From my childhood and teenage years on into my adulthood, I had grown to appreciate the fact that visits to Grandma and Grandpa had remained, like the town itself, relatively unchanged. I think I must have believed that Grandpa would always be out tending his cows and walking his dog, while inside the house Grandma would be crocheting tirelessly on the skirt and ruffle of a doll's dress. Any kind of change is hard to take, but if one can experience it gradually, the change can be more easily accepted. As I drove through Imboden that day, it seemed clear that I wasn't to enjoy the luxury of a "gradual" change, and I realized that I was vacillating between hope and fear: hoping my grandparents would be the same as they'd always been but fearing that everything I had known in connection with them was about to be transformed.

As I approached the gravel road which led to my grandparents' house, my ears began to pop as the elevation rose. I discovered that while the blacktop had been fine to drive on, the gravel had not fared so well in the previous day's snow. We were met with patches of ice and potholes big enough to swallow the front end of my car.

We made it fine for a short time, but when the car started to climb the first really long hill, the wheels started to spin, and the disconcerting feeling of being out of control overwhelmed me as my car started to fishtail. I remembered Grandpa's wise words about driving on ice: "Just forget you've got brakes." So I let the car do its thing and suddenly it stopped—leaving me sitting diagonally in the dead center of that silent, country road.

"Are we stuck?" I blurted out.

"Give it some gas, and cut the wheels toward the top of the hill," Chris suggested.

I touched the accelerator, and the car began to move, but the ice was everywhere, and once again we began to slide. Time to call out the big guns.

"Get the kitty litter," I said.

I had always heard that keeping kitty litter in your car during winter could help in case you got stuck in snow or ice. It was supposed to provide a source of traction to allow you to move the car. Sounds good on paper, doesn't it?

Chris got out of the car and began to slowly work his way toward the trunk. His movements were stiff and jerky as he tried to maintain his balance while holding on to the car. I released the trunk latch, and Chris pulled out the bag of kitty litter, then gingerly walked to the two back tires. After emptying the top half of the bag, he took a step back and called through the rolled-down window for me to move out. Tapping the accelerator gently, I could feel that the car wanted to move, but it was only the wheels spinning.

"We can't be stuck when we're this close!" I growled.

"I can't believe I brought a dog way out here," my mother muttered.

"This is solid ice," Chris was saying with disbelief in his tone. "I'm walking on a solid sheet of ice."

The stress of the situation was working on each of us in a different way. In my case, worried about my grandparents and trapped at the mercy of an icy road, I felt like I could fly apart at the seams. I needed to think in a calm, clear-headed way. What else did we have that we could use to get traction? I leaned my head out the window and called for Chris. He moved tentatively toward my door, nearly falling twice and grabbing at anything within reach for support. It was then that the giggling started.

"You look ridiculous," I chuckled out.

"This road is horrible!" Chris said, laughing. "I nearly killed myself."

"But you look so smooth," I said, breaking out in full-blown laughter.

"What did you call me over here for? Just to watch me bust my tail on this mess?"

"No, Gretzke. Here," I said, handing him one of the floor mats. "See if this will work."

"Hey that's a good idea," he said.

My mom agreed. She pulled one of the smaller floor mats from the back seat and handed it up to me. Chris put them in place under the tires and said, "Okay, try it now."

For the third time, I tapped the accelerator. I remember catching a glimpse of something moving really fast in my rearview mirror.

"Whoa!" Chris yelled.

I stuck my head out of the window and cried, "What happened?"

Chris was laughing so hard he nearly lost his balance. He crept along the side of the car to make his report.

"The floor mat idea won't work," he said breathlessly. "That thing flew out of there like it had been rejected!"

My mother and I laughed so hard we had tears running down our faces. We watched Chris, his arms flailing in quick, almost twitchy motions, walk away from the car to retrieve the rejected mats.

"They would have to land ten feet from the car," Chris moaned. "You do realize that if I fall because I don't have anything to hold on to, I'm going to slide all the way down to the bottom of this hill, and I'll be stuck there because there's no way I'm climbing back up here on this stuff!"

While Chris was braving the elements, my mother and I were still giggling. But as I wiped my face and pushed back my hair, the idea of being stuck began to sink in. I turned toward the back seat and stared at Duchy; she was sitting in my mother's lap with that *I could have told you this would happen* expression on her face. In a half-serious, half-flighty tone, I said, "Lord, what in the world are we going to do?"

It's funny the way some prayers are answered even before you give them utterance. At that precise moment, my mother looked out the back windshield and saw something in the distance.

"Someone's coming," she said.

Chris had seen it too. He stood and watched the approaching car while hugging one of the floor mats as if it were a life preserver.

The vehicle reached the bottom of the hill and then pulled over to the shoulder. Two men got out, and the driver waved his hand. He called out, "Leah?"

God's auto club, I thought as I opened my door and got out on the ice. "Yes! It's Leah. Mack, is that you?"

"Yes," came the very welcomed reply.

Mack and his son made their way up to our car. We told him we'd never been so glad to see anybody in our lives.

"I knew these roads were bad," Mack said. "I got to thinking that you might have trouble on these hills, so I came out to look for you. I've got chains on my tires so I can get around on this stuff."

Mack suggested that we leave my car on the side of the road rather than trying to get it back down the icy hill. He and Chris moved all our stuff to his car and then they threw their weight behind my Sunbird, gently guiding it over the ice to the shoulder of the road. We walked down the hill using the underbrush along the side of the road for traction and climbed into Mack's back seat. Duchy sniffed the air of that unfamiliar vehicle, thrusting her wet nose up into the front seat between Mack and his son. Mack delivered us safely, but oh-so-slowly, to my grandparents' home by way of a back road that was relatively flat and easily negotiable for a car equipped with tire chains. Given the dead stop we were at before Mack found us, just being able to move— even if it was painfully slow—was a welcome relief. Mack's presence in that place at that particular moment was nothing short of God's supernatural provision. Even now when I think back on it my faith is strengthened, and I remember that God promised in His Word that He would never leave us or forsake us (Hebrews 13:5).

Arriving at my grandparents' house was an emotional experience for me that day. Turning into the driveway, I was overshadowed by the same feeling I'd had while driving through Imboden just an hour before; it was almost eerie because everything *appeared* so normal. We saw Grandpa's pick-up truck parked, as usual, in front of the cabin. As the drive curved around toward the house, we passed the two huge oak trees and the snow-covered picnic table that sat between them. Grandma's flower bed appeared unchanged; there were tiny sprigs of the previous summer's leftovers peeking out from under their snowy veil.

Through the years, I had grown accustomed to being greeted by the excited barking of my grandparents' dog, Boots. He had been a wonderful companion and a loving pet for many years, but sadly, in 1992, he had to be put down after injuring his back in an overnight scrap with some unknown animal. The barks that greeted us that day were from their second dog, Duke, so named to be a match for our Duchy. Duke was a beautiful dog with a deep red coat and brown eyes that were so clear they almost appeared yellow. When Duchy emerged from the car, she stood looking at Duke for a few seconds, then turned abruptly away from him and headed for the door, never dreaming for an instant that she occupied the same station in life that he did.

I opened the carport door and stepped into the kitchen, and as I did so my eyes landed on Mack's wife, Betty Jo, who had graciously come to keep an eye on Grandma and Grandpa until I arrived. She smiled when she saw me and started to get up. Then she leaned over to Grandma, who was sitting in her usual chair, and said, "Look who's here."

Grandma leaned forward. I noticed she was wearing her coat, which was unusual because the house was always so warm during the day. In addition, I saw immediately that the lens on the right side of her glasses was completely missing. Her face brightened when she saw me, and she got up from her chair.

She was noticeably thinner than she had been when I had last seen her on December 1.

"Well, hello, Sweet!" she said as we embraced the way we always did.

Again, I was awash in the sensation of how "normal" everything was. Tears involuntarily pricked my eyes as I said to her, "I'm so glad to see you."

Grandpa stood up from stirring the fire in their wood-burning stove, the house's solitary yet highly efficient source of heat. He too appeared to have lost a considerable amount of weight.

"Howdy, howdy!" he said as we hugged one another. "I didn't know you were coming up today."

It was the first time I can remember putting on a false front—the brave face—for them, but it certainly wasn't to be the last.

"I came to see you! You know I love you so much that you can't keep me away."

Grandma had remained standing with a polite smile on her face as Duchy was sniffing her way around the room. I asked her, "Why have you got your coat on? Aren't you warm enough?"

"Oh, yes, I'm fine, but we're about to go."

"Where are you going?" I asked.

"We've got to be getting home," she said. "Ed, where's my purse?"

There was a strained silence. I remember being conscious of everybody looking at me, waiting for me to do something. Grandpa, who never dreamed he needed a hearing aid, had gone back to put another log on the fire, so he hadn't heard Grandma's question. I thought to myself, *What does she mean, "getting home?" Here she is, standing in what has been her living room for the last sixteen years, surrounded by all her own things, her furniture, her lamps, her pictures—and yet she's wanting to go "home" to someplace else. Where?*

I walked over and put my arm around her.

"Grandma, you're at home," I told her, fully expecting to be able to reason with her. Then I smiled and said, "Let's get your coat off."

Her face clouded over as she resisted.

"No, Sweet, I better keep it on 'cause we're gonna have to go."

Betty Jo lowered her voice and told me that Grandma had been like that since she'd been brought home on Wednesday.

"I was hoping you might be able to help her understand where she is," Betty Jo said with a frown.

Turning away from Grandma, I looked Betty Jo straight in the face. I felt like running away screaming.

"I don't know what I can do," I mumbled. "She's never been like this before."

My initial shock over encountering Grandma at that level of cognitive degradation was overwhelming. It took a long time before I came to understand the best thing I could do for Grandma was to simply agree with her, no matter how ridiculous or outlandish her statements were. I was slow to accept the fact that she really believed the things she was saying, at least in the moment.

I looked back at Grandma and noticed the missing lens again.

"What happed to your glasses?" I asked her.

"I don't know," she said. "They broke." She pulled them off and looked at them with a puzzled expression.

I turned to Betty Jo with a questioning look. She just shrugged her shoulders.

"They were like that when she came home yesterday."

The broken glasses turned out to be a blessing in disguise. I went over to Chris and said quietly, "That's how I can get them to the doctor."

Like so many folks of their generation, both Grandma and Grandpa had lived their whole lives with an aversion to going to the doctor, but I knew that after what they'd been through in Forrest City, I wanted them to be checked out by a physician. I was certain that any overt attempt to get them to a doctor would never work, but they would probably go along if I said we were going to get Grandma's glasses fixed. It was more than a diversionary tactic; I fully intended to see about getting new glasses for her, but the missing lens made it possible to avoid an argument and get them peaceably to a place where they could be medically examined.

Betty Jo began to gather her things.

"I guess I'll be getting home," she said as she patted Grandma's shoulder. "You'll be fine now that Leah's here."

"I know it!" Grandma said, looking at me with a smile. I remember thinking how I wished I could share in her optimism. In spite of everything, though, I knew there was definitely one thing to be thankful for: both Grandma and Grandpa had recognized me. After what Mack had told me on the phone the night before, I wasn't sure if they would even know who I was. Their recognition of me bred trust, and that trust made working through the difficulties that were still to come a little easier.

As the Proctors got ready to leave, I thanked Betty Jo profusely for looking after Grandma and Grandpa. I found myself at a loss for the right words to tell her just how much her kindness and help meant to me. Mack then made the offer to drive us to Walnut Ridge so I could take my grandparents to the medical center there. His kindness, like Betty Jo's, was of such a great measure that a mere "thank you" just wasn't enough to express how grateful I was. Mack's attitude was so selfless, and as I tried to express my appreciation, he would only say, "Well, we're all going to need help someday. I'm just glad I can do something for Mr. and Mrs. Meade. They're mighty nice people."

I turned to Grandma and Grandpa to begin explaining that we were going to take Grandma into Walnut Ridge to see about getting her glasses fixed. While I was talking to them, my mother began looking through the refrigerator and pantry. She made a thoroughly unexpected discovery.

"There's no food here," she said. "No wonder they're skin and bone. You're going to have to go to the store tomorrow; I've brought enough stuff to get us through tonight, though."

My wonderful mom! She had thought ahead and packed a couple of bags of groceries—just in case. It was something that had never even occurred to me. But even as I was thanking God for my mom's resourcefulness, I still had a feeling of helplessness hanging over me. It seemed that each time a new fact about my grandparents' current reality was uncovered, a new wave of despair came with it. Was Grandma so far gone that she didn't realize she hadn't even cooked a meal? Even if she didn't know she hadn't cooked, didn't Grandpa realize that she had not cooked and he had not eaten? How could so much have changed since I saw them last, and how could I have been so blind that I didn't see it coming?

I would later learn from my research into Alzheimer's disease that in the early stages, the patient actually does realize something is happening to them. They struggle to compensate for things forgotten and may even lie to cover up the fact that they can't remember something because they're afraid they'll look foolish to their family. On the flip side, it is not uncommon for family members to be oblivious to the fact that something is radically wrong. It is especially difficult to see the true magnitude of the symptoms when you don't live in the house with the dementia patient; as I mentioned in chapter one, I had the impression that something wasn't quite right, but I let it slide by convincing myself it was just garden variety forgetfulness that can occur with age. While Grandma and Grandpa had *appeared* normal when I had seen them a mere six weeks before, their empty fridge and impromptu road trip to Forrest City told a different tale; the façade was over.

CHAPTER 4

FIRST MEDICAL OPINION

A s I had expected, Grandma and Grandpa willingly complied when I suggested that we see about getting Grandma's glasses fixed. My mother stayed at their house because there wasn't enough room in Mack's car for her to go along. The ride into Walnut Ridge was almost unbearably slow since Mack didn't take the chains off his tires when we reached the highway. He said removing them wasn't worth the trouble of having to put them back on for the return trip over the icy gravel, so we puttered down the highway at about thirty-five miles per hour; all the other cars were passing us like we were going backwards.

I sat beside Grandma in the back seat, and we chatted about the things we saw along the way. I remember thinking she didn't seem so different after all, and maybe I was all worked up over nothing. Denial can seem like a happier, safer place.

We arrived at the medical center in Walnut Ridge, and since I had no idea where to go or what doctor to see, we went in through the emergency room. Chris and Mack waited with Grandma and Grandpa while I explained our situation to the nurse. She began to check the doctors' schedules to see who could help us. While scrolling down through the names on her computer, she asked that favorite medical provider question: "What type of insurance do they have?" At that precise moment, I realized how grossly unprepared I was for that particular aspect of "caregiving."

I went over to Grandma and sat down beside her.

"I need to see your insurance card," I said. Chris and I exchanged glances as Grandma began to dig through her purse. She produced a very worn wallet and began to painstakingly extract little pieces of paper from it. I looked at her face and thought to myself, *She has no idea what I'm asking for.*

"Can I have a look?" I asked cautiously. Grandma had always been fiercely private about her personal business. Because I respected that, I was unaware of which insurance company provided their medical coverage; but if I was now to assume the role which she herself had appointed me to take, there could no longer be any barriers—I would have to know everything.

I was enormously relieved when she handed the wallet over to me without the slightest hesitation. I quickly thumbed through several cards, papers, and pictures, looking for anything that resembled proof of medical insurance. The search paid off as I pulled out her supplemental insurance card.

"This is exactly what I need," I told her as I gave back her wallet. I stood up and asked Grandpa if he carried a similar card. Always agreeable, he reached into his back pocket and began riffling through his various ID cards and photos. Chris spotted the card that was identical to Grandma's, and he pulled it out, handing it to me.

"Leah needs this," he explained to Grandpa.

"OK," Grandpa said.

I gave the cards to the nurse, and we waited for just a few more minutes before she told me that Dr. Donnelly had agreed to see them. We walked through the halls that led to the internal medicine clinic, and the nurse put Grandma in one room and Grandpa in another. Chris and I waited in the hall while Dr. Donnelly made his examinations. When he was done, he asked to see us in his office.

"Your grandfather is in good physical condition," he began. "His heart and lungs sound good, and his bloodwork appears normal. A few good meals will get his weight back up where it needs to be, but he does seem to be in a confused state of mind. While he did know his name, and he knew he lives in Arkansas, he was not able to correctly answer basic questions such as, 'Who is the president?' and 'What year is this?' His recent malnutrition could account for some of the confusion, but the overall indication is that he is suffering from some type of dementia, the exact level of which would need to be determined by someone more qualified in that area than I am."

"What about my grandmother?"

"That's a little bit different," he said slowly. "She has a dangerously low potassium level, and while that could explain away some of the confusion she's experiencing, it is my opinion that there's more than just low potassium working on her." He paused before going on. "She knew her name but was unclear as to where she presently lives or what her current age is. She was also not able to tell me who is president and what year this is."

"So what is it? Dementia of some sort?"

"A more specific type of dementia, I'm afraid. I believe we're looking at Alzheimer's."

It's hard to describe just how that word hit me. In a way, I guess I expected to hear something like that; her recent behavior certainly indicated a problem that went beyond your garden variety old-age forgetfulness, but the concept of it being an actual disease—one which would never get better—was absolutely devastating. As the word *Alzheimer's* kept rattling around in my head, I realized I couldn't seem to find a place for it to land in the reasoning center of my brain. After several seconds of mental wrestling, I finally jumped back to the potassium level—a far easier issue to deal with. That issue had a tangible solution which Dr. Donnelly already seemed to have worked out.

"I'm going to advise that we admit her to the hospital and get her started on an IV drip. If we don't get that potassium level up, it could be life-threatening."

I agreed to her being hospitalized immediately. I knew she wouldn't like it, and I prepared myself for battle. We walked out of Dr. Donnelly's office and discovered that Grandma and Grandpa had grown impatient waiting on us. They had found each other and were wandering around the halls, presumably looking for me.

"Grandma," I said, walking up to her and putting my hand on her shoulder. "The doctor has told me that your potassium level is awfully low. He wants you to stay here tonight so you can get better."

"Oh no, Sweet," she said. "I can't stay here. I've got to get home."

I looked at Dr. Donnelly. He came around and stood in front of her and said, "Mrs. Meade, you're not doing as well as you should be. Just stay one night; you should be well enough to go home tomorrow."

She became the immovable force.

"No! I'm not staying here."

"Leah," Grandpa spoke up as he took Grandma by the arm. "We're going home. There's no reason to stay here. Now let's go home."

It had been a very long, stressful day, and I felt the tears beginning to brew, but I was determined to hold them back.

"Grandma, please," I began again. "I'm concerned about you, and I wouldn't ask this unless I really believed it was necessary."

"Sweet, I'm not staying in a hospital. Now let's go." She turned away from me and started down the hall with Grandpa by her side. I stood and watched them go in utter disbelief. I felt like a parent who was pitifully unable to control her own children—except they weren't my children, they were my grandparents. What category did that fall under?

I looked again at Dr. Donnelly and two huge tears rolled down my face. Embarrassed by Grandma's defiance and ashamed to death of my emotional display, my brain began to race as I searched for an alternative.

"Do you have some medicine you can give her that will help?" I asked, wiping my face.

The doctor said he could write a prescription for potassium tablets, and then he suggested we stock up on potassium-rich foods such as bananas, spinach, and raisins. While he was getting the prescription ready, his office assistant offered me a box of tissues. I smiled and thanked her, then turned to Chris.

"Will you go after them? Get Mack to take them back to the car."

As Chris turned and followed Grandma and Grandpa down the hall, Dr. Donnelly's office assistant patted me on the back.

"It's gonna be OK," she said. "It's hard with older people sometimes. They don't like hospitals."

"You're so right," I said, trying to smile. "They've never liked hospitals. They don't even want to go to a doctor's office."

After a few minutes, Chris came back. "Mack's got them," he said. "Are you OK?"

"Yes, it's just been a long day. And I'm wondering how I'm going to take care of them; they won't listen to me. How can I provide help for them if they won't work with me?"

Dr. Donnelly walked up and handed me the potassium prescription.

"It is difficult to take care of people when they don't understand what you're trying to do for them," he said.

"What worries me is *how* do I take care of them? Do I take them back to Memphis? Even if they go back to Memphis, what in the world am I going to do with them?"

Up to the time of her refusal to stay in the Walnut Ridge hospital, I had been cautiously optimistic that I could reason with Grandma; but as I left Dr. Donnelly's office, I truly felt like the weight of the world had landed squarely on my shoulders, and with less than twenty-four hours under that weight, I felt like I was going to buckle. The evidence that they were no longer able to live on their own was piling higher and higher, and that meant I was going to have to—do *what* exactly?

When Chris and I reached the car, Mack got out and closed his door. The sun had been down for some time, and the temperature, which had been cold all day, had dipped below freezing once it got dark. Before I could open the door and get into the warm car, Mack came over to me.

"She thinks you're mad at her," he said.

"Well," I paused. I suppose I was really more frustrated than mad. I felt overwhelmed.

"I'm a little exasperated," I told Mack, too ashamed to acknowledge the real emotions I was feeling.

I sat down in the back seat next to Grandma, and she looked at me with a sheepish expression.

"I hope you're not mad, Sweet," she said. I melted.

"No, Grandma, I'm not mad at you. I'm just concerned, that's all."

"Well, I'm glad. I don't want you mad at me."

"Well, promise me that you'll do something for me?"

"What's that?"

"The doctor has given me a prescription for potassium tablets that you need to take," I said. "Will you take them for me?"

"Yes, I will." Finally! A break in the heaviness. I settled back in my seat and felt my eyebrows relax a little. Chris and I looked at each other as Mack's car pulled out of the doctor's parking lot. I could see a degree of relief on his face as well.

On our way out of Walnut Ridge, we stopped by Walmart to get the prescription filled. Mack waited in the car with Grandma and Grandpa while Chris and I went in to get the tablets. As we waited on the pharmacist, we began to talk through all that had just happened.

"I can't believe how defiant she was," I said.

"I know," Chris replied. "They may be suffering with some kind of dementia, but they sure were cognizant enough to know they weren't going to stay at that hospital overnight."

"What am I going to do with them? They're obviously not right, Chris. They can't keep living on their own. How does this sort of thing happen to people?"

The questions that had been swirling around in my brain throughout the day started to come out all at once.

"Girl, I don't know," Chris sighed. "One thing at a time, though. We'll just talk to Hollis [my grandparents' attorney in Walnut Ridge] tomorrow and see what he says."

When the prescription was ready, we just paid for it out of our own pocket rather than try to fool with insurance. It wasn't that much, and we just wanted to get on the road headed back to their house and the hodge-podge dinner my mother would have ready. The drive was as slow and plodding as it had been earlier, and it seemed like an eternity passed before we pulled back up to the house. My mother was so glad to see us.

"It's creepy when you're out here alone at night," she said. "I've never been so thankful to have Duchy with me."

As Mack walked out to the carport to leave, Chris and I went out with him and offered him some cash for all the gas he'd used on us. In spite of our urging, he refused to take it.

"I'm just glad I can help. I'll come up tomorrow morning, and we'll go see if we can get your car back down that hill."

We thanked Mack again, then returned to the warm kitchen. The first thing Grandpa had done when we arrived back at the house was check on the fire. He stoked it a bit and added another log as Grandma stood in front of the "stove" (the large wood-burning furnace in the den), warming her hands. While she was rubbing her stiff, red fingers together, she announced pleasantly, "We're gonna have to go home, Ed."

I remember feeling so tired and in no mood to argue the point that this was Grandma's home, but I realized that I had to deal with this issue if we were going to get any sleep that night. As I walked into the den where she and Grandpa were, I settled on the loving-but-firm approach.

"Grandma, you're at home. Chris and my mom and I have come to stay with you and Grandpa for a few days. Everything's OK, Grandma."

The confusion on her face was evident, so Chris and Mom began to reassure her as well.

"This is where you're supposed to be," my mother told her.

"Now, who are you?" Grandma asked her.

"I'm Judy," she said. "I'm Leah's mother."

"Oh!" Grandma closed her eyes and smiled. "I didn't recognize you. How are you doing? It's been a long time since I've seen you, and you look so different."

Finding out about my mother seemed to settle Grandma down. We were able to get her coat off and seat her comfortably in her usual chair. My mother and I went back into the kitchen, and I told her all about the doctor's conclusions while she finished dinner for us. Chris turned on the TV, then sat down at the kitchen table and filled in details about the day's experience.

"It's been ugly," I said. "So ugly, in fact, that I think I'm going to have a nice, hot, soaky bath after we eat, and maybe it will all be better when I get out."

"No," my mother said slowly, "you won't do that."

I felt my eyebrows go up involuntarily.

Mom turned to face us and leaned back against the sink as she announced flatly, "There's no hot water."

Chris reacted first.

"What? Are you kidding?"

"It's true. The water heater is apparently on the fritz."

"How are we going to bathe?" I asked, shaking my head.

"I wonder how long it's been like this," Chris mused.

I went over and asked Grandpa how long the water heater had been out.

"Oh, it's fine. You can get all the hot water you need," he said.

All I could do was stare at him. I could see by the look on his face that he was completely sincere. I remember thinking, *He really doesn't know.*

Chris, thinking only of what really mattered, said, "I certainly hope everybody's deodorant is equal to the challenge," and the three of us burst out laughing—undoubtedly to keep from bursting into tears—while Grandma and Grandpa watched TV in the living room, completely oblivious to our plight.

As we were putting the last food items on the table, Mom told us that she'd talked with Dad earlier in the evening. She had filled him in on everything that she knew before we returned from Walnut Ridge and said that we'd call him again Friday night after meeting with the lawyer. In the meantime, Dad said he would begin doing some telephoning for us, gathering information on nursing and retirement homes in the Memphis area.

When dinner was ready, we crowded around the small kitchen table and filled our plates with the random assortment of foods my mother had put together. The day had been longer than we'd realized; we hadn't even had lunch. As hungry as we were, though, our appetites paled in comparison to Grandpa's. He dove into the food as if it were the first meal he'd had in days, which, under the circumstances, it probably was. My mother later remarked that watching him eat that night was one of the saddest things she'd ever seen.

"He ate like a man who was literally starving," she said. For her it was the first tangible realization that things were no longer "normal" for my grandparents. She knew what we'd been told, but seeing Grandpa eat so vigorously had a profound impact on her.

As the evening wore on, the three of us were so tired that we each seemed to be moving in slow motion as we cleaned up the dishes and put away the very few leftovers. Grandpa put one last log on the fire, and, just as he had done every night for years and years, he announced, "Well, folks, I'm gonna have to call it." He was going to call it a day, and the rest of us were only too happy to follow.

I told Grandma that we were going to bed, and as I did so I prayed that she would not get started about "going home" again. She watched Grandpa take off his house shoes and slide them under the TV stand. He turned around and looked at her as he began to unbutton his shirt and said, "Are you coming to bed now?"

"I guess I will," she said, and I breathed a sigh of relief.

She got up and followed Grandpa to their bedroom, stopping outside her door and turning around to face me.

"Goodnight, Sweet," she said, and she kissed my cheek just like she'd always done. "You have a real good night, hear?"

I put my arm around her shoulder and hugged up close to her.

"I will, Grandma, and you too, OK?"

Our precious goodnight exchange—at least that had remained unchanged. My eyes filled with tears as she turned from me and moved slowly into the bedroom. I stood outside the door and watched the two of them together for a few seconds, and in that moment, I realized how badly I wanted to keep them the way I'd always known them to be. She was turning down the bed, and he was laying out his pajamas. It was all normal; it was all a part of what normal people do. Then Dr. Donnelly's devastating diagnosis intruded into my peaceful thoughts, and the tears became so prominent that my vision was momentarily blurred.

"I will take care of you," I whispered. "I will do all I can for you. I promise. . . ."

I returned to the kitchen and heard my mother making up what was to be her bed for the night—the couch in the formal living room. She covered the cushions with a sheet and took a single blanket from Grandma's quilt box. Chris and I slept in what had always been my room—the little room with the green carpet, located on the front of the house. We crawled into the tiny double bed and turned out the light. Dark is never so dark and quiet is never so quiet as when you're out in the country. I closed my tired eyes and prayed for sleep to come. The thick, stuffy warmth from the fire in the living room began to dissipate, and as the cold settled in the room, I could feel my muscles coming down from their heightened state of tension.

"I don't know what to do for them."

"Don't worry about that. God's going to lead you and take care of you, just like He did this afternoon. Can you believe Mack just appeared out of nowhere like that?"

"That was amazing," I said, feeling slightly reassured.

"If God can do that, then we really don't have anything to worry about."

My eyes were getting heavier and heavier. "I know you're right," I mumbled.

The room was cool and dark and quiet. The high energy of the day gave in to the exhaustion of the night, and sleep finally came as I prayed in my mind the words of Psalm 138:8: "Don't abandon me, Lord. . . ."

CHAPTER 5

LEGALITIES

I was awakened suddenly on Friday morning, aware that someone was moving in the hall outside our bedroom door. The dawn was just beginning, and I could barely make out the bedroom's definition. As I listened carefully to determine who was up and functioning at an hour which shouldn't even be recognized as a respectable time of day, I realized I was absolutely freezing. I gathered the covers closer around me, and, as my faculties began to register, I could tell the noises were being made by Grandpa; he was working to start the fire for the day. Chris was breathing deeply, still asleep, and for a few seconds my eyes roamed around in the dim light. After a minute or so they got heavy again, and I must have dozed off because when I opened them back up, the room was significantly brighter, although still cold enough to make me think I was housed with polar bears.

A new day was stretching out before me, and I began to wonder what new horrors would greet me before it was over. I considered the events of Thursday, focusing on the Alzheimer's diagnosis, and I began to realize how limited my knowledge of the disease really was. It was the kind of malady I always heard people talk about, but when it came to hard facts, I actually knew very little.

As I lay in bed that morning, I had only the vaguest idea of how things would be changing for Grandma and Grandpa. They would have to be taken back to Memphis, of that there was no question. I would have loved nothing better than to be able to have a nurse take up residence with them, caring for them and protecting them in the comfort of their own home. I had no concept of how much a live-in nurse would cost, but I was certain it would be way out of the Meade budget. I also knew it would be impossible for Chris and me to pay for any of their care out of our own pocket; we were still basically newlyweds and were thankful to be making ends meet.

I began to truly consider the moral dilemma I was facing. How do you just go up to someone you care about and say, "OK! You need my help now; just come with me"? I had wondered for many months how I would know when it would be time for me to step in and begin helping them. The current situation clearly indicated the time had arrived; the problem was how to tell Grandma and Grandpa that the time had arrived. Judging from their behavior on Thursday, they seemed perfectly comfortable in their own reality. They had no idea anything was wrong.

As my thoughts were rambling, Chris began to stir. In a muffled and slurred "morning" voice, he said, "It's freezing in here."

"Welcome to the Arctic," I said. "Grandpa's fire goes out overnight, so early morning in the Meade's house feels like frozen tundra."

Chris and I dressed quickly and emerged from our glacial bedroom in the hope that Grandpa's fire had had enough time to start warming the house. I asked my mother how she slept.

"Awful," she said. "I wonder just how cold this house got last night. And that couch. . . ." She rolled her eyes.

She began to prepare breakfast, and I got the dishes out to set the table. Grandma came out of her room and smiled when she saw me.

"Well, good morning!" she said. "Did you have a good night?"

"I did. And how about you?"

"Oh, fine." She looked down as Duchy came up to her. "And how about you, little pet? Did you sleep good?" She stooped over to scratch Duchy behind her ears.

Grandpa had stepped out onto the carport to get more wood for the fire. As he came back in he smiled, realizing we were all up.

"Burrrrr!" he said as the door closed behind him. "It's cold out there."

Grandma went to her usual chair and sat down.

"You don't mind if I just sit here?" she asked politely.

I turned slightly, feeling my face fall almost into a frown. Sleep hadn't made it any better; she still didn't know she was in her own house, a fact which stung just as much that morning as it had the day before. I turned back to her and smiled.

"Grandma, you just sit anywhere you want to!"

"Thank you, Sweet." She settled back in the chair, and I realized for the first time that she was wearing the same dress she'd had on the night before.

"Grandma, didn't you wear that dress yesterday?" I asked.

She looked down at the dress.

"It's all I've got here," she said.

"Well, Grandma!" I wondered if she'd even looked in her closet. *Probably not*, I thought to myself, *since she doesn't know this is her house, she probably thinks it would be rude of her to look in the closet.*

I went into her bedroom.

"Well, she's a neat guest anyway," I said jokingly to Chris, who had followed me into their room. "She made up the bed."

I opened the closet door fully prepared to select a new dress for Grandma. Chris and I dropped our jaws simultaneously as we found that, except for the old purse which doubled as a camera bag and Grandma's strongbox, the closet was completely empty. No dresses. No shoes. Nothing.

"I don't understand," I mumbled.

"Does Grandpa keep his clothes in here?" Chris asked.

"No, he keeps his clothes in the closet in the little room next to our bedroom."

As if we were one person, we made our way across the hall to the closet in the little room, looking to see if Grandpa's clothes were still there. It was fully stocked; as far as I could tell nothing of his was missing.

"Where are her clothes?" I was dumbfounded.

"I wonder if they're in the car in Forrest City," Chris speculated.

I decided to ask Grandpa what had happened; he seemed so much clearer on things than Grandma, so I was certain I could get a straight answer out of him. I went back into the kitchen and found him pouring a cup of coffee.

"Grandpa, all of Grandma's clothes are gone. Do you know where they are?"

"They're out in the car," he said. Chris and I looked at each other. All of her clothes were stuck somewhere in Forrest City. Grandpa then looked at me with a serious expression and said, "We need to go to Walnut Ridge to get our car."

"Walnut Ridge? Grandpa, your car is still in Forrest City," I said.

He looked puzzled. I remember thinking that he must have been confused because they had spent the night in Walnut Ridge before being brought home Wednesday. Whatever the case, I was in no shape for an argument over the car's whereabouts, so I spoke quickly before he could say anything else.

"Don't worry about your car, Grandpa. I'll take care of it."

My statement pacified him for the moment, but what I didn't know at the time was that his car was to remain an issue until the day he died.

As we ate breakfast, Grandpa's fire began to thaw out the living room, and we finally started to feel warm. Before we cleared the table when the meal was over, I went to the kitchen sink with my face cleanser and a washcloth. As I splashed the icy water on my face, I began to realize how thankful I was for something I had always taken for granted: hot water running into my house.

"Me next," Chris said, standing behind me armed with a towel and a toothbrush.

Outside, Duke began to bark as a car turned into the driveway. True to his word, Mack Proctor had returned to take us back to where my car had spent the night. Before Chris and I left with him that morning, we sat down with my mother and made a grocery list. Trying to determine exactly how much to buy was the big question because we didn't know how long we'd be there. We decided to stock up enough to get us through the weekend.

"If we're here past Sunday then you can go back on Monday," Mom reasoned.

"Are you going to be OK to stay here with them today?" I asked her as we were gathering our things.

"It'll be fine. Don't worry about us here. You just do what you need to do."

My mother had never been a "country girl." I couldn't imagine what the day ahead would be like for her because sitting under a shade tree, listening to the whip-poor-will and bobwhite calls, had never been her choice for passing the time. Her generous help that day was a great sacrifice, one we couldn't have done without. If Chris and I had made that trip without her, then Chris would have had to stay back with Grandma and Grandpa while I went into Walnut Ridge alone to meet with the lawyer. My mom's help at the house made it possible for me to have Chris's support—and another pair of ears to listen to everything that was said—at Hollis's office, and for that I am truly grateful.

Just before we left, I walked out to the edge of the carport and began to scratch Duke behind his ears. I glanced out across the yard and saw Grandpa's cows gathered together by the fence. Mack came out and stood with me.

"They're starving," he said flatly.

I turned my head sharply to look at him.

"What?"

"He hasn't been feeding them. I found two of them that had already starved to death, and the rest are dangerously thin. There's no vegetation at this time of year, so if you don't give them grain, they get nothing."

I looked back at the pathetic animals, no doubt gathered at the fence in hopes of seeing Grandpa coming with their grain . . . just like he'd always done.

"His cows," I mumbled, staring at them. "He hasn't been caring for his cows. . . ."

Grandpa had always been like a mother hen to his cows. He had helped to deliver baby calves and had once sewn up a badly hurt mother cow in order to save her life following a rough delivery. Twice a day during the winter he would go out to feed, just like clockwork. He stored the grain in the cabin and had always made sure he was well stocked, not wanting to ever completely run out before spring came. Now I was being told that one of his greatest pleasures in life had been stolen from him by an unseen enemy who had attacked him right inside his own mind.

"I'll be glad to feed them if there's any grain on hand," Mack offered. "Where would he keep it?"

"It would be up in the cabin if he has any."

"I'll drop you and Chris off at your car, and after I make sure you won't get stuck again, I'll come back and take a look. If there's grain, I'll get them fed."

"That would be wonderful, Mack," I said. "Thank you."

I cannot over emphasize how much I appreciated Mack Proctor and how I thanked God over and over for having that man there just when we needed him. There was so much that he had already done and was continuing to do for us—there would have been no way we could have taken care of everything without his help. I continually stand amazed at God's ability—and willingness—to provide a perfect safety net for His people.

Chris came out, and we headed off to retrieve my car. We found it, thankfully, just as we had left it. Navigating back down the hill proved much easier than the adventure of going up the hill the day before. Mack's car separated from ours when we came to the highway; he turned to go back toward my grandparents' home while we headed toward town. After the crawling we had done the day before in Mack's tire-chain-fettered car, driving at fifty-five miles per hour made me feel like I was on the Autobahn.

We drove into Imboden and made our first stop at the local bank. My grandparents had had an account there since they'd first moved to the Ozarks. At some point when I was in my early twenties, Grandma had added my name to their checking account as a precautionary measure. She had wanted to be sure that if anything ever happened to her or Grandpa, I would be able to access their funds. Even though my name had been on the account for many years, I had never once written a check or drawn cash against it. I must confess that as I walked into the bank that morning, I experienced a rush of guilt. In my mind I was thinking, *Grandma should be doing this, not me!* I knew I wasn't doing anything wrong, and I certainly wasn't stealing from their account. For me, it was really more of the denial experience; if I went into their bank to do their business, it meant they weren't able to tend to things for themselves, a fact which I was not yet ready to face.

Adding to the anxiety of getting involved with my grandparents' finances was the fact that I didn't want anyone to think I was some cruel relative who was just going to lock them away somewhere and make off with all their money. For that reason, I maintained from the very beginning a policy of strict openness where their money was concerned. I did not know at that early date how Grandma and Grandpa would ultimately be cared for; I didn't know the extent to which Medicare and/or Medicaid would be involved. I had no idea what sort of accountability the government would require from me in the way of Meade financial records, therefore I determined to keep every receipt, deposit slip, cancelled check, and financial statement which had anything to do with their business or my handling of it.

Before we had left the house that morning, my mom, Chris, and I had decided to withdraw some cash to cover the groceries, a couple of new dresses for Grandma, the day's legal fees, and any unforeseen expenses. When Chris and I walked into the bank, I approached the available teller, explaining who I was, and briefly told her what was happening to my grandparents. She knew immediately who I was talking about and expressed her sorrow regarding their situation.

"They're such nice people," she said.

As we were talking, another bank employee asked me what was going to happen to them. I remember thinking how funny it was that they were all looking at me with such confidence, as if I had all the answers. I drew in a deep breath and tried to sound sure of myself.

"Well, they'll have to go back to Memphis with me, but. . . ." I froze for a few seconds and then blurted out, "Quite honestly, I just don't know what we're going to do."

They were very understanding, and I appreciated how kind they were. I swallowed hard and moved forward with the business at hand. I pulled out my driver's license to prove that I was who I said I was.

"I'm listed on their account," I began. "We need to get some cash to take care of their expenses and other business matters that need to be handled."

"That's no problem. How much do you need?"

We had decided to withdraw two hundred dollars, to start. For security, Chris and I divided it. He put one hundred dollars in his wallet and I put the rest in my purse. We then left the bank and started out for Walnut Ridge with just enough time to make our appointment with Mr. Hollis.

Even though Bruce Hollis had been my grandparents' attorney for several years, I had never met him. I had received directions to his office from his administrative assistant over the phone on Thursday before we'd left

Memphis. Just passing through the door caused me to yet again experience that rush of disbelief—the prick of *What on earth are you doing?*

"You must be Leah," the woman behind the desk said pleasantly. The face was unknown to me, but I easily recognized Phyllis's voice. She stood up and came out from behind her desk to shake my hand. Somehow, she looked different from the person I'd pictured when we'd spoken on the phone. She was not quite five feet tall, and she wore glasses. Her hair had once been very dark but was now a salt and pepper blend.

"Did you have a good trip up?" she asked.

"Yes, the drive up was fine; we just hate the circumstances that brought us here at this particular time."

"Oh, I can imagine. I'm so sorry about it all." She paused then said, "Well, Bruce is ready to meet with you," and she showed us into his office.

Bruce stood up from behind his large desk. He was a tall man with a balding head, clean shaven, and dressed very casually. I suppose I was expecting a Perry Mason type, complete with suit and tie, holding some sort of legal book. But whatever he may have lacked in Hollywood image he made up for in legal competence.

I filled him in on the specifics of what had happened over the last week. He listened carefully, making notes on various points.

"Well, Leah, I'm very sorry about all of this. Your grandparents are really fine people," he said with a serious tone. "And you feel certain that they are not able to continue living on their own?"

"I don't see how; I mean, they leave their house and wind up in Forrest City in a wrecked car. They have no food in their house, and even their cows are starving. She has no change of clothes and doesn't even realize she's in her own house. If everything was all right, I don't think any of this would be happening."

"Well," Bruce paused pensively. "Fortunately for them and for you, they took the appropriate legal precautions. They have each prepared a legal document which gives durable power of attorney to a specific person preappointed by them. Mrs. Meade appointed her husband to serve as her primary agent and attorney in fact, and Mr. Meade appointed his wife to serve him in the same capacity. Both of them appointed you as their only alternate agent, in the event that they were not able to serve, for whatever reason, for each other. The term *durable* indicates these papers are not affected by the incapacitation of your grandparents. At this time, I need you to go back to the clinic and get Dr. Donnelly to put in writing the fact that, in his medical opinion, Mr. and Mrs. Meade are no longer able to conduct their own business or to provide sufficient care for themselves. This will allow me to legally turn over to you the original documents which will empower you to act on their behalf."

It all sounded so clinical, and on the outside, I sat emotionless, absorbing what the lawyer was saying. But on the inside, I could feel myself crumbling. Sitting in a lawyer's office, making plans to just take over someone's life—at least that's what it felt like—it was like some insane game where a bad throw of the dice had landed Grandma, Grandpa, and me in a pathetic triangle, leaving us all to hover somewhere between living, existing, and dying.

"When you get back," Bruce continued, "we'll discuss the particulars of the power of attorney documents."

We left Bruce and headed for Dr. Donnelly's office. Chris helped me explain to the receptionist what we needed, and she got to work on it right away. While we waited, I went to a pay phone and called my mother.

"How's it going there?"

"This is rough," she began. "I can't keep up with them. He gets up to go one way and then she goes another way—I don't know which one to follow! And they want to do everything for themselves—they won't let me help them at all. I don't know how you're going to handle them." Her frustration was evident.

"Well, that's encouraging news," I said with a frown.

"A little while ago she fell," Mom paused. "Now don't get upset; she's OK. But while she was still on the floor, Grandpa came and tried to jerk her up as if nothing had happened."

"You're kidding!"

"No. I had to tell him to let her lay there for a minute to see if she was all right. She's fine, but I bet she'll be sore. She went down hard."

"How did she fall?"

"I don't know. It happened so fast, and I never saw it. I heard her call out, and then I heard her hit the floor. By the time I got to her she was flat on her back."

"But you say she's all right?"

"Yes, she seems fine. There's certainly no broken bones or anything. She's sitting in her chair right now, and Grandpa's out on the carport. Oh, by the way, Mack said there is no grain for the cows. He said he can go buy some, but it'll be tomorrow before he can go get it."

We discussed the fact that neither one of us could believe Grandpa hadn't been taking care of his cows. I asked her to tell Mack that Saturday was fine and how we so appreciated his help. Even today, I know that if it had been up to me I wouldn't have had any idea where to go to buy grain for those starving animals. That man was such a blessing.

I briefly filled Mom in on our first meeting with Bruce. I told her that after we went back to his office for the paperwork we'd stop by the grocery, and then we'd be heading to the house.

"What about getting her another dress?" Mom asked.

"It'll have to wait until tomorrow," I answered. "We just don't have time to do it all today."

I returned to Chris and found he was still waiting for the letters. I told him all about what was going on back at their house.

"Your poor mother!" Chris sighed.

"I know. She deserves a medal."

After a few more minutes the receptionist returned with two type-written letters both signed by Dr. Donnelly.

"Have a look at these and see if this is what your lawyer needs," she said.

I read both letters. Their statements were brief, but their impact was powerful.

January 17, 1997

TO WHOM IT MAY CONCERN:

RE: Edward Meade

I examined Mr. Edward Meade on 1/16/97. Mr. Meade appeared confused and has difficulty with short and long-term memory. It is my impression that he is lightly suffering from dementia and as such may not be competent to adequately care for his health.

I would be happy to answer any questions regarding Mr. Meade.

The letter concerning my grandmother was similar in tone . . .

January 17, 1997

TO WHOM IT MAY CONCERN:

RE: Clara Meade

I examined Mrs. Clara Meade on 1/16/97. She appears to have fairly advanced dementia, probably of Alzheimer's type. As such it is my impression that she is not competent to make decisions about her health.

I would be happy to answer questions regarding Mrs. Meade.

Seeing it on paper was hard. The letters were just one more piece of evidence building the case that it wasn't just my imagination running wild. The time really had come for me to fulfill my designated role for them.

Chris and I returned to Bruce's office and waited only a short time to see him. I gave him the letters, and he read them carefully.

"This is fine," he said. "Phyllis, I need copies of both these letters."

Phyllis hurried out, and Bruce began thumbing through the Meade file. He pulled out the two durable power of attorney documents. The originals were each stapled to a thick sheet of blue backing and were both one and a half pages in length. Bruce glanced over them and then folded them together and put them into an envelope. Our eyes met as he leaned slowly across the desk, extending his arm to hold out the envelope to me. I took the papers slowly and leaned back in my chair. I could feel my heart pounding, and my rib cage was actually shaking.

"Right now, you don't understand the power these documents give you," Bruce said slowly, "but you will understand over time. Your grandparents spoke to me about you. They think very highly of you, Leah. *Very* highly. And they have entrusted you with everything: their property, their money, their care. Everything."

I was not surprised by the sweeping trust they had placed in me because I knew we had shared an open, deeply loving relationship throughout my entire life. But in that moment, those documents became a sort of measuring stick which made their trust in me a very tangible thing. It showed me a more exact level of what Grandma and Grandpa had felt toward me for those many years.

"I will do the best I can for them," I said.

"I know you will. Now listen very carefully, this is extremely important. You can make as many copies of these documents as you want to. You can give copies to anyone who wants or needs copies of these documents. But. . . ." Here, Bruce paused, looking hard at me before going on. "*Under no circumstances* let the originals out of your sight or possession. They are irreplaceable. If the originals are lost, your ability to act on your grandparents' behalf will be seriously compromised."

"I understand," I said.

"Does this make us financially responsible for anything their insurance won't cover?" Chris asked.

"Absolutely not," Bruce stated emphatically. "Leah is authorized to act for the Meades as their agent but is not, in any way, responsible for anything not covered either by their insurance, Medicare, or Medicaid." He put his chin to his chest and cut his eyes over to me. "No one can legally demand payment on a Meade bill from you."

Obviously Chris was thinking more clearly than I was. The question of financial responsibility, in that capacity, had never even occurred to me.

Bruce stood up.

"If you have any questions or need my help in any way, I'm here. Just give us a call."

Phyllis came back in with Dr. Donnelly's letters. She put the copies in the file and handed the originals to Bruce.

"What do you want to do with these?" she asked.

"Give them to Leah," he told her, then turning to me he said, "They will further document your position."

Chris and I thanked Bruce and Phyllis for their help and walked out of his office. It was very cold as we walked across the street to where our car was parked. I went over to the driver's side door. I stopped and looked down at the envelope in my hand. The storm of emotion that had been raging inside of me broke, and I began to sob uncontrollably. Chris came around the car and embraced me and just kept saying, "I know, I know. . . ."

"I don't want these papers," I cried. "I don't want to need these papers! I want Grandma and Grandpa right, not all . . . not all confused and messed up! I don't want these papers! I don't want them. . . ."

CHAPTER 6

REMINISCENCE

With our trunk full of grocery bags loaded with everything from ground beef to ice cream, Chris and I began the half-hour drive back to my grandparents' home. We didn't speak; our normal chattiness was spent. It was late in the afternoon, and the events of the day had left us both feeling drained. I drove the car, staring blankly at the road as it stretched out before me.

My mind began to drift back to better times—times when I had rolled over that long road with Grandma and Grandpa and we had laughed and talked and theoretically solved most of the world's problems through lively speculation. The irony of the whole mess was that while a memory-robbing disease was the very thing that was pulling Grandma and Grandpa away from me, I felt like my memories were the only thing I had which still truly connected us to each other. As I drove the car toward their home, all thoughts of the present and the future seemed to melt away for a bit; only the past remained and was real.

"Sing that song I like, Grandma . . . that one about 'Ka-Ka-Ka-Katie,'" I used to request when I was very young, perhaps seven or eight years old.

"Ka-Ka-Ka-Katie, beautiful Katie. . . ." Off she'd go singing this little melody about some shy and stammering suitor. "When the mo-mo-mo-moon shines over the cow shed, I'll be waiting at the ki-ki-ki-kitchen door."

Her song would help pass the time as we covered mile after mile between Memphis and their cabin in the foothills of the Ozarks. I would feel the thrill of anticipation just before our arrival at "the place," and somewhere between Walnut Ridge and their house Grandpa would always comment, "You won't know the place, Sweet, 'cause I've been clearin' a lot of land and sowin' it with grass."

Chris's voice broke into my thoughts.

"Have you decided when we'll take them back to Memphis?"

I considered his question and realized that, while I knew they definitely had to go back to Memphis, I hadn't given any thought to the actual logistics. My full mental resources had been concentrated on going to see Bruce Hollis. Now that my appointment with him was over, I felt myself just drifting.

"What can we do with them if we go back to Memphis?" I asked, more thinking aloud rather than expecting a serious answer.

"When your mother talked with your dad last night, didn't she say he was going to make some calls today about nursing homes?"

I sighed deeply.

"Yes, she did. She said he was going to call Waverly to try to find out what they require before admitting someone to live there."

The concept of my grandparents living in a nursing home sounded appalling—no matter how good or bad the particular facility actually was—because no nursing home would ever be their *home* home. I already knew this because our family was no stranger to actual nursing home experience. Even as I was just beginning my journey as a caregiver, my maternal grandmother had been looking after her own mother for quite some time. Known throughout our family as Mother Privett, my great-grandmother was suffering from an unspecified form of dementia. Over the years, her condition had advanced to the point where she needed constant care. In the fall of 1996, only a few months before Grandma and Grandpa had taken off for Forrest City, my mom's mother had to place Mother Privett in a semi-private room at Waverly Nursing Home in Memphis.

Chris said meditatively, "I'm glad your dad's at least checking on it. That will give us an idea of what options are available." He paused, then quietly asked, "Are you OK?"

"Well, I guess so . . ." I answered, not looking at him.

"This is rough," he responded. "You're not alone, you know. It hurts me to see them like this too. Not as much as it does you, I know, but I hate it for them and for you. I think it's hard for your mom too."

"They were awfully good to her when Ray pulled his stunt. She has always said how she appreciated their kindness to her, and she's never forgotten all they did when she was going through what was probably one of the roughest times in her life." I felt like I could cry again, which was unbelievable after the flood of tears that had poured out in the lawyer's parking lot.

I didn't understand it then, but a unique grieving process had already started in me. One thing I learned during my tenure as a caregiver was that grief isn't tied solely to a loss through death. My grandparents were still physically alive, but their minds were changing in an uncontrollably negative way. Their lifestyle was undergoing an irreversible alteration which was going to affect the future for all of us. I was experiencing grief because all I could really do was watch as their minds were gradually slipping away.

For me, the reality was there would no longer be trips to Grandma's and Grandpa's Ozark home. Those wonderful days where we would sit and visit, then go walking in the woods with the dog and look at Grandpa's cows and examine Grandma's flowers—those were great days. Sometimes in the summer Grandpa would go into his garden and return with a generously proportioned watermelon, and as we munched we'd talk about whether or not they were ever going to have a paved road to replace the gravel, what kind of winter was expected, which of their neighbors had recently stopped by, and how high the price of groceries in Walnut Ridge had gone. I couldn't dare count how many days we'd spent like that, but I was fully prepared to argue there hadn't been nearly enough of them—not yet, anyway.

In saying these things, I do not mean to detract in any way from what my grandparents themselves were suffering. It must have been absolutely devastating for them when they began to realize something was happening to them, something over which they had no control at all. I recall a time during the spring of 1996, shortly before my marriage, when I was sitting with Grandma at her kitchen table. She had said to me, "I want to tell you this *while I still can*," followed by her pouring out a level of anguish over her son that had been unknown to me until that time. I remember hearing the words *while I still can* but taking no real notice of them. Was she trying to reach out for my help even then?

Having turned off of Highway 63, Chris and I headed down Highway 115, driving past the gravel road turnoff which was so familiar to me. We chose, instead, to go by way of the back road that Mack had used the day before. The way was longer around, but because there was still so much ice on the gravel, we opted for the route that was almost entirely flat and therefore manageable to my tires which didn't have chains.

We arrived back at their house just in time to start cooking dinner. Since my grandparents' car was still in Forrest City, the carport was empty. For the first time ever, I pulled my Sunbird right up into their parking space. Duchy was delighted to see us, and she skirted around everybody's feet as Grandpa and my mother helped us unload the groceries. While Mom and I put the food away, I told her all about the afternoon's events. She listened attentively, and when I was done she told me about her day.

"It's pitiful. She goes back and forth between thinking this is my house and thinking it's her momma's. I've tried to explain to her that it's her house, but she just looks at me funny, like she doesn't understand what I'm saying to her. She's sounding more and more like Mother Privett."

"Undoubtedly they're both suffering from the same type of thing. I just wish I knew more about how to respond to these off-the-wall things she's saying." I shook my head.

"What are we going to do about going home?" Mom asked.

"Chris was just asking me the same thing. I don't know. Let's wait and hear from Dad tonight, and we'll go from there."

In spite of their desire to get back to Memphis, I am very grateful to both my mother and to Chris for not pushing me harder on the issue at that time. My mind was so muddled by the shock of everything, it was a wonder I could think at all. Today, I am deeply appreciative for the gentle, prayerful guidance my family was able to provide for me, but at the time, my own angst was causing me nothing but frustration; every time I was asked when I was going to take them back to Memphis, the weight of needing to make that decision became more and more heavy.

In addressing this issue, I would urge people who are not caregivers themselves to be patient with the people who are. It's a particularly difficult role to fill because the weight of the responsibility is so great, and it's easy for an onlooker to become the proverbial armchair quarterback, criticizing the caregiver's decisions for one reason or another. I learned through experience that solutions to problematic situations were not always obvious to me, particularly in the beginning. I was aware that learning to cope and move forward in the new situation were two of the main goals, but making those adjustments was not as simple as moving from point A to point B. In those early days, it was a great blessing to have people who rallied around me, assuring me they believed I could and would make the choices that would be best for Grandma and Grandpa.

Mom and I were just getting dinner on the table when the phone rang. We correctly guessed that it was Dad. Mom answered and talked with him briefly, explaining what a very difficult day we'd both had. After a few minutes, she handed me the phone, and I listened while Dad told me about his nursing home research.

"Waverly's only requirement that the Meades don't presently meet is they have to have a three-day hospital stay before they can be admitted as residents. Medicare will pick up the nursing home's cost for the first sixty days; after that they will need to apply for Medicaid or pay out of their own pocket. Do you know if they have any insurance other than Medicare?"

"Yes," I answered, "they have a supplement."

My Dad said that, as he understood it, Medicaid in Tennessee would only pay a portion of the total monthly cost of living in a nursing home. That portion was to be based upon how much the individual could afford to pay.

"If that's the route you take, you'll have to talk to the people at Waverly for more details, but that's the general idea. Have you thought about what you're going to do?"

"I don't know," I said slowly. "I know they can't stay here anymore. I just don't know what to do with them! I wish somebody would tell me . . . something." I could feel myself crumbling again.

"OK, listen," Dad said, taking charge. "Why don't you come home and try to talk to someone who knows more about these things before you make a decision. That way, when you know more what can be done for them, you can just go back and get them and take it from there."

He made it sound so academic, so easy. It's fair to say that, while I didn't quite know what the answer *was*, I knew for a fact what the answer *wasn't*.

"Dad," I began, "they can't stay here alone."

"Can't you get their neighbor's wife to stay with them?"

Poor Dad! I was tired, I was frustrated, and I hadn't bathed in two days. On top of that, I was dealing with tough emotions regarding what was happening to Grandma and Grandpa. To say that my nerves were frayed was a bona fide understatement. I didn't respond at all well to his suggestion.

"I can't ask her to just stop her life and come here and babysit my grandparents!" My voice began to crack, and the tears were welling up. "Dad! You just don't understand the situation here. They weren't eating! They got in their car and wandered off! They could have killed themselves or even someone else! His cows are starving! She doesn't even know she's in her own house!"

Dad, realizing he was on the phone with an over-emotional woman who was blowing her cork right at him, calmly began trying to reassure me that it would all be OK. Unfortunately for him, I was in no shape to buy it.

"They are pitiful! This whole situation is pitiful!" My tears poured down like rain. It was the kind of crying outburst that makes you feel like you're going crazy. I remember staring hard at the floor, seemingly trying to convince the linoleum of how bad the situation was.

"All right, all right," Dad kept saying. "It's going to be all right. Now listen: you get some rest tonight and pray about this. God knows what needs to be done, and He's going to lead you through this. Talk it over with Chris and with Mom, and let the Lord lead you to the right decision. You can call me in the morning, and we'll do whatever needs to be done."

Dad probably felt like he was trying to talk someone down from a bridge, but even so his advice was sound. His focus has always been to point people to Jesus, no matter what the situation. His instructions acted on my brain and gave me a foundation on which to plant my weary feet. It seemed that all at once I came to myself and felt embarrassed by my outburst. I began wiping the tears off my face.

"OK," I said. "I know you're right."

"Now, I love you, and it's going to be OK, understand?"

"Yes, and I love you too. Thanks, Dad."

We hung up, and I had to sit for a minute and regroup. My mother came over to the kitchen table where I'd been talking on the phone. She sat down in Grandpa's usual chair and leaned toward me.

"He's not up here," she wisely observed. "He doesn't understand the magnitude of this situation. He'll understand once he sees them for himself."

I knew that was the absolute truth; my mother's words caused me to understand his handicap. From where he was sitting back home, only hearing about it absolutely minimized how ugly the whole mess really was.

"Thanks," I said.

"Let's eat dinner and try to forget about all this for a while."

When we called everyone to the table, Grandma rose slowly from her chair. She found her legs had stiffened from sitting for a long period of time, so she had to take short, jerky steps toward the table. As my mother stood by the stove, Grandma looked at her and said, "Judy, you have such a lovely house."

For a second, everything seemed to stop, and a heavy silence enveloped the room. Chris and I exchanged darting glances, but my mother just looked at her and said, "Well, thank you." Mom, having spent the entire day with them, had started to realize that correcting them only compounded the problem. A confrontation had been averted because she had wisely concluded that it just wasn't worth telling Grandma something she probably wouldn't even remember five minutes later.

For the second night in a row we all crowded around the small kitchen table for the evening meal, which was eaten relatively quickly. After the dishes were washed and put away, the atmosphere grew heavy under the realization that the evening was stretching out before us and there was absolutely nothing to do but sit and think.

Sometimes when an unpleasant task is looming on the horizon, it's easy to find oneself sitting and just staring into space. It's like the brain demands some sort of mental break, and it practically screams out, *Let me get away from this madness for even a short period of time!* As I sat and stared at nothing in particular during that long evening, I remember thinking, *Lord, You've got to show me what to do!*

I felt that my petition may have gotten as high as the ceiling—but no further. It was one of those moments when I had the impression that God simply wasn't listening. Every prayer I uttered seemed to be met with a dead silence. However, in spite of the way I *felt*, I resolved that I would continue to stand on faith, believing God would direct me in taking the next step. I confess the trust I had was based more on what God *had done* in the past, as opposed to an *expectation* for Him to act in the future. I knew this was no time to be doubting God or wondering about His ability to care for me or my grandparents, so I began to look at scriptures which focused on Him never leaving us:

And surely I am with you always, to the very end of the age. (Matthew 28:20)

I also remembered how God had promised to be with Moses and the Israelites when He said,

My Presence will go with you . . . (Exodus 33:14 NKJV)

Looking back, I can confidently say that my trust in the Lord was not misplaced; honestly, believing in the promises found in God's Word was the only way I survived in the caregiver wilderness.

After I had been pouring over the scriptures for quite a while, it still seemed like the clock was moving so slowly it would never be time for bed. As the minutes ticked away at a snail's pace, I found myself involuntarily reminiscing about times in the past when I had come over to visit with Grandma and Grandpa.

During the summer, we would go outside after dinner and sit on the carport. We'd listen to the tree frogs and various insects singing their evening songs, and we'd talk about whatever happened to pass through our minds. After it got dark, we would head inside, and Grandpa would sit in his recliner trying to stay awake—not an easy task for someone who routinely got up around 4:30 a.m. He would nod off as Grandma and I talked, then wake up and make his nightly announcement that he was "gonna have to call it," and off he'd go to bed after giving me a goodnight kiss and draping his shirt over the back of his kitchen chair. I felt a smile come to my lips as I remembered one time he went to bed, then returned about five minutes later; he walked straight over to me and said, "I forgot to get my sugar!" He then leaned down and kissed my cheek, and I remembered reaching up, hugging his neck, and kissing him back. His affection for me was deeply appreciated and overwhelmingly reciprocated.

My memories continued to ramble until Chris let out an exhausted yawn which brought me back to the present.

"Are you folks ready for bed?" he asked.

Everyone admitted to being very tired, and we each got up and went to our respective rooms. Grandma didn't mention "going home" that night, and I was so grateful to not have to fight that battle.

I went down the hall and peered around the corner into my grandparents' room. Grandpa was in their bathroom, and Grandma was sitting on the edge of the bed.

"Goodnight, Grandma," I said, smiling at her. She looked up and smiled back at me.

"Goodnight, Sweet. You have a real good night, hear?"

"You too!"

Grandpa emerged from the bathroom.

"Goodnight, Grandpa."

He looked up and walked toward me to give me my "sugar."

"Goodnight, Sweet," he said as he kissed my cheek.

I kissed him back and said, "Have a good night."

I went into our bedroom and just looked at Chris. "What in the world will I do on the day they don't remember to say that to me anymore?"

CHAPTER 7

GOING HOME

I think the most blissful time of day must be those very first waking moments when the mind is just beginning to stir. Even before one's eyes open, the consciousness begins to separate itself from sleep, and in those first few seconds, one feels that all is well with the world. Saturday, January 18, 1997, began for me that way. My eyes opened slowly, and although I could feel the extreme cold on my face, my first thoughts were calm and serene. The room was dim, and the early morning silence was heavy. No one was stirring around as of yet, although I thought it unlikely that Grandpa wasn't already awake and moving very quietly.

Chris apparently woke up about the same time I did. He propped himself up on one elbow and punched his pillow a couple of times.

"Good morning," I said quietly.

"Hi," he answered. "Did I wake you up?"

"No, I woke up on my own. How'd you sleep?"

"Not so great. I miss our bed." He paused and adjusted the sheets. "I've been wondering what today's going to be all about."

"I can't imagine. I don't want to even think about it right now." I paused and then changed the subject. "I don't think keeping that door open last night made a bit of difference—it's still freezing in here!"

I heard the faint beginnings of movement in the bedroom across the hall. The sound of a light step told me that it was Grandpa getting dressed for the day. After a minute or so, he walked by our bedroom door on his way to the living room to start the morning fire. Chris and I lay very still and listened to him moving the wood from the storage bin into the belly of the stove. Then we could hear the striking of the match and the crackling noise that came from the dried wood as it started to burn. Grandpa then passed our door again as he returned to his bedroom. The tranquility of our morning was shattered with what we heard next.

"Daddy?" Grandma's voice floated into our room. "Daddy, is that you?"

"What, Sweet?" Grandpa responded.

"Is that you, Daddy?" she asked again.

A nervous rush passed through my body which made me feel almost panicked. Grandma had *never* called her husband "Daddy." She called him "Sweet" most of the time, or "Edward" when she was upset with his driving. When she was talking about him to me, she would call him "Grandpa," but never before had she ever called him "Daddy." As I lay there listening from across the hall, I knew exactly who she was calling for: her own father, Joseph Archer, a man who had been dead for the last twelve years.

Grandpa responded to her with a gentle, loving voice, conversing with her in a non-threatening way. He didn't seem to realize who she was actually calling for, and that fact somehow added to the incident's nightmarish feel.

"Sweet, are you ready to get up?" he asked her.

There was a fairly long silence. I suddenly realized that I felt like I was watching a play. Surely these were actors playing roles, and one of them had simply forgotten the lines. I grew anxious to know what would happen next.

"OK," Grandma finally said, and I could hear Grandpa helping her move the sheets.

"Daddy," she said again. I winced involuntarily.

"Hmmm?"

"I love you, Daddy."

"I love you too," Grandpa replied.

Tears pricked my eyes with a stinging vengeance—honestly, I don't think I'd ever cried so much in my life as I did during that three-day period. Chris must have felt the anguish pour out of me because he reached over and squeezed my hand.

"Oh, God, *what* am I going to do about this?" I whispered.

Chris launched his best effort to console me.

"It's OK, it's OK. We're going to get them the help they need."

"Doesn't he know she's not talking to him?" I asked anxiously. "Doesn't he understand she's calling for her father?"

Chris sighed deeply and said, "I don't know. I just don't know."

I lay there motionless, impaired by the shock of Grandma's words. She didn't say anything more as Grandpa helped her get into the dress that was now being worn for at least the fourth day straight. As warm, salty tears rolled down from my eyes to my pillow, I heard Grandma get up from the bed and walk to her bathroom. There followed a variety of unidentifiable noises as she moved things around on her vanity. After she ran some water from the tap, it happened. She uttered those totally unforgettable words:

"These your teeth?"

Let me try to describe that moment. I was crushed by what I had just overheard, being so harshly confronted by the fact that Grandma didn't recognize her own husband; then, right in the middle of that devastating dialogue, she suddenly wanted to know *whose teeth* were in the glass on the vanity. Although I had known for many years that both of my grandparents wore false teeth, the thought of needing to identify the rightful owner of a particular set of dentures had never entered my mind. I was overwhelmed with the urge to laugh out loud.

Chris was struck with the humor of the moment just like I was, but he was afraid to start laughing because he didn't know if I had found it funny as well. Not wanting to offend me, yet feeling like he would explode if he tried to stifle his laughter, Chris held his breath for a few seconds, hoping the moment would pass. But the giggling simply would not be put down, and the whole bed began to shake as he fought back the urge to let it all out.

I turned my head to look at him, and that was all we needed. The two of us lay in that bed and laughed for a solid five minutes. The fact that we didn't want to be heard laughing only made it worse. We were biting fingers and burying our faces in the pillows in an effort to protect the early morning quiet of that house, and just as we would start to compose ourselves, one of us would let out another giggle, and the whole thing would start all over again.

The laughter proved to be very cleansing, and, oddly enough, it made the conversation between Grandma and Grandpa somehow more bearable. The pitiful pledge of love and the overwhelmingly funny question of dental ownership are bound inseparably in my memory. As strange as it may sound, I thank God for the opportunity to experience laughter on the heels of that horrible exchange. I need to be clear that we were not laughing *at* Grandma or her state of mind at the time; our laughter was an emotional outlet, a way of releasing the tensions that had built up within both of us.

As we finally began to settle down, we realized the sun had risen and its light was streaming through our window. We got dressed and went into the living room where the bustle of the day had already begun. I found Grandpa making his coffee, and my mom was preparing breakfast. Duchy was in position at Mom's feet, waiting for some scrap of breakfast to hit the floor. One look at my mother's face told me she was positively exhausted.

"I would ask how you slept, but I think I already know the answer," I said.

"That couch ought to be taken out to the back forty and shot!" she said firmly. "They've had it for longer than I've known them. It's worn out, and so am I!"

"I'm sorry. If it helps any to hear this, I really appreciate you being here." I moved a little closer to her and lowered my voice. "Did you hear them in there this morning?"

My mother seemed to go pale as she turned to me.

"Yes," she stated emphatically, "I did. It was. . . ." Her voice broke off, and I watched her face as her eyes filled with tears. When she spoke again, her voice was almost a whisper: "pitiful."

I could see how deeply my mother had been affected by the condition of her former in-laws. I got a box of tissues, and we stood there in front of Grandma's stove and cried together.

Unaware of the conversation between my mother and me, Chris came in from the living room and announced with a chuckle, "My hair is finding new directions to lay for every day I don't shower—"

He broke off abruptly upon finding two weepy women sharing a box of tissues.

"I'm sorry . . . uh. . . ." He paused, looking from me to my mother then back to me again. "What's happened?"

"Ooohh," Mom said as she wiped her eyes, "I'm just going all to pieces and wearing everybody out."

"She is not," I countered. "We were just talking about this morning."

"Oh." Chris gave an understanding nod. "That was awful. But did you hear what she said at the end of it all?" Chris recounted in detail the utterly hilarious "these your teeth" story, including a thorough description of our reaction to it. My mother laughed out loud, and I could see that she, too, needed the wash of humor to ease the anxiety she had been feeling.

"Well, bless her heart, she's just going through something awful," Mom said.

There was no hesitation as Chris and I agreed with her. Mom and I both wiped our eyes again, and then we moved on to finish preparing breakfast.

When the meal was over, I found myself looking at a day with no preplanned agenda. After we got Grandma seated in her usual chair, Grandpa walked out on the carport. It was then that Mom, Chris, and I sat down at the kitchen table to form a plan for the day.

It's hard to describe what happened to me at that kitchen table. One second, I was directionless, existing in a sort of mental fog. The very next second, I knew exactly what had to be done. The realization was so quick and logical there was no way for me to think it was anything short of the Holy Spirit doing precisely what God's Word says He will do—leading me in the exact way I needed to go. But while the decision to return to Memphis had become very clear, the plan's logistics took a little longer to work through.

"It's time to go to Memphis," I said decisively. "Dad said in order for them to be eligible to move into Waverly, they will have to have a three-day hospital stay, so that's where we'll start. We'll take them to one of the hospitals in Memphis and let the doctors there do a more thorough exam on both of them."

"So, are you going to go the nursing home route?" Chris asked.

"I don't want to," I said. "I'll fight it off until I've exhausted every other possibility. We'll just take it one day at a time. Today's project is to get them to Memphis." I took a deep breath as I turned to look at Grandma. "And I don't know how we're going to do that."

"That's the truth," Mom said emphatically. "What can we tell them? We can't just say we're going back to Memphis and they have to come along. They'll never go for that."

Once again, I was forced to acknowledge the moral dilemma which had been looming over me for months: how could I explain to my grandparents that they had reached a point where they needed my help? Everyone wants to feel they are in control of what they do and where they go; to paraphrase William Ernest Henley's *Invictus*, we each want to be "masters of our own fate" and "captains of our own souls." The trouble was obvious; dementia had rendered Grandma and Grandpa mentally incapacitated. They were no longer in full possession of their faculties, and they lacked the competence to make decisions for themselves, but at the same time, they weren't comatose. How, then, to help them?

"What if we just say to them, 'Look, this is just the way it is!'" Chris asked boldly, but a frown crossed his face as soon as he said it. "No. Too rude and confrontational."

"Why don't you just tell them you're taking them to another doctor?" my mother proposed.

"After the way they acted Thursday in Donnelly's office?" Chris asked. "That'll never fly. Maybe we could tell them we're going to get their car."

"Grandpa would go willingly," I said, "but I bet Grandma would try to stay here. And anyway, I don't want to lie to them."

"Well, you're running out of options then," Chris stated flatly. "There's not very much of the truth you can tell them and expect them to even understand, let alone cooperate with."

I really hated the validity of Chris's statement, but I knew he was right. They were past reasoning with.

"So what do you want me to do?" I snapped out irritably. "Kidnap them?"

Three days in the trenches had taken their toll. We had reached a point where we just wanted it to get better so we could all go home, and they could get back to their normal lives—even though we really knew their "normal" lives were over. Combine all of that with a lack of sound sleep, no showers, and weird food groupings, and you had three people who were moody and unraveled—and tired of playing nice with each other.

"All right, look," my mother, edgy, but taking the high road, interjected. "We need to ask the Lord to show us what to do about this." She leaned back in her chair away from the table and let her hands fall into her lap.

"Yes," Chris said, agreeing with her. "He'll have to show us what to do here."

I turned sideways in my chair and took another deep breath. In my heart, I was looking at God a little bit like a child who doesn't quite trust what she sees. My mind had become a veritable junk room of fear, doubt, heartache, and exasperation. My brain went into overdrive churning out possible scenarios to get Grandma and Grandpa on board with going to Memphis, but absolutely nothing was making sense as I strained my own imagination for a solution to the present difficulty. In a matter of seconds, my frenzied thoughts had spun out, and my mind eventually got quiet. God knew I had finally come to the end of myself, and this allowed His Spirit to softly, sweetly wrap me in His presence. He directed my weary eyes around the room until they came to rest on Grandma—*and her glasses.*

"She still needs those glasses fixed," I said slowly.

Chris's head came up quickly, and he and my mother looked over at Grandma simultaneously.

"That's absolutely it," Chris said. "Since they didn't get fixed Thursday, we can tell them we're going to take them someplace else to get them fixed today."

"That works!" my mother said.

"Wait a minute," Chris said, looking at me. "Five people and a dog can't all go back to Memphis in your Sunbird. We just won't fit."

"Oh, nuts," I mumbled.

"No, that's OK," Mom piped up. "We'll call Dad. He can bring his car up here."

"That's a great idea," Chris said.

"Yes, it is," I agreed, "especially since Dad's car is bigger. It'll be a much easier ride for Grandma and Grandpa."

Mom went to call Dad right away, and she explained to him what we had planned to do. It was arranged that we would meet Dad in the restaurant of the motel in Imboden at 11 o'clock.

"That will give Chris and me time to go to Walnut Ridge to get Grandma a new dress or two," I said.

Mom agreed.

"Oh, yes, a new dress is a must," she said with a grimace.

"And let's not say anything to Grandma and Grandpa until your Dad gets here," Chris added. "No reason to rock their boat."

We cleared the table, washed the breakfast dishes, then each took our turn in front of the kitchen sink for the daily "spit" bath. Even my clean clothes didn't feel that fresh since I wasn't actually getting a good wash-off in the shower. I did the best I could to wash my face, though, and fresh make-up on a clean face would ease the discomfort a little bit. As I blotted my face dry, I glanced out the window and saw Grandpa's cows up by the fence again.

"Did Mack happen to mention when he'd be here with the grain for the cows?" I asked Mom.

"He said he would go get it first thing this morning," she replied.

"OK," I said as I folded my towel. "I'm going to leave you some of their cash to pay him back for what he spends on the grain. Ask him how much he bought and how long it will last. I'd like to avoid being blindsided again by those cows needing feed."

"Good idea."

"Oh—and be sure to ask him for the receipt," I said.

Chris and I got into the car and headed toward Walnut Ridge for the third day in a row. We drove straight to Walmart with the intention of picking up some essentials for Grandma. We found a red dress with a light floral print, which I thought would work fine. I held it up to my shoulders and asked Chris what he thought.

"It looks a little long," he said.

I agreed, but I didn't see anything else that would even come close to something she'd wear, and she just had to change the dress she'd been in for nearly a week. I also added two packages of underwear and a pair of soft, flexible shoes to our cart. I had assumed that if all of Grandma's clothes were in Forrest City then her underwear was probably there as well. As for her shoes, the ones Grandma had been wearing were leaving red marks on her feet, and, although she hadn't complained, I thought they must be painful for her.

We paid for the dress and accessories then drove back to Imboden where we had arranged to meet Dad. When we arrived at the motel, I parked my car where he would be sure to see it as he drove in. Chris and I went into the small restaurant at the front of the building and sat down at a table. I ordered a cup of coffee then leaned back in the chair and closed my eyes.

"What have we gotten into, Chris?"

He sighed deeply and said, "Girl, I don't know, but it really is going to be OK."

"How do you know?"

"Because God's taken care of everything up to this point. And He's going to keep on taking care of everything. You've got to know that and hang on to it."

The coffee came, and I found myself intensely watching the black liquid turn to light brown as I poured in the cream, and I observed how smooth the whirlpool motion was as I ran the spoon around the cup's rim over and over. Chris, too, seemed mesmerized by the simplicity of the stirring. We sat in silence for some minutes, completely enjoying that period of time where no one wanted anything from either of us. I closed my eyes, tilting my head back to rest it against the chair. I then slowly opened my eyes and stared at the ceiling.

"They're leaving here forever today," I said quietly. "They'll never be able to come back. Not ever."

"I know," Chris responded.

All the years of "going to Grandma's" flashed into my mind in a jumbled collage. Memories long forgotten rose into focus then blurred into obscurity: the funny little barber shop in Imboden where Grandpa got his hair cut; the big, white house on the east side of Highway 63; how I had learned to drive a car by going back and forth on their gravel road as Grandpa admonished me to "keep your left foot off that brake!" Roses for Grandma's birthday and fruit baskets for Grandpa at Christmas—there really was no time in my life where I couldn't find memories of Grandma and Grandpa.

As my eyes became focused again in the present, I saw my Dad's car drive up and park beside mine. I looked resolutely at Chris and said, "Time to go."

We arrived back at my grandparents' house not very long after Mack Proctor had come in with the grain. Grandma had to be reminded about who Dad was, but Grandpa seemed to recognize him immediately, just as he had my mother. It was time for lunch, so Mom was busy in the kitchen getting the food ready. We invited Mack to eat with us, but he declined, having already had his mid-day meal.

"I'm going to wait until you all leave to start feeding the cows," Mack told me quietly. "I don't want to risk upsetting Mr. Meade."

"That's probably a good idea," I said.

I gave Mack the money for the grain and got the receipt from him. While we were talking about how much grain he'd purchased and how long it would last, Grandma got up from her chair and walked into the formal living room at the front of the house where my mother had been sleeping. Chris and I both glanced after her then looked at each other. Curious to know what she was doing, Chris got up from his chair and followed her. Some minutes went by, and as Mack and I continued to talk, Chris came out of the living room and went into the kitchen. The look on his face puzzled me, so I excused myself from Mack and followed him. I found him leaning with his back against the sink; his head was down, and his arms were folded tightly across his chest.

"What's wrong?" I quietly asked as I approached him.

He looked up at me; his eyes were tired, but I could see there was something more than just that. He looked grieved.

"She was looking in that cabinet with the glass doors, the one where she has all her dolls with the dresses she's made. She was bent over looking at them, so I asked her if she wanted me to open the doors so she could see them better. She just stood up and looked at me and said, 'No, I just want to take a last look. I'm going to have to leave here soon.'" He paused and looked me straight in my eyes. "It's like she *knows!*"

I just stood there staring for a minute. My mind was racing, wondering if she really knew she was about to leave her home forever or if she just thought she and Grandpa were about to "go home" to the mystery location she'd been pining for ever since we'd arrived on Thursday.

My mother came into the kitchen from the pantry and saw us talking. Chris began to tell her what had happened. I couldn't listen to it again, so I turned and went into the little living room and found Grandma standing by the cabinet just as Chris had said. I stood in the door and watched her for a moment, not knowing what to say to her. Then she turned and saw me.

"Hi, Sweet!" she said pleasantly.

I went over to her and put my arm around her shoulder.

"How are you doing?" I asked with false energy, demanding of my muscles to put a smile on my face.

"Oh, I'm fine," she said.

I felt the tears prick my eyes again. The lump rose in my throat, and for a second I didn't know if I could hold it in.

"Are you ready for lunch?" I asked.

We went into the kitchen, and I held Grandma's arm as Chris and my dad moved the table away from the wall. We had so many people eating that day that we needed all four sides of the table.

As we crowded around for lunch that day it occurred to me that it really was our last meal together at that table. In terms of monetary value, the table was worth very little; but thanks to our treasured memories, it was priceless. That was the table where Grandma had frequently announced, "I just can't eat," followed closely by her reaching for the pie plate or the cake dome or the cookie bag. Grandpa and I had played countless games of checkers and various card games at that table. It was the place where we had sliced watermelons, peeled peaches, snapped beans and cut cantaloupe. Every letter Grandma ever wrote to me was penned at that table. Privy to our deepest thoughts, that kitchen table was a silent listener as Grandma and I had talked late into the night while indulging together in some form of chocolate. And now, with one final lunch, sitting around the Meade kitchen table was going to quietly recede into the past and would only exist in my memory.

Despite our imminent departure, conversation flowed along surface lines as we ate, and once all the appetites had been satisfied, my mother and I cleared the table and washed the dishes. As the last plates were put away, we began to discuss how to get Grandma into her new dress.

"She'll probably need a sponge bath," Mom said.

"Yeah," I agreed. "Let's heat some water, and I'll get a washcloth and towels."

"We can go into her bedroom to do it," Mom suggested. "I imagine she'll be as comfortable sitting on her bed as she would be anywhere else."

We gathered the necessary items, and then I went into the living room to get her, never dreaming there would be a problem.

"Grandma, can you come with me? I've got a clean dress ready for you in the bedroom."

She got up and came with me willingly enough. She walked into the bedroom and looked at my mother.

"Hello," she said politely.

I deliberately chose to overlook the fact that, yet again, she didn't seem to know who my mother was.

"I bought you this new dress," I began in a cheery voice. "Let's do a quick sponge bath and then you can put it on. I bet it'll feel better than this one you've been wearing all week."

I walked over to the pan of water and put the washcloth in. As I did so, my mother stepped toward her and said, "Let me help you out of this dress."

I cannot describe the look of fear that went over Grandma's face. Her eyes got wide, and she took two huge steps backwards and drew her hand up to her throat. She looked like she thought she was being attacked.

"Oh no!" she announced firmly. "I can't do that!"

I held up the dress to show it to her. "Grandma, it's just a clean dress. I bought it for you this morning."

"Huh-uh! I can't wear that dress!" she said.

"But Grandma—"

"Forget it." My mother cut me off in a lowered voice. "She's not going to do it."

Mom stepped away from her, and Grandma slowly turned and left the room. I stood frozen, staring in shock at the empty doorway.

"What in the world . . . ?" I said slowly.

Chris came down the hall and stuck his head in the door. "You know she's back out here?"

"Oh, yes," I said with a sharp nod of my head. "She went over the wall."

"Oh," he responded.

As my mother picked up the pan of water and took it into their bathroom, he asked, "You don't want to try and bring her back?"

My frustrated mother said irritably, "No. Just let her stay in that dress."

I explained to Chris what had happened. He just sighed and shook his head.

"I'll take the dress to Memphis. Maybe someone in the hospital there can get her into it," I said, folding the garment into a small bundle.

"Speaking of which," Mom interposed, "what hospital are you planning on taking them to?"

A debate ensued as to which Memphis hospital would be the best place for us to go. Presbyterian Hospital was the one we were the most familiar with; however, I had often heard Grandma remark that she liked the Winchester Hospital, which was a little more out of the way from our route into the city. So, based purely on emotions, my first thought was to go to Winchester. My mother cautiously advised that Presbyterian might be better.

"Listen," she said, choosing her words with care, "Presbyterian is closer. We know how to get around Presbyterian. And besides," she paused, "she won't really know. . . ."

I remember staring at the floor. The reality of their situation was dawning on me once again. Mom was right; Grandma would never know.

"Yes," I said quietly. "I know you're right. I just want to do for her . . . the way she'd want things done."

"I know you do," Mom said gently, "but because she won't know the difference, it would be better to go to a place where you're familiar with the lay of the land. You're under enough pressure as it is. Don't add to that by going to a hospital you're unfamiliar with."

Anyone who has ever worn the "caregiver hat" will understand that emotions can figure prominently in the decision-making process, even though you never mean for that to happen. If you truly love the person for whom you're caring, you can be overwhelmed with the desire to do what you think they'd want you to do rather than doing what would be the most practical. I was very blessed to have my mother sharing her concerns and reasoning with me in such a logical way. Her statements were non-threatening and inoffensive as she made her point. Unable to find any better alternative, I agreed that the emergency room of Presbyterian Hospital was the best choice for everybody.

It was decided that Chris and I would take Grandma and Grandpa in Dad's car, and Mom, Dad, and Duchy would go in my car. When I explained to Grandma and Grandpa that I wanted to take them to another doctor to get Grandma's glasses fixed, they agreed at once. While Grandpa went to change clothes for the trip, Grandma sat in her chair watching Chris and Dad carry the suitcases out to the cars. I could tell by the look on her face that she didn't comprehend what was going on.

In all honesty, though, Grandpa was the one we were worried about. We didn't want him to see us packing up because we were afraid that if he saw our luggage he might realize the unnamed destination was actually Memphis. After his belligerence in Dr. Donnelly's office, we were concerned that he would argue energetically and unreasonably against going to Memphis. I could just imagine him insisting there was nothing wrong and therefore there was no reason for them to leave. Our secrecy was never intended as deliberate deception but rather a peaceful means to provide the help they truly needed.

Just as we were taking a final look around to make sure the house was locked up and lights were turned out, the telephone rang. I answered and heard an unfamiliar woman's voice.

"Clara?" the lady asked.

"No, this is Leah," I said, still unsure who I was talking to.

"Oh! Leah, this is Harriet, Jack's wife."

Jack Swain was Grandma's nephew. I hadn't seen him or his wife for several years, but I knew they had kept in touch with Grandma. She expressed surprise at my answering the phone, so I began to explain what had happened.

"Are they OK?" she asked quickly.

"Well, yes and no. We're leaving for Memphis today. There's no way they can continue living over here alone."

"Well, bless your heart," she said. "I know this is rough for you."

"Yes," I said to Harriet. "I really hate to see them like this."

"Where are you going to take them? Do you think they'll have to go into a nursing home?"

I briefly explained the plan we had outlined. "I'm just going to let the doctors tell me what they think, and we'll make some decision from there. I don't want to go to a nursing home if we can help it."

For the first time, I heard myself talking about it as if *I* were the one whose lifestyle was on the line.

Harriet sighed heavily. She paused for a minute, and then she said something which made an indelible impression on me. "What you're about to go through is going to be ugly. I don't envy you. But they love you, and they trust you. I know you'll do what's right for them."

"Well, I'm going to do my very best for them," I said solemnly.

It then dawned on me that Harriet could actually do me a huge favor. Grandma's sister, Lena, was Harriet's mother-in-law. I thought Harriet could help me out by telling Lena what was happening, so I asked her if she'd give Lena a call.

"I'd be glad to," Harriet said. "Is there anything else I can do to help?"

"Not anything I know of at the moment, but who knows? I'm having to take this deal one step at a time."

She gave me her phone number and told me to call her if there was anything she could do. I scribbled the number down and stuffed it into my purse. After we hung up, Mom, Dad, Chris, and I all gave each other a set of reassuring nods then put the wheels of departure in motion.

Grandma gathered her coat and purse while Grandpa slipped on his jacket. I pulled Mack Proctor aside one last time.

"Please look after Duke," I said quietly. "It's funny that they were out of food for themselves, but there's lots of dog food; and if you have to buy more before we come back, I'll certainly reimburse you."

I also asked Mack if he would be able to keep an eye on the house and pick up their mail. I hated for it to just pile up in the box, telling the world there was nobody home. Even though we knew bills like utilities and insurance would keep coming, we had decided not to deal with forwarding their mail until we had a better idea of what was going to happen. At that point, the most logical thing to do was take care of them first and their paper trail second. I was beginning to realize I couldn't do everything at once; some things were just going to have to wait.

Mack said he was happy to help any way he could. I thanked him again for all he'd done for us; he humbly told me not to give it another thought. I turned around to see that Grandma and Grandpa were in the car and Chris was waiting for me to get in so he could shut my door.

"Goodbye, Mack."

He gave a nod and a wave of his hand as we backed away from the house.

And so we left. Grandma sat beside me in the passenger seat, and Grandpa sat with Chris in the back. I knew I could not reveal in my face or body language that this was anything other than a normal trip into town. But for Chris, my parents, and me it was not at all normal. Our hearts were very heavy as we drove away because each of us knew it was the absolute last time they'd ever see the Arkansas home they'd worked so hard to establish.

As we headed east away from the house, we drove by the row of pine trees Grandpa had planted when I was little. I remembered how Grandpa had diligently dug each hole and Grandma had handed him one tender little plant after the other until a long strip of pines was established. The wind had been cold that day, and I remembered Grandma standing with her back to the wind and me squarely in front of her, shielding me from the frigid gusts; but I hadn't cared how cold or windy it was. All that had mattered to me was that I was there with them, doing what they liked to do.

We jostled and jolted along over that gravel road, leaving behind all that was so familiar to me. We passed by the next property over from Grandma and Grandpa—the one with the pretty pond. After that came Mack Proctor's house on the south side of the road, and then the little white church, complete with cemetery, followed by assorted barns, farmhouses, and crooked fences. Finally we came to Highway 115, and, just like the drive over the gravel, every familiar turn in the road made me feel like I was leaving something behind. Even though I knew I'd have to make more trips back to their house in the upcoming weeks, as far as I was concerned I was saying goodbye forever because I knew without them over there it wouldn't be "Grandma's and Grandpa's" anymore.

We rode through Imboden and Black Rock in silence, but by the time we approached Hoxie, a small town which adjoins Walnut Ridge, Grandpa began to ask me what doctor I was going to take Grandma to.

"Don't worry, Grandpa," I said, trying to sound confident. "It's a good place I know of, and they have very good doctors."

When we reached the Jonesboro city limit, Grandpa again asked where we were going. I wanted to avoid a scene like we'd had in Donnelly's office, so I again gave him an evasive answer. "I promise they'll take good care of Grandma. She'll have new glasses before you know it."

My answer seemed to appease him, but guilt was beginning to roll in on me like the flood stage of a river. My thoughts were in knots as I drove that car straight toward Memphis. At times, my fingers gripped the steering wheel so tightly I thought my knuckles might pop through my skin. At one point, I found my jaws were clenched tightly together and the muscles in my abdomen were flexed hard.

"I think you're going to Memphis, aren't you?" Grandpa said suddenly—his perception startled me.

I felt the rush of adrenalin shoot through my body as I searched my mind for a suitable answer. "You'll see," I said as I looked into the back seat with a forced smile.

This had to be what people meant when they used the phrase "tough love." Over the last three days, I had repeatedly evaded giving truthful answers to questions from either Grandma or Grandpa. To my mind, that was tantamount to lying. The good news for them was they weren't remembering each time it happened—but *my* memory was spot-on, and I knew *every time* I had side-stepped openly discussing what was going to happen. I have always been a truthful person, so I was agonizing over the flagrant deception in which I saw myself engaged. At that early date, I had not yet been told that "therapeutic lying" was just about the only recourse I would have to keep the peace. In the meantime, loving them meant I had to make a painfully hard decision for them: the decision to bring them to Memphis so they could receive the help they so obviously needed.

We were riding smoothly along Interstate 55, passing through Marion and then through West Memphis as we approached the Hernando de Soto Bridge. I could see the downtown Memphis skyline appear on the horizon in front of us. As we crossed from Arkansas over the Tennessee state line, I reached over and lovingly patted Grandma's hand.

"Welcome home," I whispered.

CHAPTER 8

ADMISSION

We entered Presbyterian Hospital through its emergency room doors just like we had done at the clinic in Walnut Ridge. I let Chris get Grandma and Grandpa seated in the waiting room while I went up to the nurse in the triage area. With the durable power of attorney papers and Dr. Donnelly's letters ready in my hand, I started to explain our situation to the nurse.

"So let me understand," the nurse said. "They're not here because they want to be here. Is that right?"

"Yes," I said, then added quickly, "but I am empowered to act for them. I've already had them examined by a doctor in Walnut Ridge, Arkansas, and I have his statements here." I paused as I laid the envelopes on the desk. "I'm planning to move them permanently to Memphis; we've come here as a starting point. We really need help."

The nurse seemed to grow impatient.

"Ma'am, we can't admit someone against their will. If they don't want to be admitted, there's nothing I can do."

I couldn't believe what I was hearing. Out of sheer frustration, I pushed my arsenal of papers closer to her.

"Will you please look at these letters? They are suffering with advanced forms of dementia!" I stated firmly. "They have been legally recognized as incompetent to properly care for themselves. I legally have durable power of attorney for them, and I am asking you to have a doctor look at them."

I started talking faster as my anger and frustration rose. "I can't do anything about providing care for them until someone looks at them and gives me some options. They've got Medicare and a supplemental insurance. You'll get paid, but we've got to have some help!"

To this day, I'm not sure if it was my frantic attitude that made the nurse want to shut me up or if it was the promise of sure payment that opened the door, but all at once the nurse's tune changed.

"All right," she said, glancing over the papers. "We'll get them into a room and have one of the ER staff physicians look at them."

"Uh, there may be a slight problem if you try to get both of them back here at the same time." I told her about how they had resisted the doctor's attempt to put Grandma in the hospital in Walnut Ridge, and I further explained that we had to use her broken glasses as our excuse for going to a doctor in the first place.

"Basically my grandfather thinks he's here only to be with my grandmother. He doesn't realize. . . ." I faltered, unsure if I could finish my own sentence without breaking down again. I swallowed forcibly and said, "He doesn't know he needs help too."

"OK, we'll get her back here, and you can explain it all to the doctor," she said.

I went back over to where they were all sitting. My mother came over to me and said, "I'm going to stay here with you, but Dad's taking Duchy home. He's going to feed her, and then he'll be back."

Chris came over and stood with us.

"What's happening?" he asked.

I explained the scene between the nurse and me. "She's either never been in a situation like this, or she's just crazy," I said with aggravation. "She made me feel like I didn't have any business being here."

My initial experience in the emergency room left me feeling like there was no help for us. If they wouldn't admit my grandparents, I truly didn't know where we could go next. Unfortunately that nurse had no idea what our situation was or what we had been through over the last three days, and the feeling I got from her was one of apathy; she didn't seem interested in digging deeper to find out what was going on. Today I can look back and see things with much more clarity; in truth, I don't believe the nurse intended to be rude or unhelpful. Rather, I believe she had a set protocol for ER admissions, and she was trying to use a cookie-cutter approach with me. I imagine I was as frustrating to her as she had seemed to me, but all I could feel at the time was anger and a sense of hopelessness.

As I stood between Chris and my mother to regroup, the nurse signaled to me that we should come on to the back with Grandma. I took a deep breath.

"They're ready for us," I said as I reached out for Grandma's hand.

I asked my mother to stay out in the waiting room with Grandpa while Chris and I walked into the triage area with Grandma between us. The nurse put us in a room and said the doctor would be in shortly. Someday I'm going to have to try to find out exactly how many minutes there are in a medical professional's "shortly."

While we were waiting, Chris and I were conversing in low tones. Grandma seemed unaware that we were even talking. All of a sudden, she sat up very straight and announced firmly: "Leah, I've got to go!"

She had been patient for some time, but once her patience ran out, we found ourselves racking our brains, trying to think of a reasonable and peaceful way to keep her in that room. She started to get up from the examination table, so I moved quickly toward her.

"Grandma, it won't be much longer," I said soothingly. "We just have to wait for the doctor."

"I can't sit here like this," she said in an almost whiney voice. "I'm just too nervous!"

"Well, what are you nervous about?"

"I've got to go home," she insisted. "I've got things to do!"

"It's OK, Grandma," I said quietly. I was entirely too exhausted to be very imaginative and was having a really hard time countering her arguments. I just didn't know what to say to her. She, however, still had plenty to say.

"Grandpa's gonna need supper! I've got to go home. Let's go!"

"We won't be in here very long," I said, looking over at Chris. He could see my frustration, but he didn't know any more than I did what to say to her. He put his hand on my back but didn't say a thing.

All at once Grandma calmed down. Her facial muscles relaxed, and her expression became almost tranquil. I climbed up onto the examination table and sat down beside her. I patted her knee softly; she reached over and squeezed my hand. I looked at Chris.

"Go see if you can find out what's taking so long," I said, almost whispering between clenched teeth.

He nodded and walked out. Grandma and I sat quietly for a couple of minutes, then Chris came back in with a young man who was wearing a lab coat. We spoke quietly with him, briefly explaining everything we knew about what had happened with my grandparents over the last seven days.

"Let me talk with your grandmother for a minute or so to see what we're up against, then we'll go from there," he said.

GOODNIGHT, SWEET

Chris and I stood outside the open door and listened while the doctor questioned Grandma.

"Mrs. Meade, can you tell me your first name?"

"Clara," she answered right away.

"All right," the doctor said. "Mrs. Meade, what year is this?"

"Nineteen seventy. . . ." She paused, trailing her voice. "Seven!"

"OK. And who is the president?"

"Jimmy Carter," she said confidently.

"And where do you live?"

"Over on Dunn."

While it was true that she had lived there once, the Dunn Avenue address hadn't been her home for decades.

"What city is that in?"

"Memphis, Tennessee."

"Have you ever lived in Arkansas?"

"No."

Chris and I sharply exchanged glances.

"You're kidding!" I mumbled involuntarily. Nearly twenty years of her life gone from her memory, just like that.

"All right," the doctor continued, "can you tell me your birthday?"

"August 5, 1908."

The doctor turned and gave me a questioning look. I nodded.

I am at somewhat of a loss to fully describe how I felt in that moment. It was like that whacked-out conversation had changed something in my perception; the world no longer seemed to be clearly defined. I felt like everything was blurred and confused. I rolled my tear-filled eyes up to the ceiling and carefully observed the bland, yellow tiles that lined the walls from the ceiling down to the floor. For several seconds, I breathed in long, deep breaths. The situation was so unbelievably ugly; in front of me was a once clear-thinking woman who was apparently losing her mind, but only in certain areas. It made me think of a puzzle on a table that is violently jarred causing various pieces to fly out in all directions. Some parts of the puzzle remain together on the table, but the jolt has left huge gaps in the picture.

"Thank you, Mrs. Meade," I heard the doctor's voice say. "I'm going to go out here and talk with your granddaughter for a minute. You just rest." The doctor came out and shut the door. "I'm going to have to get a specialist out here from the city's mental and behavioral health facility. The situation is very serious, but it's not something I'm qualified to deal with."

"How long will it take to get someone out here?" Chris asked.

"We'll make the call right now and ask them to send someone immediately."

The doctor walked away, leaving Chris and me to just look at each other.

"This could get ugly," Chris said. "I don't think she's willing to wait."

I honestly did not know how we were going to keep Grandma calm. I finally took a deep breath and looked at Chris. "Would you please go out there and tell my mother what's going on? Then come back, and, I guess. . . ." I stopped in mid-sentence, attempting to suppress the weepy lump in my throat, then continued. "I guess we'll just have to wait it out. We aren't really loaded with options here."

Chris walked away, and I turned back toward her door.

"Oh, God," I said with a tight grip on the door handle. "Oh, please, God. Help."

I pushed the door open and saw Grandma lying down on the table right where the doctor had left her. I didn't say anything at first; I was hoping she had gone to sleep. But as I approached her, she turned her head toward me.

"Hi, Sweet," she said.

"Hi there," I said, smiling back at her. "How are you feeling?"

"Oh, fair," she said.

I pushed some of her hair away from her forehead and smoothed it back along the curve of her face. She raised her hand to me and asked me to help her sit up.

"Sweet," she said once she was upright, "Grandpa's waiting and I'm gonna have to go."

"Well, Grandma, we've got to wait on another doctor. Chris has gone out to the waiting room to let everybody know what's going on. Grandpa will be fine, don't worry."

The talk continued in the same manner for the next hour. Grandma would flare up with argumentative revolts followed by periods of complete calm. Chris would tell her it was OK, then I would tell her it was OK, and so on and so on. Quite frankly, that roller coaster ride was on my nerves to such an extent that I thought at any moment I might scream out, "Stop it!" I truly don't know how much longer I could have sat in that room with her. I was so relieved when a nurse came in and told me that the medical social worker had finally arrived.

I found her waiting for me at the nurses' station. She told me her name was Patricia and that she was here to evaluate Grandma's mental status. Once again, I had to go through the story of everything that had happened to my grandparents during the last week. After getting all the facts from me, she went in to talk with Grandma. The conversation with Patricia was about the same as the one Grandma had had earlier with the doctor. While they talked, I went out front to tell my mother what was going on.

"You've got to do something with Grandpa," Mom said rather frantically. "He's getting very anxious. He keeps saying, 'What's taking so long?'"

"He's not the only one who wants this over," I said with aggravation in my tone. "I'll do everything I can to speed things along."

I went over and stood by Grandpa, putting my hand on his shoulder. "Grandpa, it won't be much longer," I said. "The doctor's in there with Grandma right now."

I knew Patricia wasn't a doctor, but I felt like Grandpa would accept that term more easily than if I told him Grandma was in there with a "medical social worker." I hated the misnomer; it left my integrity feeling battered, but because Grandpa had proven himself so short-tempered in Walnut Ridge, I felt I had precious little choice.

Grandpa's eyebrows came together as a frown crossed his face, and he said, "Well, I sure wish they'd hurry with her!"

I just looked at him, and I remember thinking how unlike him that was. He had always been an extraordinarily patient man who was very "go with the flow" about everything. I correctly concluded that his anxious attitude was the result of his own level of dementia. An earmark of the debilitating disease from which he was suffering was a high state of agitation in which nothing ever happened fast enough.

"I'll go see if I can hurry them up," I said as I smiled at him and patted his shoulder.

I walked back toward the room and found that Patricia was outside the door talking with Chris. She saw me coming and took a few steps in my direction.

"Mrs. Stanley, your doctor in Arkansas was right. Mrs. Meade is suffering with what appears to be Alzheimer's disease. Because of it, she is going to require fairly constant care for the rest of her life. My recommendation is to admit her to Presbyterian's Psychiatric Unit which is located in this building. They can give you a more complete diagnostic work-up. If you'll just come up to the nurses' station with me, we can get the process started."

I asked Chris to stay with Grandma, and I followed Patricia. She introduced me to another nurse who was going to handle the admission paperwork. She also introduced me to another ER physician, Dr. Weston, who would be working with Patricia during Grandma's admission process. Dr. Weston was a pleasant, soft-spoken man who made me feel less like an irritation and more like someone whose family genuinely needed help.

"Now, let me understand," the admitting nurse started, "you're her granddaughter, not her daughter. Is that right?"

"Yes, that's correct."

"But you have power of attorney?"

"Yes."

Another nurse came over to Dr. Weston. "Do you want me to get Mrs. Meade's vitals?"

"Yes," he said. He then rattled off a string of other medical tests he wanted her to schedule for Grandma.

"Now, Mrs. Stanley," Patricia cut in. I turned my head back to her. "I'll need to make copies of the legal power of attorney document that you have for Mrs. Meade."

I began to fish for the document in question while the admitting nurse continued filling out Grandma's chart information.

"What is Mrs. Meade's religious preference?" she asked.

"She's Baptist," I said, looking at her. Then, turning my head back to Patricia, I said, "What about my grandfather?" And for the second time, I had to explain to Patricia what his situation was all about.

"Dr. Weston!" The nurse who was supposed to be getting Grandma's vitals was back. "Mrs. Meade is in a highly agitated state. She's refusing to cooperate."

"She doesn't want to be here in the first place," I told the doctor. "She— doesn't understand."

"What do you want me to do with her?" the vitals nurse persisted.

"Let's give her a sedative," Dr. Weston said.

"Mrs. Stanley, what is Mrs. Meade's date of birth?" Patricia interjected.

I turned my head sharply back to her. "I'm sorry, do what?" I blurted out.

It was chaotic, utter madness. I felt like I was on a nightmarish carousel ride which was going faster and faster and faster. It was also very hot in that ER, I remember, and it was very loud. Too many people asking too many questions. On top of it all, my concern for Grandpa was starting to boil over.

"We've got to get my grandfather back here too," I said again.

Patricia looked at me. "Where is he right now?" she asked.

"He's in the waiting room with my parents," I said.

The madness suddenly stopped. The admitting nurse, the vitals nurse, the social worker, and the doctor all stared at me. I scanned that sea of eyes, gazing from one to the other with a questioning look on my face. What had I said that caused them all to stare at me like that?

"Your *parents*?" Patricia asked. "You mean their child is out there and *you're* the one back here handling all this?"

"Uh," I stammered. "No, uh, no. You don't understand. You see. . . ." I trailed off for a moment. I don't think I had ever truly known what it was to be ashamed until that very second.

"Their son is my father," I stated hesitantly, "and he's . . . gone."

The dam suddenly burst, and the sobs came uncontrollably. The shame and humiliation of Ray's abandonment, of both me and my grandparents, flooded to the surface. I cried hysterically. In that instant, I was overcome by the rage I felt toward Ray. His selfish behavior was responsible for landing me in the appalling position in which I found myself, and at that moment, I didn't believe I could ever be free enough from that shame to forgive him for his extraordinary offense.

"He's just gone," I sobbed. "He just left one day. His own parents don't know where he is—nobody knows! My mother and step-father are out there with my grandfather," I gulped between sobs, "and we need help!"

Who can account for what will make people suddenly want to work with you? All at once, hands were on my back and voices on all sides were saying, "It's OK," and "It's going to be all right." I was mortified and embarrassed by my outburst, uncontrollable though it was. I wiped my eyes rapidly with a tissue which had somehow made its way into my hand. As strange as it seemed, my emotional eruption had apparently opened the door to the help which we had come there for in the first place. These people who had been shuffling me around like a rag doll just a few minutes before now couldn't get enough of wanting to help me as I struggled to regain my self-control.

I didn't realize in the midst of the chaos that Chris had walked up behind me. He saw the crowd gathered around me but didn't know that anything was wrong, having completely missed my breakdown. His immediate concern was elsewhere.

"Um, could someone come and help me with Mrs. Meade?" he asked. "She's getting to where I can't control her."

The vitals nurse looked at Dr. Weston again. "I'll get the sedative," she said as she turned away.

"What happened to you?" Chris asked, staring at my face.

"I had to explain to them . . . about Ray."

He just put his arm around me and whispered, "I'm sorry."

"Me too," I said with hostility, realizing that I was still very angry.

The vitals nurse came back with a hypodermic needle which she was pointing up at the ceiling; it was filled with a clear liquid. She looked at Dr. Weston. "What do you want me to tell her the shot's for?"

Without a moment's hesitation, he smiled and said, "Tell her it's a load of B1."

"She'll never go for that," I said. Once again, I felt overwhelmed with the feeling that I could not lie to my grandma. Even in that bizarre situation, I couldn't handle her being deceived.

"She did say her head was hurting," Chris offered.

"Then tell her it's to help her head stop hurting," I said decisively. I could live with that because I reasoned if she could get to sleep, then her head would not be hurting anymore.

The nurse walked away to perform her task, and I turned back to Dr. Weston. "What about my grandfather?"

"We'll get him back here and explain to him that his wife has to be admitted."

"He'll have a fit," I said with certainty.

"Well, we're agreed that we want to get him into the hospital so he can be checked out by the same doctor who examines your grandmother, right?"

"Yes," I said, wondering where he was going with his statement.

"Well, then, we'll get him back here and explain to him that his wife's not well and she has to be admitted. If he puts up a fight, then we'll give him a sedative too."

It made perfect sense. I knew the sedative wouldn't hurt him, or Grandma either, and it would make the job of getting them both admitted to the hospital easier on everybody.

"I think that's a good idea," I said.

"We'll wait for Mrs. Meade to fall asleep before we try to deal with her husband," Dr. Weston suggested. The doctor looked around for the vitals nurse who had administered the shot. He asked her what Grandma's status was.

"She's fighting it, but her head is nodding up and down," she said.

Dr. Weston looked at me and smiled. "Don't worry. She'll sleep, and she'll feel a lot better tomorrow morning."

I walked over to her room and took a peek through the partially cracked door. Sure enough, her chin was resting on her chest. Suddenly she pulled her head up and looked at the ceiling as she struggled to fight the drug's affect. It was an extremely hard thing to watch. My mouth fell open, and my eyes filled with tears. Guilt was taking yet another merciless punch at me. I thought to myself, *Look what you've done to your grandmother! You call this "love"?*

Chris had gone out to the waiting room to get my mother. The timing was excellent; my Dad had just returned from taking Duchy home, so he was able to sit with Grandpa.

"What's going on?" Mom asked.

"They've given her a shot to make her sleep," I said, still watching Grandma. "She's fighting it. This is so pitiful; just look at her!"

"Listen, listen to me," Mom said quickly, fighting back her own tears. "She's all right. She's going to be fine. She'll have a good night's sleep, and she'll feel a lot better tomorrow."

"I know, I know," I said wearily.

"Listen, I'm serious!" Mom looked directly at me. She tried to smile as she said, "She's going to have *good* sleep!"

I half chuckled. Chris agreed with Mom. "Yeah, girl, she'll feel *all* better tomorrow!"

Mom went back out to tell Dad what was happening. Dr. Weston, Chris, and I stood and just talked for a minute.

"You know," Dr. Weston began, "you're lucky. You've come in here with all the right papers in legal order. Because of that, you'll be able to take proper care of her. You're lucky she thought ahead and did this. Let me tell you, we have people come in here all the time just like your grandmother, and we can't do a thing for them because they haven't appointed anyone to make decisions for them."

"Well, she's always been a very careful person," I said.

Chris glanced down at the doctor's pocket. He saw the top of a book sticking out. "Are you studying Spanish?" Chris asked.

Dr. Weston pulled the book out. It was, indeed, a Spanish-English dictionary. "Yeah," he said. "So many of our patients who come in here are native Spanish speakers. I just thought I should learn how to communicate with them."

"Leah and I met in college in a Spanish class," Chris said.

The doctor and Chris began chatting together about things unrelated to the events that had brought us to the ER. I didn't feel very chatty myself, but, oddly enough, I appreciated being able to listen to what amounted to a normal conversation. After a few minutes, Dr. Weston suggested we move away from Grandma's door and go up front to begin working on Grandpa.

"It might be better if Mr. Meade doesn't see you when we bring him back here," he told me. "That might keep him from associating you with his being admitted to the hospital. If he thinks you're doing this, he might refuse to work with you in the future."

I was so relieved to hear that I didn't have to do the dirty deed myself. I never wanted Grandpa to equate me with anything negative in his mind. On top of that, I was already hurting so badly over what Grandma was going through I didn't think I could stand to watch Grandpa get upset.

"We'll have the sedative ready, just in case," Dr. Weston said.

"I'm almost certain you'll need it," I told him. "I hope you won't have any trouble giving it to him. He *really* does not want to be here, and I know he won't stay without a fight."

"In that case, I'll have the staff prepare soft restraints as a precaution," he said.

"Soft restraints?" I asked, puzzled.

"Yeah, it's not as bad as it sounds. The nurses will be able to restrain his hands and feet on the stretcher. It won't hurt him, but it will help keep him safe during the administration of the sedative."

My mother came back in from the waiting room. She said Dad would send Grandpa back when they called for him, and then he'd come join us.

"You guys wait here in my office, and I'll let you know how it goes," Dr. Weston said. "I'm going to go ahead and have your grandmother transported upstairs to her own room."

The doctor's "office" was basically a glorified broom closet. The small desk was covered with papers and charts and manila folders. There were Coke cans and ink pens scattered around, and a jacket was hanging on the back of the door.

As I stood with my eye peering through the door jam, I could just see down the hall toward the waiting room. It seemed to take forever, but I finally saw Grandpa walk by with Dr. Weston.

"They've got him," I mumbled. "Oh, please, God, please, please. . . ." I honestly didn't know what to ask God for. I was so spent that all I could say was, "please."

Time passed very slowly after he'd walked by that door, and the not knowing was getting to us all. What was happening? Was he throwing a fit? Was he calm? Did he hate me for this?

"Mrs. Stanley?" Dr. Weston pushed the door open.

"Yes? How did it go?"

"Well," he paused, "we did have to restrain him."

I drew in a breath. My face fell, and my shoulders sank. Dr. Weston continued. "This is going to be very hard, but I need for you, if you can, to come over and reassure him that everything is all right. He's worried about his cows and his dog. Does he actually have cows?"

"Yes," I said slowly as a tear fell. "He—they were starving because he hadn't been feeding them."

"Oh," the doctor said. "Do you think you can come tell him it's all OK? He knows you, and he'll trust you."

I looked him straight in his eyes. I could feel the muscles in my face working. I looked at my mother, then over at Chris. "Yes, I can," I said in a voice that was little more than a whisper.

We walked out of his office and spotted Dad waiting for us. He joined us as we followed the doctor, putting his arm around my shoulders.

"It's going to be OK, you know?" he said.

"Yeah," I said, wiping more tears away. "I know."

We walked around to the triage area where a group of curtains were drawn, separating the beds from one another. Dr. Weston motioned me to the one Grandpa was in.

I came around the corner, and there he was. That sweet, gentle man whom I loved so dearly was tied to a stretcher. His head was up, and he was working his hands frantically. Our eyes met. Tears rolled unchecked down my face.

He looked at me with the questioning look of a child. Mom, Dad, and Chris stood at his feet, and I walked up on his right side. Dr. Weston stood across from me. I could hear my mother crying.

"What?" Grandpa said in a quiet voice.

"Oh, Grandpa—" I broke off because my voice choked. "It's OK, Grandpa." I was weeping openly. I just wasn't able to stop.

"I've got to feed my cows," he said.

"Grandpa, I'll take care of everything. Please don't worry. I'll take care of your cows."

"Duke's got to eat."

"I'll make sure he eats . . . please don't worry about it. You just stay here with Grandma. She needs you."

He laid his head back. Dr. Weston and I looked at each other, and he gave me a nod. I put my hand on Grandpa's hand.

"I'll see you tomorrow. I love you . . ." I whispered.

I walked away slowly; I felt like the heaviness of grief had taken root. I was sure I'd never get over what had just happened.

CHAPTER 9

SEVEN AND NINE

A s I look back on it now, I know God was present with me even in the midst of that horror; He was holding me up just like He promised He would. As difficult as those hours in the emergency room were for me, it was—and still is—a great comfort to realize the situation posed absolutely no challenges to the Holy Spirit. He alone knew the intensity of the anguish I felt that night, and He alone was able to sustain me through it.

Only time has been able to separate me from those painful events of January 18, 1997, but even now as I read God's Word, I encounter phrases which seem to literally leap off the pages at me because they relate so clearly to what I personally experienced.

> *And the Holy Spirit helps us in our distress. For we don't even know what we should pray for, nor how we should pray. But the Holy Spirit prays for us with groanings that cannot be expressed in words. And the Father who knows all hearts knows what the Spirit is saying, for the Spirit pleads for us believers in harmony with God's own will. (Romans 8:26-27 NLT)*

The circumstances I faced in that emergency room had forced me to experience agonizing pain on a number of fronts, not the least of which was the discovery of a previously unknown level of rage directed at my biological father. My having power of attorney for my grandparents was undeniably tied to Ray's willful disappearance, and only when I was bluntly confronted with having to explain his selfish behavior to a group of strangers did I come to realize the force of unresolved fury which was deeply embedded in my heart. When I walked out of the emergency room that Saturday night, the concepts of forgiveness and emotional healing weren't even on my radar. I was so angry that Ray had made the choices he had made, and although I tried to convince myself that I wasn't upset about his abandonment of *me*—only that of his *parents*—I was still ruthlessly chewed on by an unrelenting hatred which had roots reaching all the way back to my infancy. For many months after the humiliating breakdown I experienced in front of those doctors and nurses, my mind would only acknowledge the tragic consequences of Ray's abandonment of Grandma and Grandpa—I never entertained the idea that I was also wounded. A time had come in their lives when they needed their son, but he was nowhere to be found. How could any pain I felt even begin to compare with that?

Ironically, while I was outraged at Ray for putting me in the position I was in, the other side of the coin was that I felt very proud to be able to serve my grandparents as their caregiver. I loved them so dearly, and therefore I gladly took on the mantle of responsibility for them. I wanted to do everything possible to provide the care they needed with the dignity and respect they so richly deserved, but my emotions regarding their situation were highly diversified. I honestly hated myself for what I'd done—taking them away from their home, authorizing a doctor to sedate my grandmother and allowing my grandfather to be restrained on a gurney; yet running parallel with that hatred was a sort of "hopeless helplessness," the knowledge that there was just nothing else I could have done. The topper was having them admitted to a *psychiatric* floor, of all places—that was more than my brain was able to process. I thought about how Scarlett O'Hara in *Gone with the Wind* was always saying she'd think about the bad things "tomorrow." I found myself agreeing with that fictional heroine; some stuff in life is just too painful to deal with in the present tense.

I'll always remember the image of Grandma fighting that sedative, and I've never been free of the memory of seeing Grandpa tied to that stretcher. And as long as I live, I'll never forget how I felt about basically deceiving my grandparents to get them admitted to that hospital. Although my honest intention was to get new glasses for Grandma at some point, I had known all along that what we were going to do was something far more than an eye exam, and the product of our "trip to the doctor" would be much more than just a new pair of glasses. I found myself grappling with the fact that communication with Grandma and Grandpa was never going to get any better. I was slowly coming to understand that it would, in fact, get worse over time. I speculated about whether I was going to wind up telling them lie on top of lie until every word I spoke to them would be so full of deception that the truth would no longer be identifiable.

I imagine every caregiver goes through a sort of rationalization process in which they attempt to validate the deceptive things they say to their afflicted loved one. Pacifying statements like, "It would only upset them to know the truth," or "They'll never understand even if I explain," will attempt to vacuum the caregiver's conscience, but the sacrifice of integrity can leave deep wounds which remain painful long after the individual being cared for has departed this life.

All these issues were passing through my brain on Sunday morning as I sat alone in the living room of our apartment. Chris had gone to teach his Sunday school class, but he planned to return home after it was over and not stay for the service. As for my attending church, I believe I could have jumped up to the moon more easily than I could have gone to church and behaved normally that day. I sat very still for a long time, just staring out into space. It seemed I couldn't even talk to God that morning; I felt so utterly spent. I didn't want anything to eat, I didn't want to shower and get dressed, I didn't want to do anything but just sit. I guess I was in some sort of shock because when I woke up, I felt numb, and I had been moving around in a slow and lethargic way since the moment I had gotten out of bed.

As I sat regarding the events of the previous three days, I repeatedly found my eyes wandering over to an 11 x 14 portrait of Grandma and Grandpa which they had given me for Christmas in 1991. That photograph showed them exactly the way I'd always known them to be. Bordered by a lovely cherry frame, they remained blissfully unchanged, and it occurred to me that looking at that picture was as painful as it was pleasant.

The phone rang sharply and drew me out of my somber thoughts. I didn't want to answer, but I thought it might be the hospital, so I decided to grab it before the machine did.

"Mrs. Stanley?" a man's voice asked.

"Yes?"

"I'm Dr. Carlton calling from Presbyterian Hospital. I'm a psychiatrist, and I've just been talking with your parents."

It was the first of many times that mistake occurred. I corrected him gently, trying not to sound like a smart-aleck. "Actually, they are my grandparents, not my parents," I said.

"Oh, I beg your pardon. Your grandparents. I see."

It occurred to me after I spoke up that it probably didn't matter to him one way or the other. I guess it just felt good to speak the truth.

"How are they this morning?"

"Well, I don't have anything really new to tell you. It's all stuff you probably already know. I understand you've already had them looked at by a physician, and he's told you that your grandmother is suffering with Alzheimer's disease. Is that right?"

"Yes, that's what Dr. Donnelly said."

"Well, I can confirm his findings. I gave her what we call a 'twenty-point quiz' this morning. It's very basic information: *Who is the president? What year is this? What is your address?*—that sort of thing. Now if you or I took the quiz, we'd probably score in the eighteen-to-twenty range. Someone in their early to midseventies might score between fifteen and seventeen. Your grandmother scored a seven.

"Oh. . . . my . . ." I responded.

The "seven" had the same effect on me as the letters from Dr. Donnelly had had. It was a numerical representation of the level to which Grandma had fallen, making her disease a very tangible thing.

"I'm sorry to have to tell you that. I know it's not a pleasant thing to hear."

"No, it's not," I said. "Well, at least she has my grandfather with her. Hopefully he'll be able to help us work with her after I explain things to him."

"Actually, Mrs. Stanley, I wouldn't put too much stock in his help at this point," Dr. Carlton paused. "You see, I also gave him the 'twenty-point quiz' and he only scored a nine."

"A nine?"

"Yes, ma'am. So, you see, he's really not very much better off than your grandmother."

Well, there's just no way to describe how those words hit me. They were piercing. They slapped me hard and then pressed like a tremendous weight. Despite all the madness that had taken place since Wednesday evening, I had been harboring a feeling that somehow Grandpa was mentally better than Grandma. I felt in some indescribable way that I could still "reach" him. Now I was learning that he, too, had been pulled away from me. The realization was abrupt: for all intents and purposes, I had been left alone to handle things for both of them. I flashed back to the multiple conversations we'd had regarding what to do *if* something ever happened to them. With a wave akin to panic, I found myself hoping I'd been listening really well because there would be no more talking their care over with them. Not ever.

"Well," I said, fumbling for the right response. I wanted to sound like I had my act all together, but I really don't think I fooled the doctor for even a minute. "I don't know what to say to that. A nine. He just seemed . . . well . . . I don't know. I thought he was better than a nine, somehow."

"Is your grandfather a very talkative man?"

"Oh, no," I said with a smile.

Dr. Carlton explained that people who are quiet by nature can go for months or even years without their relatives suspecting there's a problem. It seems that even bold symptoms of dementia can stay hidden indefinitely beneath a blanket of silence. Only when the disease has progressed to a fairly advanced stage would the victim's actions begin to overrule the facade of what appears to be normal on the surface.

"What sort of recommendation can you make as far as their care goes?" I asked.

"Well, your grandmother's condition is going to necessitate some kind of professional care. We have a number of medications which can help the symptoms of Alzheimer's, but there is nothing yet that will stop the disease. We're scheduling a battery of tests for both of them, and we'll be better able to give you some direction after we get the results back."

Dr. Carlton went into a fair amount of detail regarding the specific tests they would be administering, and he asked several questions about Grandma and Grandpa. He explained that the more correct information he had, the easier it would be to sift through the delusional statements being made by my grandparents. He wanted to know where they had lived, what their lives had been like, what they had done prior to retirement, and if they had any living siblings. After effectively beating around the bush for some minutes, Dr. Carlton finally asked point blank, "Do they have any living children?"

I knew what he was looking for. He wanted the answer to the same question that had been asked by the social worker the night before. It seemed that everybody wanted to know why the *granddaughter* was taking care of these people. I determined I wasn't going to fall to pieces like I had in the emergency room, so, like a dancer at a masquerade ball, I placed a stoic mask up to my face and began to tell the doctor all about Ray. I remained very matter-of-fact, almost cold, but somewhere in my brain I could still feel the burn of shame and embarrassment. I concluded by petitioning the doctor not to discuss the issue with my grandparents.

"He's done so much to hurt them already," I said flatly. "I see no reason to go digging up this painful part of their lives." In that moment, I was overwhelmed with the need to protect them from any more heartache. I felt like I had to stand in front of them in a guarding posture, spreading my arms apart as wide as I could.

For the first time in my life, I began to realize how "works" driven I was. I would really believe I was trusting God, but I was still planning my next three moves, trying to do everything myself. It was like I wanted to make God proud of me—*Look, God, I'm flinging myself in front of my grandparents! I'm going to protect them!* The truth was (and still is), I can't earn God's favor with my works—and if I *could* have protected Grandma and Grandpa from anything, it would have been from the dementia itself. But God's Word beautifully expresses the care and protection He provides for us:

> *He will cover you with His feathers, and under His wings you will find refuge. (Psalm 91:4)*

Only His arms could spread wide enough to cover all of us. While my love for my grandparents prompted me to protect them as much as I could with my limited capacity, God's inexplicably deep love and compassion for all of us prompted Him to protect us with His infinite ability. The great God who knew no limits was watching us and protecting us all the time.

Before we hung up, Dr. Carlton assured me that he would leave well enough alone where Ray was concerned. "It's absolutely shocking what some people do, though," he said.

I called my mother after I got off the phone with Dr. Carlton. I gave her the details of my conversation with him, explaining the tests they were going to run on Grandma and Grandpa over the next several days. I held it together until we started talking about the overall picture. The events from the previous week were bad enough, but when I started to consider the unknown future we were facing, my eyes welled up with tears, and I started asking that futile question that situations like this provoke: *why was all this happening?*

"They've dealt with so much pain throughout their lives already because of Ray," I said as I wept. "Why are both of them having to experience this degrading disease on top of all that?"

My mother, like me, had no solid answers. She, too, was confounded by the enormity of the situation. "I don't know why. It's one of those things we may never know the answer to."

That response was completely unsatisfactory. So I pressed . . . as if that would do any good.

"But I know God loves them; why is He allowing them to be like this? Why?"

"The world's not a fair place," my mother stated flatly. "Christians are not exempt from trials—Jesus told us that in John 16. As to the "why" of this particular trial for them, well, we just don't know. But the fact is that even though it's happening, we have to remember God is greater than all of it. He's still in control, no matter what it looks like."

"Well, it looks ugly," I said aggressively. "Grandma, sitting there, trying to fight off a drug-induced sleep, and Grandpa—" I broke off sharply as the lump rose in my throat. "They tied him to a stretcher like they thought he was crazy—and *I'm* the one who said it was OK!" I was crying so hard I felt like I might choke.

"It's not your fault!" my mother said strongly. "*He* fought them, *he* wasn't able to listen to reason. They had no choice—and neither did you!" She began to weep with me, and for a while, neither of us could say anything.

"If he could only understand," I said at last. "I would never have let them tie him down. I would never have done this." I sighed heavily as I wiped the tears from my cheeks.

"I know that," my mother said in a still weepy voice. "And those doctors and nurses in that ER knew that. But you just had no choice."

I guess anyone who's ever endured any kind of negative experience inevitably asks the "why" question. Ironically there is rarely a clear-cut answer, so people wind up trying to make peace with their particular situation as best they can. As a believer in Jesus, I knew the only place I would find any peace at all was in God's Word. When my mother and I hung up, I picked up my very worn copy of *The Living Bible* and began to leaf through the scriptures. I happened upon Psalm 139; I've had that psalm marked as a personal favorite for many years. As I skimmed down through its twenty-four verses, my mind was wandering, and I wasn't paying very close attention to the words I was seeing. But when I came to verse 16, my eyes were suddenly riveted to the page. I had to read the words over and over again to absorb their meaning:

You saw me before I was born and scheduled each day of my life before I began to breathe. Every day was recorded in Your Book. (Psalm 139:16 TLB)

If these words were true, and I'm sure to this day that they are, then it meant God had the lives of both Grandma and Grandpa completely mapped out from start to finish. In that moment, I began to cling to those words as I groped toward legitimate acceptance and personal healing; God had not been caught off guard. He had known what was coming down the pike.

It occurred to me that God's foreknowledge of our situation allowed Him to uniquely equip me to handle what was coming. I mused over Psalm 119:105 which says, "Your Word is a lamp to my feet and a light for my path." I felt encouraged to know that no matter what took place, God was going to be directing me through His Word. He always had; why should this situation be any different?

I checked the time and realized Chris would be back from church soon, and I still needed to shower before we could go back up to the hospital.

I was just finishing my make-up when he came in. We ate a bite of lunch together while he told me about how folks at church had expressed concern over the events that were turning our lives upside-down.

"It got a little awkward, though," Chris said. "People kept wanting to know why your parents weren't handling it . . . you know?"

"So what'd you tell them?" I asked, feeling my tiny appetite slip away.

"Well, just the high points. Enough to make them be quiet!"

Explaining Ray had always been rough enough, but as people began hearing about my grandparents' circumstances, I could assess very quickly whether or not they truly understood all the dynamics that were in play. Interestingly I found the ones offering the most advice were the individuals who had never dealt with a situation like mine. I knew they meant well and they just wanted to help, but wow, how I wished they would just stop talking! Those early days of decision after decision were so difficult, and when people wanted to critique my actions without necessarily having all the facts, I found myself wanting to forcefully push them away because it was obvious they had no idea what they were talking about. They were the ones who had a knack for oversimplifying the situation, and they often wound up saying things that left me feeling frustrated and miserable. It was very easy for them to tell me what I "ought" to be doing or to let me know in some round-about way that I wasn't handling a specific issue the "right" way.

I eventually crawled into a hole where I decided people couldn't understand the way I felt because they weren't me and they weren't wearing the decision-maker hat. And so ensued the pity-party reaction: *No one understands me!* I thank God for the Holy Spirit and His patience in developing me through the ups, the downs, the kudos, and the criticisms. I came to see—over a long period of time—that I couldn't fault people just because they weren't walking out my journey; that would be judging them the way I perceived they were judging me. I eventually learned it was better to disclose only minimal details to those people who were blessed enough to have never been in my shoes.

After Chris and I finished our lunch, he went to change out of his dressy church clothes into jeans and a turtleneck. It was midafternoon when my parents and my maternal grandmother, always known to us as Mother Marine, arrived at our apartment. The five of us piled into my dad's Taurus, and we headed out to Presbyterian Hospital. I remember being so full of anxiety, wondering if Grandma and Grandpa would remember the events of Saturday night. *Would they blame me? Would they ever forgive me?* I just wasn't sure what I'd face when I saw them.

As I walked down that long path that connected the parking garage with the main part of the hospital, I sensed that my breathing was rapid, and my eyebrows were pushed involuntarily together. When the elevator doors opened on the psychiatric floor, we got off and saw a set of glass doors which had to be buzzed open by someone at the nurses' station. As I looked through the glass to see if anyone was there, Grandma and Grandpa suddenly crossed my line of vision down by the nurses' station at the opposite end of the hall. A wave of relief passed over me; apparently the sedatives had worn off, and they were fine—just like everyone had assured me they would be. I pressed the intercom button and waited for a reply.

"Yes?" a voice squawked from the box on the wall.

"I'm Leah Stanley, and I'm here to see my grandparents, Edward and Clara Meade."

I could see the nurse straining her eyes to look at us.

"How many of you are there?" she asked.

"Five," I answered.

"You can't all come down here at the same time. Come on through the doors, and I'll send someone down there to meet you." The door buzzed as she finished her sentence. We walked in and followed one of their staff into a small waiting room.

"You can come down to see them two at a time, or you can bring them down here," he said.

"Why don't you and I go get them and bring them here?" Chris asked.

We all agreed that was the best thing to do, so Chris and I followed the orderly down to their rooms.

"Can you tell me how they did last night?" I asked.

"They did just fine," he said. "It was funny, though. They were placed in separate rooms, right next door to each other. Early this morning, he woke up and came out into the hall looking for her. He found her and sat down in the chair in her room. We found him leaning on his elbow, dozing, and we tried to get him to go back to bed, but he wouldn't hear of leaving her. I guess they've been married for a long time, huh?"

I quickly counted up the years. "They celebrated their sixty-fourth anniversary this past Christmas," I said proudly.

"Whew!" the orderly said. "That's a long time. They would really feel lost without each other."

We turned the corner at the nurses' station and started down another hallway. About halfway down, the orderly showed us into a room off to the left. Grandpa was sitting in a chair against the wall, and Grandma was lying on the bed.

"Well, good afternoon!" I said, smiling as brightly as I could.

"Hello, Sweet," Grandma said.

"Howdy, howdy," Grandpa said as he stood up.

I stood squarely in front of him, searching his eyes for any sign of hostility. The words, *Please, Grandpa, please forgive me!* were screaming so loudly in my head that I thought the whole world must have heard them. But there was no hostility. There wasn't anything but love in his eyes. We hugged affectionately like we had always done, and then he offered me the chair he had been sitting in. For the first time since being diagnosed, the dementia had done me an indescribable favor. I honestly don't think he remembered the stretcher incident because he never once brought it up—not then, not ever.

I turned and walked over to Grandma who was trying to sit up. Once she was steady, I leaned down, and we hugged that tight, clinging hug like we had always done. All my life I had treasured those hugs, but from that day on, they meant more to me than ever before. In a mere five days I had become acutely aware that our time was nearly gone—how many more hugs were left?

Chris spoke up and told them that my parents and Mother Marine were waiting to see them down the hall, so Grandpa started toward the door. After I helped Grandma to her feet, she reached for her coat.

"Grandma, you won't need your coat. It's not cold in the hall, and we're not going outside," I said.

She looked at me with that absent look that had recently been so prevalent on her face. "I've got to put it on for when we go home," she said.

Chris and I looked at each other. "Oh no!" he muttered under his breath.

Grandma swung the coat around and put her arms through the sleeves. Involuntarily I found myself helping her get it on straight. I looked at Chris.

"Well, all right," I mumbled. "Wear the coat."

We walked back down to the waiting area, and everybody smiled as greetings were exchanged all around. When we sat down, though, the atmosphere grew heavy pretty fast because beyond "hello," nobody was sure what we actually had to talk about. Our standard "go-to" subjects like Grandpa's cows, his dog, Grandma's flowers, and her latest handiwork projects were out because absolutely nobody wanted to broach the subject of the life they'd left behind. It came as a relief that Grandpa seemed fairly clear-minded as he asked Dad about his job, but Grandma seemed to be in the same fog she'd been in since we'd first seen her on Thursday. The longer we talked, the more at ease we felt; we had verbally groped along until we found a few non-threatening subjects to banter back and forth. A sudden change occurred, though, as Grandpa scooted forward to the edge of his seat, cleared his throat, and said, "Leah, I think I know where we left that car."

My eyes darted to meet his fixed stare. He looked anxious. In my peripheral vision, I could see that all eyes moved from him to me with a bizarre blend of curiosity and tension. I leaned forward and placed my elbows on top of my crossed legs as I looked at him. "Where is that, Grandpa?"

"It's in that parking lot," he said rather indecisively.

"In Forrest City?" I asked, unsure what parking lot he was talking about.

His eyebrows came together. "No," he said slowly. "We haven't been to Forrest City."

Chris lowered his voice and cautioned me not to argue with him. I nodded in agreement.

"Well, don't worry about your car, Grandpa. I'll take care of it," I said with a smile. I was trying so hard to appear calm, but the truth was I was almost panicked because I just didn't know what to say to him.

"Well, we need to get it. I'm afraid the battery might be dead," he persisted.

"What makes you think that?" I asked with a questioning look. This was a new concern; there had been no previous indication of a battery problem.

He looked down at the floor as his brows moved together again. The strained silence told me he didn't have an answer to my question. He seemed mentally stalled in a way I didn't understand. All at once he reached into his pocket and pulled out a ring of keys.

"I've got the keys here," he said, looking at me intently.

I held out my hand for them, and he surrendered them immediately.

"All right, Grandpa. I'll go get your car," I said slowly.

"Do you want to go right now?"

"No, I'll get it a little later. And anyway, you need to stay here with Grandma."

He seemed to relax a bit, sitting back in his chair. The air almost crackled in that room as Mom and Dad, Mother Marine, and Chris all looked from me to him. Was the "confrontation" over?

"We need to get it back," Grandpa said firmly.

"We will, Grandpa. I promise you. I'll take care of it."

We all sat silently for a moment or two, and it was during that tense time of searching the deepest part of my brain for a conversational topic that I realized something very pathetic: dementia robs its victims not only of their memories but also of their ability to converse normally, even with those people whom they know very well and love deeply.

After a few more minutes of reaching for conversation, we announced it was time for us to go. So Chris and I walked my grandparents back down to Grandma's room. I told them I'd be back to see them the next day. It was really weird, but neither one of them acted like it was strange that I was leaving them there. I took it as the blessing it was and didn't question it.

Just inside Grandma's door I hugged her very tight. "I love you!" I said as I looked her straight in her eyes.

"And you know I love you, Doll," she answered with a smile. "I couldn't love you any more if you were my own daughter."

I turned to Grandpa, and we embraced. "I love my grandpa!"

"I love my Leah too!"

As we walked back down the hall, Chris commented on how strained the conversation had been.

"Yes, I know it was," I said, "but no matter how strained it ever gets or how much conversation is to be lost between us, they'll never fail to hear me tell them how much I love them. They'll hear me say those words until they are both gone."

CHAPTER 10

FAMILY VISIT

My eyes flew open as the ringing of our telephone jarred me out of my sleep. It was Monday morning, and Chris, having planned to return to work that day, had already left. I was grateful he had not tried to wake me up because I was just exhausted. I blinked two or three times, trying to clear my blurry eyes as the phone continued to ring. Although I coughed and cleared my throat as I awkwardly reached for the receiver, it was still obvious I hadn't been awake for very long.

"Hello?" I managed to say.

"Leah?" A woman's voice came over the line. It was vaguely familiar to me.

"Yes?"

"Leah, this is Lena," she said. "Hon, I hope it's not too early for you, but I'm nearly crazy to find out what's going on with Clara."

I should have anticipated hearing from Grandma's sister once she got the news from her daughter-in-law, Harriet. Lena was very distressed, frantically asking multiple questions. As we talked, I remember thinking how hard it must have been for her to hear about the mental spiral Grandma was in. Lena and her much-loved older sister had grown up together, double-dated, married, and had raised their children at the same time. Over the years, Grandma had often told me about her high regard and deep affection for Lena. Despite my own grief, I was so very sorry to have to tell Lena about the destructive toll which Alzheimer's had already taken in her sister's life. It became obvious to me that the dramatic change I had been witnessing was going to reach far beyond my immediate family.

And so it began to dawn on me that this was another aspect of being a caregiver: keeping the family informed. My appointed position had placed me in a communication loop wherein I would have to repeat the Meade story and prognosis each time initial contact was made with various family members. As long as Grandma and Grandpa lived, I would be the family's "point person," serving as the liaison between the Meade physicians and the extended family. Never before had it occurred to me that having power of attorney on their behalf would branch off into all of these other areas; it was turning out to be so much more than just making decisions for my grandparents—as if that hadn't been enough to cope with. There was a distinct lack of appeal in having to rehash everything with distant family members who were practically strangers to me.

In the five days since receiving the phone call that had started it all, I had lost count of how many times I'd just broken down in tears; I didn't see how I was going to be able to talk about such a sensitive subject with so many different people. Ultimately I was glad to serve my grandparents by providing care for them in their later years, but in those early days when the future was so uncertain and I was still personally going through the adjustment phase, even simple tasks like keeping folks informed felt like something to be shied away from—avoided altogether, if possible.

As Lena and I continued to talk, she began to move away from the emotional responses to the much more practical questions regarding what was going to happen next. What did I plan to do with them? Would they ever be able to go back to Arkansas, or was I planning to take them into my own home?

"I really don't know what we can do yet," I said with a sigh. "I'm just going to wait for the test results, and then I'll talk with the doctors about the available options."

But Lena was thinking ahead in a way that had never even crossed my mind; she introduced a totally new perspective to the problem of providing care for my grandparents.

"If they stay in Memphis, what's going to happen to their property in Arkansas?"

What indeed? I thought rapidly for a few seconds, but no light bulb went off over my head. I told her honestly that I didn't know.

"You be careful!" Lena warned. "If they have to go on Medicaid, the State of Tennessee may make you sell that property. I don't know how their wills read, but you could wind up losing everything they've always meant for you to have."

"Oh," I said with exasperation.

"Maybe the medical social worker you were talking about might be able to help," she said firmly. "You need someone who can tell you what your rights are."

As our discussion was winding down, Lena stated that she and her son, Philip, and Grandma's younger brother, Joe, would all be going up to the hospital that evening to visit Grandma and Grandpa. I told her Chris and I would meet them there.

When Chris got home from work that evening, we spent some time mulling everything over once again, and before the conversation was finished, I grew misty eyed. I truly don't think I had ever cried so much in my whole life. My constant state of weepiness made me feel like I was constitutionally weak. So much had happened in such a short period of time, and all I seemed to be able to do about any of it was cry. Forget fight or flight; I needed a third option code-named, "water works."

"Do you think I'll ever cry all this mess out?" I asked Chris.

"It's good for you to cry," he insisted. "It's helping you to release all the tension that's come as a result of the situation."

"I guess I'm tense because I don't know what I'm going to do with them," I said, shaking my head.

"On that note," Chris said, jumping up to collect some pieces of paper he'd come in with, "I had a few minutes this morning, so I did some looking through the phone book. I looked up 'retirement homes,' and I got the names of several different ones located throughout the city. I figure it won't hurt to call them."

"Well, it's another option, I guess. But we'll have to do it later because right now we've got to leave to meet Lena."

Once more we turned our car toward the hospital which was serving as a temporary home for Grandma and Grandpa. When the nurse buzzed us in, we were told that my grandparents already had visitors. We followed the orderly down the hall to a different visiting room from the one we'd been in the day before. As we were walking, I asked how they were doing.

"They're fine. They've just eaten dinner. He ate real good, but she really didn't eat much. After two or three bites, she says she's full. Even if we coax her, she won't eat much more than that."

"She was probably waiting for dessert!" I said with a half-smile.

"Well, there was Jell-O on her tray, but she didn't touch it," he said.

"It wasn't chocolate. Just not the same in her book—or mine!"

Chris and I grinned at each other because we both shared Grandma's passion for chocolate.

"What about their medical tests?" I asked. "How did they do?"

"Well, when they come to get him he goes by himself just fine, but he won't let us take her without him. He's awfully protective of her."

"Yes, he certainly is," I said as tears sprang unexpectedly into my eyes. It was somewhat of a relief that these tears were rooted in my appreciation of Grandpa's devotion to his wife rather than the tears of heartache I'd been shedding for days.

As Chris and I came around the corner into the visiting room, I saw immediately that Grandma was sitting beside Lena and was having what appeared to be a pleasant chat. Grandpa, Joe, and Philip were all standing a few feet away, talking as if they had bumped into each other at the mall.

I found I was very glad to see Lena. I couldn't even remember how long it had been since I'd last seen her. It was so refreshing to talk with her because she didn't seem changed the way Grandma did. The visit was a pleasant one, even though it was evident that Grandma wasn't altogether "there," so to speak. I guess by Monday evening I was growing more accustomed to seeing her with that absent look on her face.

Lena spent a lot of time telling Grandma all the latest news from her family, with Philip interjecting a word here and there to help complete the stories. Grandma seemed to be enjoying the conversation when suddenly she straightened herself up and turned sharply toward her sister.

"Lena, tell me," she said very deliberately, "how's Lester doing?"

An uncomfortable silence fell over the room like a heavy blanket. Lena just looked at her sister for a few seconds, then cut her eyes over to me. I stood looking at Grandma, and as I did, I realized that my head was slowly shaking back and forth.

"Clara," Lena began, "Lester died."

I knew for a fact Grandma had been told that her brother-in-law had died. Over the past two years, her repetitious statements to me regarding Lester's death had been one of the very earliest indicators that something wasn't quite right with her. But when Lena told her that Lester was dead, a frown crossed Grandma's face, and she shook her head as her glance fell to the floor.

"I'm so sorry," she said slowly. "I'm sorry I couldn't be there for you."

"It's all right," Lena said stiffly. "I know you were with me in thought."

Lena looked up at me, and I could tell by her expression that she wanted me to either explain the madness or fix it. Unfortunately I was not able to do either one. Philip, feeling the awkwardness of the moment and wanting to help, bent over toward Grandma.

"Aunt Clara, did Momma tell you that my wife, Doris, just passed away?"

Once again, a wave of grief swept over Grandma's face, and she expressed her sorrow. "I don't think I ever knew your wife," she said, looking up into Philip's face.

"Yes, you did!" Philip said boldly. "We visited with you lots of times."

Indeed, they had visited with her on many occasions, but the blunt confrontation with that fact seemed to upset Grandma. She looked clouded and disoriented. "I don't know," she said as her eyes met mine.

In that moment, it seemed she became my own child, and that child of mine was hurting because she was rattled by confusion and embarrassment. My heart just broke for her, and I knew I had to either make it better for her or I would just die. I moved swiftly to her side and put my arm around her.

"It's OK, Grandma. Everything is just fine." Tears blurred my vision as I hugged up close to her. She reached out her hand, patted my face, and smiled.

"You know you're my heart!" she said as we held on to each other.

Chris gently deflected the rigidity of the moment by starting to talk with Philip about his recent loss of Doris. As the conversation moved along, the tension began to recede, and Grandma once again sat back in her chair.

Aside from that one difficult moment, the evening went along very pleasantly. After a while, Lena announced that she was ready to leave. Joe approached me as Grandma and Lena were saying their goodbyes.

"I'm going to give you my phone number, and I want you to call me if there's anything I can do for them."

I pulled a piece of scrap paper out of my purse, and he dictated his number. After we chatted briefly about the situation as a whole, I thanked him for coming up to see them.

"I know it means so much for her to get to see you," I said.

Lena came over to us as Joe turned toward Grandma to say goodnight.

"She's just pitiful," Lena mumbled. "I can't bear to see her like this."

I could do nothing more than tell her I felt the same way. "It's the worst nightmare I've ever had," I said. "I just keep hoping I'll wake up from it and find her normal again."

"Well, I sure do understand that. Listen, you take care of yourself and don't worry about things. They trust you, and I know you're doing what's right for them."

I so appreciated Lena's words of encouragement. Even though my immediate family had been very supportive, it was good to hear the confidence of someone who hadn't been in the thick of things from the start.

Joe and Philip came over to us, and we exchanged our goodbye hugs. Lena joined her brother and her son who were moving toward the door. All at once, Joe turned around and came back over to me.

"I want to give you my phone number just in case you need to reach me," he said.

I stood frozen for a few seconds. Very slowly I could feel my eyes grow wider, and my mouth was wanting to drop open. My thoughts began to run wild—he sounded just like Grandma; did he realize what he'd said? Did anyone besides me realize what he'd said?

"You gave it to me earlier," I said slowly. I watched him carefully, and for a fleeting second, I could see a trace of the blank confusion on his face which I had been seeing in such abundance on Grandma's.

"I did?" he asked as his eyebrows moved together.

I reached into my purse and pulled out the scrap of paper and read off the number he'd given me. He nodded and smiled.

"Well, that's right," he said, apparently unaware that he had given it to me himself only a few minutes before. "Now, you be sure to call me if they need anything, hear?"

I assured him that I would, and then I watched the three of them walk out the door. Chris came and stood beside me. All we could do was look at each other.

I learned several years later that Joe did succumb to the same debilitating disease that had ruined the latter years of his father's life and had most recently taken hold of his older sister. It was my understanding that he regressed to an almost infantile state of existence before he was finally laid to rest in 2003.

For the first time, the prospect of Mack Proctor's words, "We're all going to need help some day," came into a frighteningly clear focus.

We got home from the hospital well after nine o'clock, and all I could think about was going to bed. Chris checked the answering machine and listened to one message from his mom, Sarah. She asked us to let her know when we got home because she wanted to come by our apartment for a short visit. Chris gave her a call, and a few minutes later we heard a knock at the door. As soon as she came in, she walked directly to me and handed me a folded package.

"This is for you," she said.

My first thought was she was giving me something for my grandparents; they had been the sole recipients of my thoughts, concerns, and energy for nearly a week, so it never occurred to me the package might be for me. I unfolded the paper and drew out a medium-sized gift box. I looked up at her with curiosity; she was smiling. I lifted the lid from the box, pulled back the crisp, white tissue paper, and saw a small black handbag with a silver heart-shaped button over the clasp and a silver chain for the shoulder strap.

"Well, this is so pretty, thank you," I said, looking up at her again. I was still not sure of the occasion, so I quipped, "Late Christmas present?"

She chuckled and said, "No. This is just a little something for *you*. You've had a hard week, and sometimes a person just needs something nice."

It was a simple gesture, but it meant more to me than I could put into words at the time.

"I really appreciate this," I said quietly, "especially in light of all the ugly that's happened over the last five days." I pulled the purse from the box and stretched the shoulder strap out to its full length. "It's very pretty, thank you so much."

After she left, I told Chris, "This was really thoughtful of your mom."

"Well, she likes giving gifts, and right now there's not much she can do to help with your grandparents," he said. "She wanted you to know she's sorry about what's happened and that she's here for you."

I pulled the tissue paper stuffing from the bottom of the new purse, then began moving things from my old purse into the new one. As is typical when a woman changes purses, I found I was discarding the obvious junk while keeping the valuables. In his masterpiece, *The Hunchback of Notre Dame*, Victor Hugo observed that "as the purse is emptied, the heart is filled." I couldn't help but think about the importance of a purse and what a woman typically carries in her purse: that which is valuable. I regarded Sarah's gift as very fitting and timely, because the new purse would provide a safe haven for things of value, not only to me but also to my grandparents—Medicare and insurance cards, their checkbook, and not least, the power of attorney documents. I found that as their caregiver, I was pulling those kinds of things out of my purse—"emptying" it for them—as I took on the tremendous responsibility of providing care for them, and in doing it, I found my heart truly was filled—with love for them.

I snapped the clasp shut and tried it out on my shoulder. It was a perfect style and an excellent size, and I carried it with gratitude until I wore it out completely.

CHAPTER 11

EVIDENCE AND DENIAL

Wednesday, January 22, 1997, marked the one-week anniversary of my tenure as caregiver for my grandparents. In the six days that had passed since I had received the phone call that started it all, I felt like I had lived an entire lifetime, aging prematurely to a level of knowledge usually reserved for those who were decades older than I was. Never at any time had I cried so much, felt so isolated, or been so boldly confronted with the reality of loss. On and off throughout the day, I reflected on the fact that I really had been totally unprepared for what was coming. One week before, I'd had a completely normal existence; I was working, I was making weekend plans with friends, and I was enjoying life with my new husband in our first apartment together. In only six days, my world had been dramatically reshaped by the muddled rambling of my grandparents, so much so that I now considered the line which lay between fact and fiction to be virtually obliterated.

In addition to being a milestone for reflection, January 22 also marked the first of several trips I made back to that house on the ridge in the foothills of the Ozarks. Even before we had returned to Memphis with Grandma and Grandpa, I knew that I would have to go back to their home fairly soon for a number of different reasons, not the least of which was to get the rest of Grandpa's clothes.

As for Grandma's wardrobe, I had tried to give one of the nurses the dress we'd purchased for Grandma in Walnut Ridge, but she still wouldn't have anything to do with it. Realizing Grandma wouldn't wear anything but what she actually recognized to be her *own* clothes, Chris and I had driven over to Forrest City on Tuesday afternoon to pick up their abandoned car from the wrecker service company that had been holding it for more than a week. I drove it back to Memphis and, at least for the time being, parked it in the lot behind our apartment building.

The contents of the back seat had revealed tangible proof of the chaotic mindset that had pushed my grandparents to leave their home in the first place. We found all of Grandma's clothes heaped on the floor of the backseat—quite out of character for a woman who had always been neat and orderly. We found one of Grandma's dolls and a purse containing several cards and letters, some of which were from me and some from Lena. I came across a framed photograph of Grandma's parents and another one of me with Duchess. I also found our wedding invitation that we'd mailed to Grandma and Grandpa the year before. It was pressed against a photograph of me in my wedding dress. I remember the pictures had made me smile and cry all at the same time because I realized that even in her jumbled mental state, she had recognized the people in the photographs to be among those whom she loved.

By mid-day Wednesday Chris and I were on the road into Arkansas once more. As anxious as I had been to get up to Grandma and Grandpa on January 16, I was all the more dreading the January 22 trip because I knew we were going to a place that was home to no one except a lonesome dog and a handful of undernourished cows. As we made our way north on Highway 63, the landmarks I had always found so familiar seemed to be glaring at me with cold, angry eyes. Driving into Imboden was especially hard because it seemed that the town itself was refusing to look me in the face.

This place knows, I thought to myself. *This very town knows Grandma and Grandpa are never coming back. And I'm the one who took them away. . . .*

We went in by way of the gravel road I knew so well because we could see that all the snow and ice from the previous week had melted away, even from the grass and the trees. As we approached the long hill that had stopped us cold the week before, we actually managed to laugh a little as we remembered the spinning wheels and flying floor mats, passing with ease the very spot where the trouble had started. That bumpy thread of a road curved and twisted past acres of pastureland and countless rolls of hay on the various farms that had been maintained by the same families for years. As the Meade place came into view, it all looked the same. The curved driveway, the two huge oak trees with the picnic table between them, Grandma's flowerbed. But it was not the same, because absolutely no one came out the kitchen door to greet us. No one.

I drove right into the carport, and we watched Duke as he came out of his dog house and stretched. We could see there was water in his bucket and food in his dish, so we knew Mack Proctor had been looking after him—not that I ever doubted he would.

After our two-and-a-half-hour drive, my body was ready to get out of the car and stretch, but my mind wasn't so eager; I just sat there for a minute, maintaining a tight grip on the steering wheel. I was still trying to comprehend the fact that nobody was there. I sighed heavily and looked over at Chris.

"They're not here," I said. "They'll never again come out onto this carport to greet me. Never again."

Chris's sympathy for my feelings was priceless to me. By his own admission, he had never lost anybody close to him, nor had he ever been through anything that even resembled my present situation. But he knew me, and he knew by my words and by the look on my face that I was hurting very deeply. I cannot thank God enough for providing Chris for me during that awful time. He helped cushion the blow of the realization that my grandparents were not where I wanted them to be. He never tried to explain it away; he didn't try to make me laugh. He allowed me the dignity of experiencing my own pain, wisely accepting the fact that there was nothing he could say that would make it any better. He gave me his support and graciously allowed the necessary tears to fall. As a gesture of love and pure kindness, he simply put his hand on my knee and said quietly, "I know."

I remember the wind was so cold when we finally did get out of the car. I scrambled to unlock the carport door to get us out of the freezing blast. We stepped into the kitchen, and I was bluntly struck with the fact that it was also cold inside the house. Grandpa hadn't been there to keep the fire going, so it had burned out sometime on Saturday, leaving no evidence of its existence but the cold ashes in the stove.

"Listen to the quiet of this house," I said in a low tone. "There's no life here anymore." I looked at Chris with a pained expression. I could feel the bitter sense of loss just as surely as if it was a heavy coat draped over my body. I had never known that air could be so thick and still. I felt like the house itself was in shock; even the furniture seemed to implore me to give some explanation for Grandma and Grandpa's prolonged absence.

"I wonder if death is any worse than this," I said as I looked around.

"Don't start thinking like that," Chris admonished me sternly. "They're not dead, so don't think of them that way."

"I know," I said with a sigh. "But that's what this seems like—a death."

"Well, I guess in a way it is. It's certainly the death of the lifestyle you were used to with them."

I laid my keys down on the kitchen table and gradually walked into the living room, stopping in front of Grandma's recliner.

"So many memories," I said slowly as my eyes roamed from floor to ceiling. "Do you know that Grandpa built this house himself, from the ground up?"

Chris smiled as he regarded the living room. "That's amazing."

"I know. I wouldn't even know where to begin to do something like that," I said.

I looked over at the beautiful crystal hurricane lamps that Grandma had placed symmetrically on either end of the sideboard. "Her brother Ralph gave those to her for Christmas not long before he was shot down," I said. "She always treasured them because they were the last thing he ever gave her." I turned suddenly and looked at Chris. "Do you think they'll be safe here?"

"What do you mean—safe?" he asked with a puzzled look.

"This house is sitting out in the middle of nowhere. When word gets around that nobody's living here, and you know it will eventually, what will happen to all their things? Somebody could just come in here and help themselves!"

Chris looked around the room with a frown. "Yeah," he said, "I see what you mean. Well, we've already asked Mack to keep an eye on things. Beyond that, there's not very much we can do."

The concept of being unable to stop those who would plunder the personal effects of my grandparents left an exceptionally bad taste in my mouth. I had to agree, though, there was no way I could adequately shield a house that was nearly one hundred miles away from where I lived. I knew my first duty was to provide care and protection to Grandma and Grandpa themselves, but as I looked around the house, glancing over their belongings, I felt tremendously helpless because of my inability to provide proper security. It wasn't like they had anything of any great value, but what was theirs was theirs. At last I had to shrug my shoulders in what felt like defeat because I had obvious limitations. Chris suggested that we stop worrying about those things that were beyond our control and set about doing the business that had brought us there in the first place.

He began to gather all of Grandpa's clothes, including pants, shirts, socks, and underwear, packing them in paper grocery sacks that we had found in the utility room. While Chris sorted clothes, I began sifting through the papers and postmarked envelopes that Grandma had been uncharacteristically stuffing into kitchen drawers as well as every other nook and cranny imaginable. The sheer volume of paper was even more evidence of her diminished mental capacity; the Grandma I had always known was of the mind that business should be handled immediately, and all junk mail should be tossed into the stove and burned up.

I worked my way from the kitchen toward the back part of the house. I finally wound up in the front bedroom unlocking Grandma's cedar chest, the formal seat of all Meade business. In it I found records of all kinds, including their auto and homeowners insurance, life insurance, as well as their bank statements and bills from the utility and phone companies. I started to notice some of the bills were stamped, "past due." I continued to dig and found a notice that property tax payment was due, but I saw no corresponding evidence that it had actually been paid. I also found checks in Grandma's handwriting that were dated as recently as December 1998 but only half filled out. Her handwriting on one such check was so distorted, I was unable to decipher the name to which it was made payable; another check reflected a dollar amount and bore Grandma's signature, but it was made payable to no one.

As I looked at paper after paper, I began to comprehend just how deteriorated Grandma's mental status had become *right under my very nose*. I stood there, shaking my head back and forth as recent memories from my own mailbox began to flood my mind. Just one month earlier, I had received two different Christmas cards from Grandma. The first card was addressed to me in a normal fashion, complete with return address, but absolutely nothing had been written on the card inside the envelope. The second card had arrived several days later, also addressed to me in a completely normal way, but inside the card she had written, "With all our love, Granddad and Mom." In all the years she had been sending me cards, never once had she deviated from signing off as, "Grandma and Grandpa." I sat down on the edge of the bed and considered the situation. My eyes roamed aimlessly around the room until they came across a photograph of Grandma. I stared longingly at the picture, wanting so badly to communicate with the woman inside the frame.

"I didn't know," I said to the picture. "I didn't know you needed my help this badly."

I remember gazing back over the mound of papers, and it occurred to me that the half-written checks and unpaid bills seemed like something a person who was half asleep would do—like when you're reading a book and you doze off. The book slumps down on your stomach, your head tilts gently to one side, and if someone tries to talk to you, you sort of mumble a half understandable string of words. That was what talking with her had felt like too. Sentences sometimes remained unfinished, and the faraway look she gave left you half expecting her to just doze off. The utter sense of hopelessness produced by that train of thought brought me to tears—again. But sitting on the bed at Grandma's empty house wasn't getting us anywhere, so whether I went into a sense of outright denial or just felt like I couldn't take it anymore, I rose abruptly from the bed and with a quick, sweeping motion began to empty the contents of the cedar chest into a large box. I decided I would sort through those papers later, some other day, not now.

I returned to the living room and began to go through the mail mountain, getting rid of the obvious junk and putting everything that looked to be of legitimate importance in a designated spot. As the afternoon wore on, though, I found that I was making very little headway. Even when Chris began to help me, the task was daunting; it appeared there was no end in sight.

"We're going to have to pack all this stuff up and take it home so I can go through it properly," I said as I sat back in my chair.

"Yeah," Chris agreed. "We could be here for days just trying to separate the real mail from the heaps of stupid mail! She must have been on every mailing list in America for her to get all this junk."

We began to dump the papers into assorted boxes, grocery bags, and anything else we could find to make transporting it all to the car a little easier. When everything was gathered up, I took the separated pile of junk mail and other throw-away papers to the stove, lit a match, and burned them up. I didn't want to leave identifying papers in the unattended house, thus making it possible for someone to steal my grandparents' respective identities. In the absence of a shredder, burning the junk paper seemed like the next best thing I could do.

As we were stacking the boxes and bags by the door, we heard the sound of a car coming up the driveway. Chris glanced out and saw Mack Proctor. We took the opportunity to thank him again for his watchful eye over Duke, the cows, and the house.

"Oh, I'm just glad to do it," he replied. "Well, tell me how Mr. and Mrs. Meade are doing."

We filled him in on everything that had happened since we'd last seen him. Mack told us that some of his neighbors were already beginning to ask him about my grandparents. "Folks around here know that something's changed. I'm coming up here a couple of times every day, checking on the dog and taking care of the cows. Word of a change gets around fast in a place like this."

"Yeah, bad news always seems to travel fast, no matter where it is," I said with a slight chuckle.

As Mack got ready to leave, we thanked him again for all his kindness.

"We just couldn't have done all this by ourselves," I said.

Chris agreed.

"We really appreciate you putting yourself out by taking care of things on this end. It makes handling the business in Memphis so much easier to know that you've got us covered over here."

Giving Duke a gentle pat on the head, Mack went to his car. After he drove away, Chris and I loaded our car with Grandpa's clothes and the Meade paper stash. We then spent a few minutes with Duke, petting his back and scratching his ears as we tried to assure him that everything was going to be OK. Finally we decided we were ready to hit the road for the long ride home.

As we approached the bank in Imboden, it occurred to me that I should stop in again, this time to discuss the procedure for closing out my grandparents' account and moving their money to our bank in Memphis. It turned out the process was simpler than I thought it would be.

"You can authorize a wire transfer from us to the bank of your choice in Memphis," the teller explained.

I suddenly remembered something that had been long tucked away in the back of my mind. I knew Grandma had set up savings accounts for each of her three grandchildren. She opened one for me when I was born, and a second account was started ten months later when my half-brother Anthony Raymond, Jr., was born. A third account was established a few years later following the birth of Ray's second son by his second wife, my half-brother Duane.

Now that my grandparents were incapacitated, I knew at some point I would need to contact Tony and Duane. If the bank in Imboden showed active savings accounts for my half-brothers, then the time for contact would clearly be sooner rather than later. The problem was I didn't have an address or a phone number for either one of them; I didn't even know if they were still living in the midsouth. I gathered my thoughts and began to explain to the teller about the savings accounts.

"Can you look under the Meade name and see if my grandparents have any other accounts set up?"

"Certainly," she replied. She typed in the necessary information, and we waited while the computer searched the records.

"There is another account here," she said. "It has your name on it, but that's all I see. I show no record of an Anthony, or Tony, and nothing for a Duane Meade either."

"Well, I know she had them set up. She told me so years ago." I sat momentarily puzzled. "I guess that means she's already given them all the money that was in their accounts."

When we got back in the car, Chris asked, "Have you thought about how you're going to get in touch with Tony and Duane?"

"Well, I know I need to do it; I'm just not sure how to go about it." I paused pensively. "I guess I'm going to have to get creative and figure something out."

Tony and I had always gotten along reasonably well on the few occasions that we had been around each other. I understood from Grandma that Ray's disappearing act in 1985 had hit Tony extremely hard. I felt great sorrow for him on that account because the grief of paternal abandonment was something that I, too, understood; but Tony had it worse than I did because he actually grew up into his teen years knowing Ray as his father.

My relationship with Duane, however, was practically nonexistent. I had spent very little time around him when we were children, but I had always believed that he didn't like me at all. Grandma had chalked it up to his being a very quiet, introverted person, but I had perceived it as contempt.

Driving mile after mile, I continued off and on to mull over what to do about contacting my half-brothers. I finally concluded that getting Grandma and Grandpa settled was the top priority of the moment; I would try to figure out how to reach Tony and Duane when I had more information about the permanent arrangements. In hindsight, I really wish I hadn't waited as long as I did, but driven by my discomfort in the relationship and, frankly, my fear of the unknown, I put it off for a full five months.

When we arrived back in Memphis in the early evening, we decided to make a brief stop at the hospital to see how Grandma and Grandpa were doing. On our way down the hall, we passed by the dining room where Chris spotted a checkerboard, so Chris asked Grandpa if he wanted to play a game. As they were setting up the board, I leaned over to Chris and asked him to let Grandpa win. I didn't mean any disrespect toward Grandpa or his capability to play the game; I just wanted to lift his spirits and put a smile back on his face. The fact was that Grandpa had always been able to play checkers very well. Chris later admitted to me he thought like I did, that Grandpa would be terrible given his present mental capacity, but it turned out that he played rather well, legitimately winning the game as Grandma and I sat together looking on.

The next day, I spoke happily to Dr. Carlton about the game's outcome. "I was pleasantly surprised that he was able to play so well after all that's happened," I said in an uplifted tone.

"Well, that's understandable, but don't allow yourself to think too much of it. He probably learned to play checkers many, many years ago. The thing about dementia is that it starts out robbing its victims of only recent memories. Those things that were learned in childhood or even early adulthood may take a little longer, but eventually they too will go the same way. If he lives long enough, the time will come when he no longer understands the concept or strategy of checkers."

The doctor was right.

Ever since receiving Lena's call on Monday morning, it had become a normal part of my day to be awakened by a ringing telephone. As news of my grandparents' situation circulated among the family, I had been getting more and more phone calls from some close—and some not so close—relatives within the Archer and Meade families. By Thursday morning, I had repeated the story of the trip to Forrest City and its consequences so many times that I jokingly told Chris we should just put it all on our answering machine and then turn off the ringers to our phones.

But the voice that greeted me from the other end of the line that morning was not a relative. The young man identified himself as Richard, a medical social worker with Presbyterian Hospital. He informed me that my grandparents would be released from the hospital on Friday, and he wanted to know what, if any, plans we had made for their care. Although I had known their release was forthcoming, I hadn't realized it would be as early as Friday. I sat up in bed to collect my thoughts so I could rationally discuss the tentative plans we'd made.

"When I spoke with Dr. Carlton on Wednesday, he indicated that my grandfather is functioning at a somewhat higher level than my grandmother," I told Richard. "Based on that information, my husband and I are going this afternoon to look at a retirement home. I'm hoping my grandfather will work with us once I explain to him that Grandma's health requires that she stay here in Memphis."

Richard was very encouraging; he agreed that if Grandpa could be made to understand the necessity of caring for his wife, then a retirement home would be perfect for them. We talked for some time about the available options, and then Richard alluded very gently to the fact that the day might come when my grandparents would require assisted living.

"The good news about that is most retirement homes have assisted living facilities on site so if that ever becomes necessary, you could just move them into a new room over on the assisted side."

I appreciated Richard's pleasant manner and tactful choice of words. We continued to talk for several minutes, and then, very slowly, he maneuvered the conversation around to ask me a rather personal question.

"Tell me, Mrs. Stanley, how are *you* doing?"

I found it difficult to answer his question. In my mind I was thinking, *What does it matter how* I'm *doing?* The whole situation, as I saw it, was only

119

about me doing the best I could for Grandma and Grandpa; to my mind, *they* were all that mattered, so I paused at his question and sighed heavily before I spoke again.

"Well, this has been challenging," I said, very matter-of-factly, "but I'm getting through it, sort of one step at a time."

"You're going through some difficult stuff," he said. "Sometimes it's hard to handle all the things that go along with being someone's caregiver. The pressure can leave people feeling overwhelmed."

Richard was one of the first people I'd talked to outside of my immediate circle who acted like they really understood my predicament.

"Yes," I said stoically. "It's very difficult for me to see them like this." I could feel my jaw tighten as I fought to keep it together.

"I just want to let you know that it's OK—normal, even—for you to feel that way," Richard continued, "and there is help available for you if it gets to be too much. The Alzheimer's Association has a lot of information that you might find helpful, and many churches throughout the city offer counseling programs and support groups."

I thanked Richard and told him that I was a member of one of those churches with a great counseling department, and I had already been planning to make an appointment as soon as things with Grandma and Grandpa were permanently settled. Richard said he was glad to hear that.

"It's highly unusual for someone in your age bracket to be handling this kind of situation, and that just adds up to more stress for you. That's another reason we want you to know that support is available."

After Richard and I hung up, I became consumed by the thought of Grandma and Grandpa being released from the hospital the very next day. My thoughts ran rampant as I showered and dressed because the pressure was on to find a place that would be suitable for them. I truly had a lot riding on the fragile idea that Grandpa was in better mental shape than Grandma. I hung suspended between believing we could convince Grandpa that staying in Memphis was the best thing for Grandma, yet knowing in the back of my mind he'd never believe it.

Throughout the week Chris and I had engaged in prolonged speculation about what the best care options for Grandma and Grandpa really were. We talked about the possibility of selling the Meade place in Arkansas, something which the durable power of attorney documents gave me the authority to do, then using the proceeds to buy a home for them in Memphis. Because we had heard stories about Alzheimer's patients just wandering off, many times with tragic results, Chris and I reasoned the only way Grandma and Grandpa would be able to live in suburbia would be for us to move in with them. Doing that would have meant resigning from my job so I could look after them full time. Chris shot that idea down before it ever got off the ground.

"What happens when they die?" he demanded.

I saw the validity of his argument. According to the Meade wills, their "estate" was to be divided into equal thirds between my two half-brothers and me. If I sold the Arkansas property and used the money to buy a house in Memphis, we could then move in and take care of my grandparents. However, upon the deaths of both grandparents, Chris and I could be uprooted from the place we would have been calling home so the property could be sold and the inheritance disbursed. Using the same scenario, it was equally possible that Chris and I could keep the new Memphis house if we bought out my half-brothers, thereby providing their inheritance; but even that seemed far-fetched for the life season we were in. Chris and I had only been married for eight months, and at that time we weren't ready for the financial commitment of owning a home.

We also took into account the information we'd been gathering about Alzheimer's disease. Historically, if an Alzheimer's or dementia patient lives long enough, it is highly probable they will require round-the-clock nursing in a long-term care facility.

"You'd be giving up everything," Chris argued. "Your career, your every waking moment, everything! And to top it all off, they might wind up having to go into a nursing home anyway." He paused before going on. "And what if we ever have children? How could you be both full-time mom and full-time caregiver? It just won't work."

So we initiated the search for "Plan B." We discussed their taking up residence in a nursing home, but only briefly. The idea of putting Grandma and Grandpa in one of those places was so unpalatable I couldn't even talk about it seriously. Long-past memories of other family members having to be put into nursing homes plagued my thoughts. One of Grandpa's sisters had been placed in a nursing home in Memphis when I was in my midteens, and Grandma and Grandpa were going to pay her a visit. I went along with them in blissful ignorance, but I came away very disturbed by the experience. I remember seeing people wandering aimlessly through the halls of the facility. I specifically remember one pitiful old man in a wheelchair who was repeatedly asking for a cigarette. When we left the building, I told Grandma that it was one of the most unsettling experiences I'd ever had.

"It was a terrible place!" I told her energetically when we got into the car. "They're all just waiting to die!"

"Yes," Grandma had replied in a very matter-of-fact tone, "those places are terrible."

I never forgot the way she looked as she agreed with me about that place, and even though she had never made me promise I wouldn't put her in a nursing home, I think I must have somehow vowed to myself that I'd fight with all I had in me to keep her and Grandpa out of any place like that.

"A nursing home is not where they need to be," I argued to Chris. "The doctors are telling me that Grandpa is doing better than Grandma. So if he can understand she needs medical attention, maybe he'll agree to stay."

In fact, Grandpa *was* better than Grandma, but only marginally so. The truth, which I was so blatantly refusing to see, had already been revealed in Dr. Carlton's "twenty-point quiz." Grandpa's score of nine in relation to Grandma's score of seven told the real story. Despite Dr. Carlton's warnings, I wanted to believe that Grandpa would agree to stay in Memphis for Grandma's best interest. I guess I thought that if my will for it to work was strong enough, then it *would* work. To be sure, denial is a dangerous companion because it is powerfully deceptive, able to push a person well beyond the limits of logic and sensibility.

And so, we continued to work our way through the available options, talking next about retirement homes. These are facilities in which people live independently, but they have neighbors who are close by so help isn't as hard to find in the event of an emergency; it's sort of like apartment living for seniors. Furthermore, as Richard had pointed out, most retirement homes have a wing reserved for people who require assisted living, complete with a nursing staff on duty twenty-four hours a day. Chris helped me out tremendously by calling a number of retirement homes whose names he'd found in the phone book.

Several of the facilities he contacted said they didn't have any availability, but finally Chris reached the Manders Retirement Home resident manager, who indicated they did have a one-bedroom unit available. She invited us to come over Thursday afternoon for a tour. I was eager to visit the facility; I wanted so badly for it to be right for Grandma and Grandpa. I latched on to Manders Retirement Home to justify the hope that there could still be life outside of a nursing home for my grandparents.

When Chris and I finally stood in the actual apartment space, I surveyed it with great satisfaction, believing that it was an ideal location for Grandma and Grandpa. Manders was set back off the road in a rather secluded area, a feature which pleased me because it meant that Grandpa and I would still be able to go out for walks just like we'd always done. It seems I was absolutely determined to hang on to the semblance of what had been normal for them—and for me. In hindsight, I can see that I was being very foolish. The overwhelming evidence of the change that had occurred in them positively screamed that a retirement home would never work; nonetheless, I walked very purposely through the unit's small kitchen, living area, and vastly oversized bedroom. I especially liked the fact that the bathroom was equipped with a pull cord which would sound an alarm to bring help if one of them fell. In a pitiful attempt to disavow the horrible experience of the last two weeks, I accepted the apartment on behalf of my grandparents.

With my decision firmly made, I wrote a check from the Meade account to cover their rent for all the days remaining in January and the entire month of February. The resident manager even offered to let Grandma and Grandpa use one of the facility's furnished apartments for a couple of nights, just until we could get their own furniture moved in and properly set up for them.

On Friday, January 24, 1997, my parents met Chris and me at the hospital to help us move Grandma and Grandpa over to Manders Retirement Home. Checking them out of that hospital was almost like closing on a house; I had to sign their names over and over, and right behind their names I had to sign my own name, writing, "legal power of attorney" after each signature. Once all the paperwork was completed, Chris and I met with Richard to go over my grandparents' charts.

"Other than the dementia, your grandfather is in relatively good health for his age, but Dr. Carlton indicates that your grandmother's heart is very weak. Because of that, he has ordered in-home nursing for her which will be paid for by Medicare. Once your nurse and home health aides are assigned, they'll be checking in with you at Manders."

A home health nurse was even better than I'd hoped for, and for the first time in days, I really began to think that everything would be all right for Grandma and Grandpa. We thanked Richard for all his help as we gathered my grandparents' things. We took everything down to our car, paid for our brief parking stay, and then drove around to the front door while Mom and Dad brought Grandma and Grandpa down to meet us.

One of the nurses tried to get Grandma to ride down in a wheelchair, but she would have none of it. Mom later told me that she too had tried to convince Grandma that the wheelchair would help her. After repeated attempts to get her to ride, Grandma stopped in her tracks, turned a frustrated face to my mother and demanded, "*You* ride in it!" And so, the Meade entourage arrived at our car, having been chased all the way from their rooms by an empty wheelchair.

CHAPTER 12

ANGER AND GUILT

O ur arrival at Manders was hampered by having to wait for the resident manager to find the keys to the available furnished apartment. Grandma and Grandpa sat rather impatiently in the lobby with my parents for several minutes until Chris and I finally came back to take them to their temporary room. When Grandpa saw me, he got up and announced that he and Grandma needed to be getting home.

"Grandpa," I said, guiding him toward the elevator, "I've got a surprise for you! Just come with me."

His brows stayed furrowed together, but he walked along with me and got into the elevator without comment. When we walked into the apartment, both he and Grandma just looked around for a few minutes, moving slowly through the living room like two goldfish in a new bowl. I pulled Grandpa aside and began to explain to him that Grandma was going to have to stay in Memphis because of her heart condition. I never discussed her mental status with him at all. Although Grandpa firmly took the position that there was nothing whatsoever wrong with Grandma, he didn't make any protests about staying in the apartment . . . at least not then.

We turned on the TV and got Grandma seated comfortably in one of the living room chairs. Once they seemed settled, Chris and I brought in their clothes from our car, and Mom and I began to separate them into light and dark loads to wash. We spent the better part of the day running to and from the laundry room down the hall; every piece of clothing they owned needed washing. Around 5:00 that afternoon, I went downstairs to request that two dinner trays be brought up to their room. Grandpa ate with a very hearty appetite, but Grandma would hardly touch her food.

As the evening wore on, folks were getting tired. My parents left, and after I finished folding the last of their freshly cleaned clothes, I helped Grandma get into her nightgown. I remember she seemed very tired, so I helped her get into bed.

"Goodnight, Grandma."

She looked up at me with weary eyes. "Goodnight, Sweet," she said with a smile.

"I'll be back tomorrow to see you," I told her as I leaned down to kiss her cheek. "Sleep well. You know I love you."

"Thank you, Sweet. And you know I love you too, hear?"

Before we left, I told Grandpa I had requested the dining room staff to bring two breakfast trays up to their room on Saturday morning, and the same was to be done for lunch and dinner. "You just stay here and take good care of Grandma, and don't worry about anything," I said. "I'll be by tomorrow to see you."

We hugged at their door and said goodnight, then Chris and I walked out. The second he was out of my sight, anxiety began to set in, and the farther down the hall I walked, the more upset I got.

"What if they won't stay there?" I mumbled. "What if they wander off? What am I going to do about them?"

Chris spent the rest of the night trying to assure me they would be all right, but deep in my gut I wasn't convinced. So I moved on to another tactic.

"Oh, God, you've just got to take care of them! You just can't let them wander off. Please make them stay there!"

It was interesting how my "bargaining with God" started right then, rather than a few days before when I was trying to figure out where they should go after leaving the hospital. I was so caught up in the swirl of trying to "do" something that I wasn't taking the time to find out what God wanted me to do.

In fact, my own apprehension should have been a red flag to me, but I was a castaway floating in a sea of denial, aware only that it was my will for Manders to be the right place for Grandma and Grandpa. But side-by-side with my stubborn determination was a nagging panic over them which absolutely refused to let me have any peace, so I was pleading with God like a bratty child, essentially demanding that He watch over them and make this work. Rational thought, it seemed, had completely escaped me; in my foolishness, I was failing to take into account that God actually did have a plan—but it appeared I was going to have to hit rock bottom before I would be ready to cry out in submission to Him. I was moving ahead without looking into His Word or taking any legitimate time in prayer.

But God is still God, and He's able to work things out His way for His glory—even when we are behaving imprudently. I can say this now because it's been my genuine experience: when I was trying so hard to make Manders be the right place for my grandparents—one of my most foolhardy moments—Jesus never stopped loving me or withdrew His Spirit from me. Instead, He took the time to make the necessary course corrections. Just to be clear, though, His goodness to me has absolutely nothing to do with *me*. I haven't earned His love or His favor; it's entirely His own goodness. He's willing to work with anyone, and in my case, He graciously waited for me to see that trying to do this caregiving thing on my own was as futile as chasing the wind.

I was very nervous and upset when Chris and I left Manders, but as we got in the car, I began to realize we had another pressing matter that was competing for our attention. We had to finalize plans to rent a U-Haul moving truck and drive over to Arkansas to pick up the furniture which Grandma and Grandpa were going to need for their new digs in Memphis. Two of our close friends, Karen Caldwell and Jimmy White, had very generously offered to go with us to help move the furniture. Karen and Jimmy were engaged to be married in May, so most of their weekends were spent planning their wedding and looking for a place to live. The gift of their time and help during the turbulence of those early caregiver days truly meant the world to us.

Chris called Jimmy to settle the details of the Saturday road trip, and after they hung up, I called my mother in a rather agitated state to ask her if she and Dad would mind going over to Manders to check on Grandma and Grandpa the next day.

"We'll drop by and stay with them for a while," my mother assured me. "Mother Marine also said something about going by for a visit."

"That's great," I said with a weary smile. "The more the merrier, I guess."

I knew I was doing all I could, and I was truly thanking God for all the people who were helping me, but the nagging fear that Grandma and Grandpa might not "stay put" was like a lead weight on my shoulders. At last I resolved in my mind that most likely they wouldn't try to go anywhere after dark. In fact, while I was lying wide awake and feeling as jittery as if I'd had an espresso shot, they were probably already asleep. Finally, with clenched teeth and knitted brows, I turned out my bedside lamp. As my conscious mind settled down, allowing drowsiness, then sleep to come, my subconsciousness came alive with vivid, agitated dreams.

All the stressful events I'd been living since January 15 came awake in my mind, and they danced across my mental stage to some horrible dirge. All night long, it seemed, I wandered the halls of Presbyterian Hospital with Grandma and Grandpa in tow. They followed me like children up and down escalators, around corners, and down long hallways, going somewhere and nowhere all at the same time. I was aware of being so tired, but I also knew I had to keep going, keep moving. Suddenly Grandpa was in front of me, his face just inches away from mine, and in a rage he screamed, "Take us home!" The image was so powerful that it jerked me out of my sleep as the first light of dawn was filling our bedroom.

I sat up and rubbed my eyes, trying hard to clear my mind of the dreams that had haunted me throughout the night. Chris was just barely awake, but somehow he knew I was upset.

"What's the matter?" he asked in a muffled voice.

"Oh, nothing," I said in a dry, morning voice.

I ran my fingers through my tangled hair, stopping them just as my hands met in the back of my head. Then I leaned forward until my elbows landed heavily on my knees.

"What are you doing awake this early?" Chris persisted as he turned over.

"They want to go home," I said slowly.

"Who does?"

"Grandpa was yelling at me to take him home."

"When? Last night?"

"No, just now. In my sleep. They want to go home, but I won't let them."

Chris stacked two pillows together and leaned back on them. "It was just a bad dream," he said. "It wasn't real."

"Oh, it's real, all right," I said with surprising force. "Real and ugly."

Chris was still trying to wake up, so he didn't say anything more. I could feel my limbs beginning to race with adrenaline as I contemplated all that had to be done before nightfall.

"Come on, let's get this day started," I said. "The sooner it starts, the sooner it will be over."

Karen and Jimmy arrived at our apartment shortly after 7 a.m. We went through the McDonald's drive-thru for breakfast, and then I stopped at a grocery store to buy a fruit basket for Mack Proctor and his family. I just had it in my mind to do some little something to say "thank you" for all they'd done for us. After we topped off the gas tank, I merged with the west-bound traffic on Interstate 40, crossing the Mississippi River for the fifth time in ten days.

We had been told by the truck rental company that we would only be allowed to drive the U-Haul for a predetermined number of miles; after that, we would begin paying a "per mile" charge. For that reason, Chris and I thought it would be better to save mileage by renting the truck in Jonesboro, the halfway point of the drive, then after the move was complete, we could just drop the truck off at a U-Haul rental location in Memphis. After all the rental papers had been duly signed, Chris and Jimmy climbed into the truck and followed my Sunbird the rest of the way to my grandparents' house.

It seemed funny to me, making that drive with Karen under those circumstances. Not that her going with me to see Grandma and Grandpa was all that odd—my grandparents had played host to all three of my close girlfriends on many occasions. Throughout the years, Karen, Lisa, Julie, and I had made several trips up to that house on the ridge. We enjoyed canoeing on the Spring River, which was only about a half hour from my grandparents' home. We'd drive up and spend the night with Grandma and Grandpa, then go canoeing the next day. It was a nice arrangement for me because I got to enjoy the best of both worlds—time with my friends and time with my grandparents.

But my trip on January 25, 1997, was unlike any I'd ever made with Karen because I knew Grandma and Grandpa wouldn't be there to receive her the way they always had been before. How would the absence of Grandma and Grandpa affect my friend? I wondered if she would feel the gaping emptiness the same way I had. Jimmy wouldn't feel it because he'd never been there before, but for Karen, surely for Karen it would be different—and just thinking of that difference made my heart ache because it reminded me *again* of what had been lost.

We drove up to my grandparents' bleak and lonely house under a gray sky which gave no hint of the sun's bright light. The inside of the house was ice cold just like it had been when Chris and I had arrived three days before, but the chill that had been so troubling to me on Wednesday seemed to somehow match my frame of mind on Saturday. The necessary work that had brought us up there was enveloping me with a cold and bitter sense of guilt. I was there to pick and choose the various furniture items, pictures, and accessories that were to be placed with Grandma and Grandpa at Manders, but I was struggling with exactly how one chooses which items will go and which will stay out of a collection that took a lifetime to amass. Their bed would have to go, of course, and their living room chairs, along with the kitchen table. But what about the sideboard with the hurricane lamps? What about her china cabinet which contained the bulk of her spoon collection? What about the cabinet he'd made to display the gold-plated mechanic's tools which had been presented to him for excellence in his work? The apartment at Manders simply didn't have room for everything they owned; all the same, I knew that leaving any single piece behind would make me feel as if I was tearing away an essential part of who Grandma and Grandpa fundamentally were.

The job had to be done, though, so I forged ahead. On the outside I stoically chose what items should go, but on the inside I was crumbling with each uncertain choice. It was strange, because I had believed nothing could ever be as hard as taking my grandparents away from their beloved home, but that afternoon I was finding out that dismantling the appointments of their house was almost as difficult. It was like the things had taken my grandparents' place, and by removing them I was removing my grandparents all over again. Every item had been placed by Grandma and Grandpa just exactly where they had wanted it; who was I to come in and destroy the order of their home?

Karen and I watched as Jimmy and Chris loaded piece after piece into the truck, and when all the large pieces had been successfully moved, Karen helped me take down a lifetime of photographs from one of the walls in my bedroom. Among them was a picture of Grandpa as a very young man, another was of me as a baby, and still another was of Tony and me when we were very young children. One by one we pulled them down, and Karen wrapped them gently in towels so they would be protected during the trip back to Memphis.

At one point, as everybody stopped to take a breather, we saw Mack Proctor drive up. I gave him the fruit basket, telling him how much we had appreciated all the help both he and his family had been to us. He accepted it, but still refused to admit that he had done anything special. We chatted for a while about my grandparents and that wonderful place out in the country which they'd called home for so many years, and as our discussion worked its way around to the house itself, Mack took the opportunity to tell me he had noticed several places on the roof that were in need of repair.

"I haven't been up there to take a close look, but I've noticed some spots where the shingles appear loose or missing altogether. If it's not dealt with, you could wind up with a leak that could do a lot of damage inside the house." He glanced around, then added, "And, you know, come summer, all this grass will need to be mowed."

I looked around that vast lawn, and I remembered what a job it had been to cut, even with a riding mower.

"Oh, my goodness," I mumbled.

"I'd be glad to keep it mowed for you," Mack said. "I'll need to use your grandfather's equipment, of course, but there's no reason I can't do it for you, I mean, since I'm up here and you're not."

Once again, Mack's generosity came to our rescue. I told him that his taking care of the Meade yard would relieve a tremendous burden from my shoulders. By mid-July, after he had been mowing their yard for several weeks, I wound up telling Mack I wanted to give him the John Deere tractor and all its implements as a gift from us, even though I felt like it was a woefully inadequate attempt to thank him for everything he'd done. He protested, as I knew he would, but I insisted, pointing out that the power of attorney documents gave me the authority to do whatever I needed to do with their property. And since Grandpa was no longer going to need it, I couldn't imagine anyone else I would rather see with his tractor.

Just before he left, Mack said he was going to need more money to buy additional feed for the cows. I asked Mack if he could go ahead and buy everything he needed, then mail me the receipts and I'd put a check in the return mail. He said he'd be glad to. As he drove away, Jimmy came up and began patting Duke's back.

"What are you going to do with this fellow?" he asked.

"I don't know yet," I said. "Grandma and Grandpa can't have him at Manders, and our landlady won't allow pets in our apartment. My mother can't take him because Duchy would have a fit. We'll just have to figure something out."

As the afternoon progressed, I found it was like taking a trip down memory lane, sifting and sorting through all the things of my grandparents' lives. Memories dating back to my toddler years tumbled in on one another, each making me smile or cry, sometimes both at the same time. All at once I happened upon an extra pair of Grandma's glasses. I put them in my purse and decided I'd give them to her when we got back to Memphis. I didn't know how long it would be before I could actually have Grandma seen by an eye doctor, so I figured an old prescription with both lenses was better than the newer one with only one lens.

After we had carefully gone through each room of the house, I finally concluded we had packed up everything Grandma and Grandpa would need in their new home. With a last look around, I made sure all the doors and windows were locked, then Karen and I waited in my Sunbird for Jimmy and Chris to seal the doors of the truck.

The drive home seemed painfully long, but I was very thankful to have Karen's company in the car. She let me talk out some of what I was feeling, and, just like Chris, she didn't try to explain it all away or oversimplify the very serious issues I was facing. That day, just like so many times before, I greatly appreciated her faithful listening ear.

When we arrived at Manders, we immediately began to unload everything. I had decided to just get everything inside the apartment for the night and save the unpacking and arranging for the next day. Once the last pieces had been removed from the truck, the four of us went by to see Grandma and Grandpa. I found Grandma to be indifferent to her new location, but right away Grandpa wanted to know when I was going to take them home. I did everything I could think of to settle his mind, assuring him that he wouldn't have to stay in *that* apartment for very long. Our visit was fairly brief because it was late in the evening and we still had to drop off the truck. Our very long day drew to a close as we arrived back at our apartment where, after receiving our sincerest thanks, Karen and Jimmy said goodnight. Once I got inside and settled down, I called my mother to check on how Grandma and Grandpa had done that day. The report was not favorable.

"Grandpa is really agitated," she said.

My face fell, and I sank back into the couch cushions. "How bad was he?" I asked.

"Well, bad enough," Mom said. "Mother Marine got there before we did, and she said he was very angry and demanding to know where you were. She tried to calm him down, but it was not good. She didn't stay very long."

"I can't blame her," I said with a heavy sigh. "I just appreciate her going by there in the first place. And you too."

"Well, I'm glad to help, but I'm really beginning to wonder how long he'll stay at Manders."

She had put into words exactly what I had been thinking all along. As I hung up the phone, I was overcome by an aggressive combination of rage and disgust. I felt like if I didn't do something physical I might fly apart. I wanted to throw glass against the walls; I wanted to yell at the whole world about how ridiculously unfair this whole situation was; and I absolutely craved the opportunity to slap Ray's face for going off and doing his own thing instead of staying put and seeing to his rightful responsibility.

Those violent, aggressive, useless thoughts were churning wildly in my mind, but my body sat motionless on the couch, blatantly refusing to vent the genuine feelings I was experiencing. I knew that I would get up and go quietly to bed, not breaking any glass; I would yell at no one and wouldn't swing my fist at so much as a pillow. I would suppress my base emotions and carry on as if I didn't have a care in the world.

Because I was being driven by nothing less than guilt, I was absolutely refusing to admit that I was horribly angry about being saddled with the tremendous responsibility and, yes, *the burden* of caring for Grandma and Grandpa. Having to actually admit that I saw it as a burden was more than I was ready to deal with; it would have crushed me beneath a load of shame and remorse, the likes of which I couldn't even imagine. I had already felt extreme levels of guilt when I drove them away from their home, and when I authorized the hospital to give them both sedatives, and again when I saw my grandpa tied to a stretcher. Four days later, guilt had rushed over me with a new intensity when I found the jumbled and confused records of their household business—why hadn't I realized something was wrong? How out of touch was I? Another hard hit came when I removed their personal belongings from the house that my grandpa had built. And now, here was my own conscious mind trying to make me admit the fact that I felt angry because I was having to care for my grandparents.

I was angry. I was very angry. I was angry at the disease that was robbing me of my grandparents. I was angry about my own ignorance of things like Medicare and other forms of insurance for the post-sixty-five crowd. I was angry at myself because I hadn't been able to recognize that the strange things Grandma had been saying were actually legitimate signs of a debilitating disease. But underneath it all I was becoming increasingly aware of a very targeted fury directed at their son because he had so contemptuously abandoned them, apparently not caring that one day they might need his help.

Ironically, at the time I don't think I fully realized how angry I had become, or how compartmentalized that anger was. I had just assumed that what I was feeling was fully directed at Grandma and Grandpa personally. But because I didn't want that to be true, I wasn't overly eager to admit it out loud. And so, as I said, I got up quietly and went uneventfully to bed . . . while my temper simmered. . . .

CHAPTER 13

FAILURE

On Sunday morning, I was back at Manders bright and early with my mother, shuffling furniture around and doing some heavy-duty cleaning prior to bringing Grandma and Grandpa into their new home. My Dad and Chris had gone to church to teach their respective Sunday school classes, but both had said they would join us later in the morning. We also had help from Grandma's niece, Peggy, with whom I had spoken just prior to my grandparents' release from the hospital. When I told her about the plans to move them into Manders, she offered to come and help my mother and me get everything ready. It was an unexpected gesture, but one we deeply appreciated.

Peggy's gracious offer to help caused me to once again feel the breeze of encouragement; it was an opportunity to reflect on the sheer number of people who had selflessly extended their hands to help my grandparents and me. I really struggled to find words adequate to describe how thankful I was for all the assistance and support I had been receiving since day one. During that entire season of graduating from grandchild to caregiver, my thoughts had been skewed at best, but even then I had some vague understanding that only Jesus could provide me with such a thorough ring of support; I could see that Jesus, the Living Word, was doing exactly what He said He would do:

Your Word is a lamp for my feet, a light on my path. (Psalm 119:105)

He really was highlighting the path ahead of me; everything that was happening was somehow being overseen by Almighty God, and He was continually showing Himself faithful by providing the help and the direction I needed just when I needed it. Now, as to my listening and following those directions . . . well, I was still somewhat lacking in those areas.

After the cleaning had been done and all the furniture had been properly placed, we brought Grandma and Grandpa into the tidy apartment, and I held my breath as I waited to see what their reaction would be. Grandma sat down in her recliner, but I could tell by the blank expression on her face that it was only because she was tired, not because she recognized the chair as her personal property. I looked at Grandpa and watched him walk around slowly, surveying the furniture carefully. He even bent over one of the end tables to take a closer look at it.

"See, Grandpa," I said with a smile, "I've got your own furniture here for you. You have your own chair, and you'll be able to eat your meals and drink your coffee at your own kitchen table. Now you can feel right at home. What do you think of that?"

"It's nice," he said, looking at me. "It's real nice, but this isn't our furniture."

My jaw dropped as Mom and I looked at each other with wide eyes. I think it's fair to say that neither one of us expected that response—at least not from *Grandpa*.

"Yes, it is, Grandpa," I said, trying not to sound panicked. "It is your furniture."

"No," he said, looking it over again, "this is not our furniture."

My mother stepped up to the plate. "Why do you think this isn't your furniture?"

He turned toward her and smiled. "No," he said in a pleasant but decisive tone, "it's not ours."

"But Grandpa—"

"Where is our car? We need to get it so we can go home."

And so it started up again—the same discussion we'd been having about their car. I assured him I would take care of it, but he wanted to get it right away. I told him that now wasn't a good time, etcetera, etcetera. We were so relieved when Chris and Dad finally came in because their arrival successfully drew Grandpa's attention away from that car.

The little living room seemed almost overcrowded as Mom, Dad, Chris, Peggy, Grandma, Grandpa, and I all settled in for a Sunday afternoon visit. Peggy proved to be a marvelous guest for Grandpa because she was able to get him talking about generic, benign things which held his interest. After about an hour of rather relaxed conversation, she announced that she had to leave. As I walked her to the door, I stated again how much we appreciated everything she'd done. Shortly after her departure, Dad also decided to head home since Grandpa appeared to be more settled than when he'd first arrived.

While my parents chatted briefly in the doorway about what time Mom would be getting home, I suddenly remembered the old pair of glasses that I had brought back from Arkansas for Grandma. I went to get them and encouraged Grandma to trade them out for the broken pair she was wearing.

"Oh no, Sweet," she said firmly. "I can't wear those glasses."

"But Grandma, these are *your* glasses. They're an old pair of yours, and I believe you'll be able to see out of them much better than the ones you're wearing."

She looked up at me with a determined expression and stated belligerently: "Those are *not* my glasses!"

It was incredible, because even after all I'd been through, I was still shocked by the level of agitation Grandma would demonstrate toward me from time to time. In truth, the real problem was that I had, in a purely psychological way, refused to accept the legitimacy of the Alzheimer's diagnosis as an explanation for the behavioral changes Grandma had displayed. I wanted so badly to believe the doctors had exaggerated the significance of her symptoms, even though I could clearly see it all for myself. I simply had not been able to take in the idea that those symptoms were tell-tale signs of an insidious disease that would keep marching forward until my grandma was gone. But all the denial in the world couldn't get me away from the fact that everything I had learned about the indicators of Alzheimer's disease read like a laundry list of Grandma's symptoms: disorientation as to time and place, severe memory loss, dysphasia (inability to find the right word), and *abrupt changes in mood.*

So, as I stood there, holding that pair of glasses out to Grandma, I felt somewhat dazed as my brain searched in vain for an explanation, other than Alzheimer's, for her antagonistic attitude.

Maybe she's just tired, I thought, *or maybe she's upset by the move. Or maybe it's malnutrition.*

Maybe, maybe, maybe.

My mother, seeing the stupor I was in, intervened. "Don't push her," she said quietly. "Just let her wear the broken glasses for now. We'll try again later."

I went into the tiny kitchen and tossed the glasses on the counter. I thought I would jump out of my skin as I stood there, wondering if that was how she was going to act for the rest of her life. The problem was that my subconscious removal of the Alzheimer's diagnosis from Grandma's behavioral equation had left me with *no* logical explanation as to why she couldn't understand that it was me, Leah, her own granddaughter, and that I only wanted to help her. I paused before the sink, wringing my hands and shaking my head, muttering to God under my breath that the whole screwball situation was just one big mess. While I was stewing around, shamelessly expressing my annoyance to the kitchen appliances, I noticed Chris out of the corner of my eye as he moved in a deliberate way toward the front door.

"Where are you going?" I asked irritably.

"Someone's knocking!" he said defensively.

"Oh," I said, pretty embarrassed because I realized that my own anxiety had drowned out the sounds of the world around me—and because I realized I was acting like a jerk.

Chris opened the door to a tall, dark-haired woman who pleasantly announced that she had been assigned as Mrs. Meade's home health nurse. I screwed a fake smile onto my face and introduced myself.

The nurse spent quite a bit of time with us that day, getting to know Grandma while I sat seemingly chained to the kitchen table, filling out enough papers to keep even the most fastidious bureaucrat happy. As I had expected, the home health agency needed copies of Grandma's durable power of attorney document as well as her Medicare and supplemental insurance cards. The nurse also showed me a care plan she had worked out, explaining the agency's time with Grandma would be evenly split between herself and a home health aide who had already been assigned to our case. I was so glad to see that Grandma apparently liked her new nurse, freely surrendering her arm for a blood pressure and pulse check, then accepting a thermometer in her mouth without the slightest hesitation.

Just as I was signing the last of the papers, my mother had an idea flash into her mind. She grabbed the old pair of glasses from the kitchen counter and thrust them into the nurse's hands. "See if you can get her to wear these," she said, briefly explaining what had happened earlier.

The nurse walked over to Grandma and boldly pulled the glasses from the lab coat pocket she'd just sneaked them into. "Mrs. Meade, let's see if these glasses won't do better for you."

To this day I'm not sure if it was the nurse's confident manner or the starched white medical uniform that did it, but Grandma took off the broken glasses, laid them in her lap, and reached for the pair in the nurse's hand. She put them on and pronounced them perfect. I just pursed my lips and shook my head.

"Well!" Chris said, looking at my mother and me as he raised his eyebrows sarcastically. "Wonder why *we* didn't think to do that?"

The nurse smiled and quipped that it was the uniform. "The lab coat does wonders!" she said. She packed up the newly signed papers and then said goodnight to Grandma and Grandpa. I walked her to the door, and as we stood outside in the hall, she turned a serious face toward me and asked how I was doing.

"You're the second person to ask me that," I said with a smile. "Do I just have the look of someone who's about to break under the pressure?"

"No, but you're in a devil of a position," she said in a grave tone. "Being a caregiver isn't easy no matter which way you cut it, but your problem is compounded because you're looking after two people, not just one. I'm as interested in your well-being as I am in your grandmother's."

I let down my guard somewhat, admitting to her that I was going through one of the toughest things I'd ever endured in my life. She recommended at once that I go see a counselor; I told her that I did plan to see a professional counselor through my church once Grandma and Grandpa were settled.

"That's excellent," she said. "It's very important for people who are dealing with these hard issues to know there are professionals who can help. You're not alone on the front lines, although I'm sure that's how you must feel."

I thanked her for being so understanding, and I told her how glad I was that she had been assigned to Grandma's case. We said goodnight, and I went back into the apartment. As I closed the door, my mother walked up to me, holding the broken pair of glasses. With a wry smile, she said, "Who'd have guessed she'd listen to a nurse?"

"Well not me, that's for sure. The way she's always hated members of the medical profession, I'm truly surprised that she didn't throw a fit the minute the nurse walked in." I paused, covering my mouth as I yawned aggressively. "I'm just glad she's finally got a decent pair of glasses. And now that she's got them, I just want to go home and go to bed."

"Yes," Chris said with a tired sigh, "let's go home. They'll be all right for tonight."

We gathered our things and said a warm goodnight to Grandma and Grandpa, and then three exhausted people left Manders with tentative plans to return the following day.

On Monday morning, Chris left for work at his usual time, but I remained at home making phone calls. I contacted their phone and electric companies, their life, health, and homeowners insurance companies, as well as the Post Office. I methodically informed each organization of the changes that had taken place, giving them my name and contact information, directing them to send all correspondence and outstanding bills to me for immediate payment. I had a legal pad on the desk in front of me, and its pages were filled with notes of what each company needed in order to get all the business transferred over to me. Some needed copies of the power of attorney documents while others were going to send me the specific forms that I needed to fill out, sign, and mail back so I could be authorized to handle the business in question. I felt like a circus performer who was trying to spin a record number of plates under the "big top" as my overwhelmed brain was trying to sort out just exactly who needed what. As I surveyed the list of people with whom I'd spoken that morning, I felt a small sense of relief that I was finally taking some tangible steps toward getting the Meade business back on track.

After a quick lunch, I met my mother in the parking lot of Manders, and as we walked up to my grandparents' apartment, I told her that, ironically, dealing with their business had actually taken my mind off of worrying about what Grandma and Grandpa themselves were up to.

Grandpa opened the door to my knock, and he smiled when he saw that it was us.

We went in and hugged both Grandma and Grandpa, asking how they were doing and if they had slept well the night before. As I walked by their bedroom door, I was shocked to see that *all* their clothes were loosely folded across the top of their bed. I looked at Grandpa and realized he was wearing his brown zip-up jacket as if he was getting ready to go outside.

"Grandpa," I asked, looking back at the pile of clothes. "Why are all of your clothes on the bed?"

"We need to take them with us," he explained. "You need to take us to our car so that we can go home."

My mother and I exchanged a quick glance.

"Now, Grandpa," I said as calmly as I could, even though I could feel the frustration starting to build, "you don't need your car."

He looked at me anxiously. "Now, I had that car, and it got left somewhere. I want that car."

"Grandpa, I told you the other day that you can't go back to Arkansas. You've got to stay here and take care of Grandma. She's—not doing well."

"There's nothing wrong with her except that she needs to go home," he said with definite conviction. "Now get me that car."

"Grandpa," I hesitated, not really sure what to say to him as he was growing more and more demanding. "I promise you don't need that car."

In one quick, unexpected action, Grandpa violently grabbed my arm and shook me with a hard jerk. "Where is it?" he demanded angrily.

I stared at him with wide eyes as a wave of adrenaline shot through my body. Never in my life had I ever seen Grandpa behave in such a manner. His body language actually seemed threatening, and the expression on his face was frightening as he held my arm so tightly that my hand began to throb.

My mother, standing several feet away at the time, couldn't believe what she was seeing. She moved quickly toward us, and the three of us stood there, entrenched, while Grandpa's eyes locked intensely with mine. I hesitated only a second, then broke under his glare, blurting out the truth.

"It's wrecked, Grandpa!"

"Wrecked?!"

I'd never heard such rage in his voice.

"*Who* wrecked it?"

Tears stung my eyes and the lump in my throat almost choked me as I finished telling him the ugly truth. "*You* did!"

He stared in disbelief. "I did?" he said in a frustrated tone as he let go of my arm.

"Yes, Grandpa, you did, when you were in Forrest City."

He stared at me with his brows pushed together like he was mad at the world, but at the same time, there was a look of confusion in his eyes that just made me weep.

"We haven't been to Forrest City," he said slowly.

"Yes, Grandpa, you have," I said as the tears fell. "You had a flat tire, and the sheriff had to take you and Grandma to Walnut Ridge. It was a mistake, Grandpa. You never meant to go there."

He turned away from me, and I could absolutely feel the wheels of his mind trying to turn. It was obvious he had no memory of the events I was describing to him. A heavy silence fell over the room as I, too, turned away, forcefully shutting my eyes and involuntarily putting my hand over my mouth. I was utterly shocked by the fact that I'd had to tell him *the truth*.

"We need our car so we can go home," he repeated in his normal voice. "Do you have the keys?"

I turned back to face a man who was completely changed. He wasn't the raging intimidator from the moment before. He was just Grandpa again. My eyebrows moved slowly together as I realized that the angry confrontation we'd just had was completely gone from his mind. I drew a deep breath, afraid to even speak for a few seconds.

"I'll get it, Grandpa," I said slowly. "I'll take care of it."

He nodded slightly and turned toward his chair. He sat down and put his hands on his knees, glancing around calmly as if nothing had happened.

I looked at my mother and just shook my head; then I went into their bedroom and began to re-hang all their clothes. Mom turned on the TV for them and then came in to help me, but we worked in silence; both of us were more than a little rattled by the scene that had just taken place. On the outside, I was calmly hanging dresses, shirts, and pants; but inside my mind I was frantically trying to make sense of Grandpa's behavior. It didn't help that

I still had not fully accepted his mental capacity as being almost as poor as Grandma's, although I do remember thinking to myself, *He's acting just like her.*

If I couldn't get Grandpa to understand that he had to stay there with Grandma, then that would mean . . . I didn't know what that would mean. I didn't *want* to know what that would mean. So I just hung those clothes one piece at a time, and as I did so, I again stuck my head as far down in the sand as I could get it. By the time Chris joined us when he got off from work, I had convinced myself that Grandpa was merely making his own adjustments to his new life in Memphis. *A little more time*, I told myself, *and he would be fine.*

Chris's arrival preceded that of Grandma's new home health aide by only a few minutes. She was a very polite woman who told us she would be helping Grandma with her hygiene needs such as bathing, brushing her teeth, and combing her hair. I was delighted to have her help, and I introduced her to Grandma at once. Grandma was polite enough at first, but she established her position quite firmly when the aide asked her if she was ready to take a bath. She looked coldly at the woman and responded by uttering a shocking and racially insensitive phrase. I was horrified.

I can still see her sitting there with that look of proud innocence on her face. The aide took it in stride, but when I walked out into the hall with her, I apologized over and over. She assured me it was all right and urged me not to give it another thought.

"A lot of people in her age bracket just have that mentality," she said with a smile. "I don't take it personally."

As we lay in bed that night, Chris and I talked it over.

"I wanted to melt into the floor when she said those words!" I told him, shutting my eyes in an effort to block it out.

"I can't believe the aide didn't deck her right then and there," Chris said.

Realizing that was true, I felt a wave of dismay wash over me as I contemplated the various other things that Grandma or Grandpa might say, and I told Chris that I wouldn't be surprised if other similar statements were forthcoming.

"Well," he responded, "it's like the health aide said: they're both in the age bracket where they have certain racial opinions. Unfortunately the disease they've both got seems to remove all sense of social awareness. I guess that's why the aide can take it so well, because she realizes it's the disease talking."

In a drowsy voice, I agreed with his statement, but my eyes were growing so heavy that I knew any further conversation would have to wait until the next day. I made a last adjustment to the covers and finally gave in to the sleep which both my mind and my body were craving. As tired as I was, I thought my sleep would be heavy enough to drown out the nightmarish images which had been recently plaguing me in the wee hours of the morning, but I was wrong. That night was again restless and broken by bizarre dreams and periods of wakefulness—a tribute, I'm sure, to the constant and intense stressors that had been recently incorporated into my life.

When morning came on Tuesday, Chris got up at his usual time and departed for work. It was quite a bit later that I was able to drag myself out of bed, and almost immediately I began to go through the boxes of papers we'd brought back from my grandparents' house the week before. As I sifted and sorted through the mounds of junk mail, my phone rang. The call was brief, but its impact reverberates in my mind to this day. I terminated the call with my thumb, and without putting the receiver down, I immediately dialed Chris's office.

"We've got to go to Manders," I said in a monotone voice.

"What's wrong?" Chris asked anxiously.

"The resident manager just called. She tells me that Grandma and Grandpa are in her office, demanding that she get them a van so they can take all their furniture and go home." I paused, fighting back the tears as the repulsive truth slapped me squarely in the face. There could be no more denial. The facts now had to be faced and accepted as they really were. Manders was not the right place for them. It had *never* been the right place for them. I cleared my throat very deliberately and said quietly, "I've failed miserably here. There's only one place they can go now."

CHAPTER 14

VIVIAN

I was glad my dad had already looked into Waverly Nursing Home; even so, the difficulty of making my first call to them left me absolutely numb. My thoughts were jumbled as I realized I was going to have to blaze new trails through my neural network, trails that would hopefully lead to some form of acceptance when it came to seeing my grandparents in a nursing home.

Even in the face of all that had happened, I found my mind was still wildly searching for *any* option other than a nursing home to provide their care. I was uselessly and foolishly revisiting previously discarded ideas like, *Maybe we could buy a house and move in with them*. From there I would quickly jump to any one of a dozen reasons that wouldn't work: *They'll constantly be demanding that I take them "home"* or *None of us have enough money for that*. I would then leap to, *Maybe we could hire a round-the-clock nurse to move in with them*, followed quickly by, *Oh yeah, they have no money for that*. Same old thoughts . . . nothing new here. The only new thought was the realization that I was backed into a corner, and the only way out was through Waverly. So, fully convinced there were no other choices, I sat down at my desk and slowly dialed the number to the last resort.

My call was routed to a woman named Audrey, a social worker who handled admissions. She was kind and extraordinarily helpful as she explained that yes, they did still have an opening for a couple. I began making notes of the various papers they required in order to admit Grandma and Grandpa as residents in their facility. Audrey described to me how life in the nursing home would work for them, including food, laundry, hygiene, and medical care. She also explained about their money.

"If your plan includes getting them on Medicaid, then by law each one of them is permitted to keep up to two thousand dollars in a checking account, so that's four thousand dollars for both of them," she said.

My eyebrows pulled together involuntarily as I contemplated the slightly more than eleven thousand dollars they had in their checking account. It seemed ironic that they didn't have enough money for private nursing care, but they had too much money for a nursing home.

"Well, that overage will have to be spent down," Audrey said. "You can purchase things they may need like clothes and any furnishings they might want in their room to make it more like home for them. You could also use it to prepay funeral expenses."

That was something I hadn't thought of. Somewhere in the back of my mind, I seemed to recall that Grandma told me they had already made their funeral arrangements, but in the vast mound of papers I had retrieved from their house, I hadn't seen anything to prove it—something else for me to look into.

"You can also use their money to pay their monthly housing at Waverly," she said. "Their private insurance and Medicare will pay a portion of the cost, but not all of it. Once their money runs out—meaning when they get down to the allotted two thousand dollars per person—then you can apply for Medicaid from the State of Tennessee."

Audrey explained that their out-of-pocket monthly payments would be several hundred dollars per person, even with insurance helping out. It wouldn't take long for their money to disappear at that rate, so making sure the funeral plans were finalized began to sound like a really good idea.

"What about their monthly Social Security checks?" I asked.

"Those you will essentially sign over to Waverly," she answered quickly. "It's considered payment toward their care."

It sounded so simple: "payment toward their care." Logically—financially—I understood the nursing home would be providing a level of care I couldn't give them myself. And when I considered the cost of food, beds, utilities, medical equipment, and staff on duty, the extremely high price of nursing home care made sense, but it just felt like this impersonal institution was going to take everything: their money, their resources, their—

Then it hit me: their house and their property.

"What about their home? They have some land and a house in Arkansas. What's going to happen with that?"

"Well, there are some options," Audrey began. "You can sell it outright and then spend the money down toward their care, or you can rent the property to someone and use the rental income toward their care. Once they are accepted on Medicaid, the social worker assigned to their case can give you more specific details."

My first thought was that renting sounded like the best way to go. By renting the property, it appeared I could actually protect it until after they were deceased, at which point I could sell it and divide the proceeds between my half-brothers and me—just the way Grandma and Grandpa had directed in their wills. However, as I turned the possibility over in my mind, it didn't take long for me to realize I didn't know a soul to rent it to. The only people I knew over there were Mack and Betty Jo Proctor, and they already had a house.

"Well, I'm glad to hear there are some options, but I'm also glad I don't have to deal with that today. Right now, the most pressing matter is to get them over to you as quickly as possible." I paused a few seconds, considering how I should broach another subject that was weighing heavily on my mind. "I have one question about security," I began. "My grandfather doesn't want to be anywhere but his home in Arkansas. As for Grandma . . . well, the truth is she doesn't know where she is. But Grandpa—are you going to be able to keep him there? I mean, actually inside the facility?"

My question felt like it rambled on and on, and I wasn't sure I'd even made my point when Audrey said confidently, "There's a code you have to punch in to exit the facility because there is actually an alarm on the door that will sound if it's pushed open. If he tries to leave without entering the code, we'll know about it."

It was both reassuring and unsettling at the same time. The feeling washed over me again that I was doing a horrible thing—*locking* my grandparents in a facility where they wouldn't be free to leave, but I also knew they simply weren't able to continue living on their own. All the competing thoughts turned my brain into a synaptic arena where notions and ideas became gladiators; every thought seemed to be fiercely clashing with every other thought, and guilt was the bloody aftermath.

Audrey picked up on my hesitation. She assured me that, given their present states of mind, Waverly was a good place for them.

"What you have to realize is that Alzheimer's disease never gets better; it actually progresses and gets worse over time. We have the professional staff and facilities to provide the level of care they'll need as time goes by," she said. "It would become increasingly difficult for you to keep both of them at home."

I knew she was right, but I still hated it.

When Chris and I arrived at Manders, the resident manager met us as we walked in the door. She pointed out Grandma and Grandpa who were waiting just inside the lobby. They stood up as soon as they saw me.

"They are verrrrry serious about going home," the manager said, almost under her breath. "They've asked for a van for their things. At one point, she asked me where she could get a 'streetcar,' and your grandfather has absolutely demanded that I call you to come and get them."

She looked exasperated as they walked up. I hugged them both, but before I could utter a word, Grandpa said very seriously, "Sweet, we've got to get home."

"I know, Grandpa," I said, sounding more weary than I meant to. "I've got everything taken care of." I turned to the resident manager and told her I had made all the necessary arrangements to move them to Waverly. She closed her eyes as she slowly nodded, obviously confident it was the best move.

"It will be the weekend before we can get all their things out of the apartment," I said.

The manager said that was no problem. She turned to Grandma and Grandpa and warmly shook hands with both of them, saying what a pleasure it had been to meet them, and she wished them "the best of luck in the future."

Our ride to Waverly was uneventful; Chris drove, and we chatted with Grandma and Grandpa about ordinary things like the weather and the sights we saw along the way. When we pulled into the parking lot, we met my parents. My mother's face looked pained with grief. She couldn't even say anything but put her hand on my arm as a gesture of support. A slight nod was the only response I could give.

We walked in, and after a brief wait, we met Audrey. She took Chris and me into her office, and we began to swap our documents—mine she had to make copies of, and hers I needed to sign. I signed two copies of every document—one in Grandma's name and the other in Grandpa's—the agreement to abide by the terms of residency, the choice of a physician, the approval for them to receive medical care, the papers that identified me as their legally recognized agent-in-fact, and a whole slew of other pages which became one long, carbon-copied blur.

"We're almost done," Audrey said with a smile. "We have this one last sheet which deals with emergencies." She placed two copies of the same document in front of me. "In the event they are found unresponsive, do you want us to resuscitate?"

I heard the question clearly, but after it was asked, the sound of it just seemed to hang in the air, ringing in my ears. The shock of it—the reality of the need to ask it—rendered me speechless. The only response I had to prove

I wasn't completely unconscious were the tears that fell heavy and hot down my cheeks. Before I could gather myself to even acknowledge I'd heard the question, I realized Chris was answering for me.

"Yes," he said.

Immediately I began to sob because I knew that wasn't the right answer, but all I could do to correct it was to shake my head vigorously back and forth. I *knew* the answer; Grandma and I had discussed it at length on several occasions, and they had actually spelled it out in their power of attorney documents. She had always emphatically stated that neither she nor Grandpa ever wanted to be "brought back" if they were found not breathing or with no pulse. I knew I had to be true to their wishes.

Audrey had given me a tissue, and as I wiped my eyes, I managed to groan out, "Do *not* resuscitate."

And with that, Edward and Clara Meade became permanent residents of Waverly Nursing Home, effective January 28, 1997. After I had managed to compose myself, I suggested to Audrey that she take them to their room without me so we could avoid what might be an ugly scene. She agreed, and we went back into the lobby where Grandma and Grandpa were waiting with Mom and Dad. Audrey began talking to them, directing them to the door that went into the facility proper. They went with her easily enough, never turning around to look at me or ask me anything. It was one of the most painful, yet oddly uneventful, experiences of my life. I stood and watched them go while my mother wept silently, pulling a tissue from her purse. My dad put his arm around my shoulder and assured me this was the best thing—the *right* thing—and Chris quickly agreed with him.

In spite of how painful it all was, I truly felt more secure leaving them at Waverly than I had felt when they spent their first night at Manders. I knew that here they would be safe; they wouldn't be able to just leave their room and wander off to who knows where. I told Chris what I was thinking and asked him if he thought I was crazy.

"I actually had the same thought," he said.

"But it still doesn't seem like 'home'," I told him. "It seems like a hospital. Tile floors, those cheap, ethereal landscape paintings all down the hall. And the rolling pill trays and linen hampers. Oh, and the big, fat nurses' station in the middle. Real homey." I could feel my agitation beginning to rise.

"Well, there's only so much they can do," Chris answered. "I mean, a huge part of what they do *is* medical."

"I wonder what the real 'bells and whistles' nursing homes are like?"

"People who can afford the bells and whistles can afford to bring private nurses into the comfort of their own homes," Chris answered dryly.

"Well, that wasn't an option for them," I snapped back, "so because they don't have boatloads of money, they get stuck in the clinical, tiled, hospital-wanna-be that smells worse than a public restroom!" I was too mad to cry and too agonized to argue.

I stared blankly out the window as we drove back toward Manders to pick up Grandma's and Grandpa's clothes. We were going to run them back to Waverly before going home for the evening; that way they would have clean clothes, and it would be one less thing to deal with as we moved the furniture out exactly one week after we'd moved it in.

"I'm sorry," I mumbled to Chris as we opened the door to their empty apartment.

Chris closed the door and pulled me close to him. I hugged him back as he assured me he understood.

"This is intense," he said.

"Yes, it is, but you haven't done anything to deserve being talked to so ugly," I responded.

"Well, I forgive you," he said with a slight chuckle, "but, if I may suggest, without sounding like I think you're out of your mind, it might not be a bad idea for you to talk to a counselor. This has been very stressful; it would be for anybody. It might not hurt you to just talk it out with someone."

I had been telling people I would see a counselor once I got them settled. So, now they were "settled" at Waverly, but still I wrestled with the notion of making an actual appointment. It had sounded a lot better when I perceived it as something I would do later, in the future; part of me wanted to blow Chris's suggestion off, using the excuse that I really didn't have time for all that right now. Too many details to see about, too many phone calls to make, etcetera. But there was also a certain appeal—sitting down with someone and pouring it all out. I had actually seen a counselor when I was in my early twenties because I had come to realize I held a great deal of hostility toward Ray and his abandonment roadshow. Vivian Holmes, a counselor on staff at our church for many years, had spent a lot of time with me as I worked through my unresolved anger and hurt. Before Chris and I began dating, I had developed the generalized notion that if men treated women the way Ray had treated my mother, then I figured staying single was a better idea. Vivian had gently and lovingly walked me through the maze of lies which I had accepted as truth about how men and women should treat each other. As a result of our time together, I was able to let down my walls and allow my relationship with Chris to grow and develop.

I walked into Vivian's familiar office with the oversized desk and the comfortable chairs that sat at a slight angle toward each other. Before sitting down across from me, Vivian shut her door and tilted her blinds up like she always did.

"So what's up, girl?" she asked as she settled into her chair.

I drew in a breath to speak, and it was like my cork popped. I began by telling her everything that had happened since the first call from Mack Proctor, and I concluded with the most recent event of watching Audrey walk Grandma and Grandpa into what was undoubtedly going to be their final home—a point on which I suddenly became fixed.

"I'm twenty-nine years old," I blurted out. "At twenty-nine, ordinary people are looking forward. I just got married. I'm at the beginning of everything, but I've been suddenly thrust into their reality, and now everything looks like it's just going to . . . to end. It's like life is over; everything is paused and still and waiting."

"What do you feel like you're waiting for?" Vivian asked gently.

I stared blankly for a few seconds, and then I looked straight into her eyes. "We're going to die. Not today, maybe, but it's where we're headed." I leaned forward slightly in my chair as my feelings rose intensely. "I have this thing about hands," I said, almost breathlessly. "Hands in a casket. You know how you go to a funeral and the person is laid out with their hands folded neatly—too neatly—across their stomach?"

Vivian's expression matched my intensity as she nodded slightly.

"Have you ever noticed the hands? They look almost plastic. They look dead. Weird. Not natural. Not warm and touchable. Not the hands that pushed your hair back or touched your cheek with a loving pat. They're disturbingly still, dead hands. It's like the fingers have been glued together or sprayed with some kind of creepy glaze. They're dead, and they won't return the squeeze from your own hand anymore."

I paused, a little astonished at the words gushing out of my mouth. What was wrong with me? It was like some kind of macabre dam had burst. "I found myself looking at Grandma's hands the other day," I continued forcefully, "and then it came over me that one day those hands were going to be dead. Dead Grandma hands. Those wonderful, warm, soft hands that have made me quilts and doll dresses and flipped pancakes for me and stroked my hair and pulled me to her for those tight, squeezy hugs she gives."

All at once I stopped. I leaned back against my chair and looked around the room, finally letting out a long, slow sigh. Vivian just waited silently until my gaze met hers. Then she leaned toward me, placing her elbows on her knees and holding out her hands, palms up with fingers spread wide apart.

"Leah, someday these will be dead hands," she said very matter-of-factly, "but right now they're living hands that can still hold yours—still reach out to you with a loving touch. They're still warm and vibrant. Your Grandma and your Grandpa are still living—and so are their hands. You're experiencing a great loss that's coming in stages, and it's left you devastated. Your feelings are perfectly normal because you're experiencing them being 'gone' in the sense that they're not mentally who you've always known them to be. Someday they will be gone physically too, but that day's not today. Embrace them where they are today, Leah. Touch them, love them, enjoy them, remember who they were. Don't put them in that casket before it's time. Grieve the loss of what was, but seize every day you still have with them. Allow the nursing home to 'care' for them and you just love them. Your love for them honors both God and your grandparents. And yes, you *are* at the beginning of your life, and you need to understand that if your grandparents were in their right minds, they wouldn't want you to give up your season of life to be immersed in theirs."

She paused and reached over to pat my hand gently. "Honor them by loving them, overseeing their care, and by living your life in a way that makes you part of their legacy."

CHAPTER 15

THE NEW NORMAL

S aturday morning found us over at Manders for the last time. With Jimmy
and Karen to help us again, we reloaded all the Meade furniture and their
personal items, then set out for their house in the foothills of the Ozarks.
Duke seemed pleased to see us as we pulled up. We immediately went to
work unloading the furniture. Everything went back into the house except for
Grandma's rocking chair along with a few of her photographs that we were
going to carry back with us for her to have at Waverly.

At some point in the early afternoon, I stood on the edge of the carport
and spent a substantial amount of time petting Duke. As I leaned over and
rubbed his neck, I glanced out behind the house toward the cabin and saw
the little shed with the feeding trough and the deeply grooved remains of a
salt lick. I saw the barbed-wire fence and the gate which was securely shut.
I saw the tattered remains of a roll of hay and the tree line at the back of
the property. What I did not see, however, was even a single cow. Mack had
taken care of getting them sold for us, but their absence made the back of the
property look like a ghost town.

It hadn't always been like that. I smiled slightly as I recalled the image of
Grandpa carrying two weighty buckets of cow feed, walking stiffly toward the
trough—something I'd seen him do hundreds of times over the years during
the winter months. All the cows would gather at the point where Grandpa
first began pouring the feed into the trough, then they would follow each
bucket as he walked from one end of the shed to the other.

I used to help him feed his cows when I was there during Christmas break. I remember being astonished at how heavy the buckets were when they were loaded with the grainy substance that always reminded me of birdseed. I also used to chuckle at how eager the cows were to get to the grain—no matter who was pouring it. Clearly not domesticated animals, the cows displayed no affection toward the hand that fed them, but there were times when I could literally feel the ground vibrate as they aggressively pushed their way toward the food itself. Grandpa had to keep a watchful eye out to make sure all the cows were able to get to the trough. He would talk about how some of the bigger ones would try to block the smaller ones, so he would reach over the rail and give them a gentle but firm nudge to back off. And when the food was gone, the cows meandered off toward the roll of hay while Grandpa returned the buckets to the cabin—his makeshift storage room for the cow feed.

I found the memories come tumbling back into my consciousness as I looked across that yard, scratching Duke's ears, but the present circumstances made it feel like the whole world was upside down; the cows were gone, Grandma and Grandpa were gone—sort of. They were gone from their home, but as Vivian had pointed out, I could still go see them and talk to them. Glancing down at Duke, I felt somehow like I owed him an explanation.

"They just couldn't stay," I said quietly as I looked into his eyes. "I didn't ever want to take them away from here. And I know they love you and miss you."

He sat quietly at my feet, wagging his tail slightly as his gaze met mine with an intelligent intensity. It almost broke my heart to think how lonely he must have been after they left.

The kitchen door swung open, and Chris came out to the carport. A few seconds later, Jimmy and Karen walked up from the van.

"Have we got everything?" Chris asked, reaching down to pat Duke's head.

Jimmy pointed up to the cabin. "Is there anything in there you might want to get?"

I stood up straight and looked at the lonely cabin. I hadn't even considered going in there since the whole thing first started. "I don't know," I stated flatly. "I guess I better check."

I started out across the yard, walking under the two huge oak trees, past the picnic table set between their large trunks, and approached the door to the screened-in porch on the west end of the cabin. I fumbled in my pocket for Grandma's keys. After a couple of wrong tries, the right key slipped into the lock, and the bolt slid back. The door swung open, and I had to adjust my eyes to the dark room.

I wasn't sure how long it had been since I had last seen the inside of the cabin, but it remained largely as I remembered it—a small, rectangular space with a window in the back and another in the front. The one room served as living room, kitchen, dining room, and bedroom. In the northeast corner, Grandpa had framed out a small, perfectly square bathroom. In front of the bathroom just under the back window was a make-shift couch where I used to sleep before the house was built. In the corner across from the bathroom was a well-worn double bed, and just a few inches from the foot of the bed under the front window was the tiny kitchen table. The cabin's bit of a kitchen was in the corner, diagonally opposite the bathroom, and just inside the door to my left stood the old black pot-belly stove, complete with its metal funnel that ran up through the ceiling. Straight across from the door in the corner next to the bathroom stood a cedar armoire which Grandpa had built for use as a clothes closet.

The smell of the cedar armoire combined with the ashes of wood burned in the stove brought a flood of wonderful childhood memories. In a flash, I could almost see Grandma standing at her sink, rinsing some boiled potatoes, then turning to amble over to the pot-belly stove to stir some green beans or butter beans or maybe check the reheating progress of the pot roast left over from lunch. She'd glance toward me and say, "Get your drink, Sweet; supper's almost ready!" Then she would put her head out the door and call loudly, "Edward! Supper!"

I would scramble to help her set the table with those blue-green and brown glazed pottery plates she had. While we moved food from the stove to the table, we'd compare notes on our respective books which we'd spent the afternoon reading. Grandpa would come in and start to wash up at the sink, scrubbing all the way up his forearms nearly to his elbows. We'd sit down to eat, and Grandpa, always thin as a rake, would get a good portion of everything on the table, and no matter the season, he'd wash his meal down with a cup of black coffee. Grandma would slide her plate away from her space at the table and declare that she just couldn't eat, all the while eyeing the dessert selection.

"Whew! This place is a dusty mess!" Chris's voice brought me back to the present.

The room was indeed a mess, with empty bags of cow feed stacked on the couch and the scant remains of grain scattered along the floor. Cobwebs had forged new connections between the ceiling and the walls, and my eyes caught sight of a fair-sized hole in the wall situated between the armoire and the bed. I couldn't imagine what had happened there. Grandpa kept his tractor parked in the garage, which was attached to the cabin behind that wall. Had he rammed the tractor through the wall? Had someone tried to break in? And who could even guess how long it had been that way?

My eyes roamed around the dim room until they settled on a little cedar box with two bears and a baby duck stenciled and painted across the front. It was sitting in front of the bathroom door, old, unused, and long-forgotten. It was my toybox, the one Grandpa had built for me when I was still an infant.

"I'll want to get that," I said immediately, pointing in the general direction.

Chris could see at once what I was going for, so he and Jimmy walked over and gingerly began scooting it out of the corner so they would be able to lift it.

"I think I'd like to get Grandpa's cedar armoire too," I told them.

As Chris and Jimmy carried the last piece off to the truck, Karen and I locked the cabin door and started back across the yard.

"I guess I'm silly," I said with a smile, "but I figure if we ever have children, they'll need a toybox. Seems funny to be thinking like that after only being married for eight months—*and* with everything that's going on right now."

"It's not silly," Karen said. "The box is handmade by your grandfather, and it'll mean a lot for your kids to have the same toybox you had."

Duke welcomed us back to his part of the yard, wagging his tail expectantly. I felt like I wanted to cry because I couldn't believe I was about to leave him alone again. Even with Mack looking after him, it just wasn't the same as having his own people there with him. Jimmy, as if he was reading my mind, suddenly spoke up.

"I hate to leave him here again."

"I know what you mean," I said, "but I don't know what I can do."

Jimmy was affectionately scratching Duke's ears, and Duke was leaning into Jimmy's leg.

"Well," Jimmy hesitated, the wheels of thought spinning in his mind. Then his expression changed, and he spoke with conviction. "Well—he's going home with me!"

My eyes grew a little wider. "Really?!" I said. "I mean . . . really?"

Jimmy was already getting his leash off the stob (pole). "Yes," he said firmly. "Really. He can live with my mother—she's going to want a companion after Karen and I get married, and Duke is perfect. He's going home with me today!"

And without the slightest hesitation, I was thrilled to consider the adoption complete.

By the time we made it back to Memphis Saturday evening, we had just enough time to drop off Grandma's rocking chair at Waverly before returning the U-Haul and calling it a night. I went to bed exhausted, and I woke up Sunday morning feeling a little bit like the U-Haul had run over me.

When we got to Waverly that morning, I had the distinct impression I was reliving my last discussion with the resident manager at Manders. One of the nurses caught me in the hall and began telling me all about the Meade doings at Waverly since they'd moved in.

"Mr. Meade doesn't want to stay here at all," she said, leaning slightly forward with her hand over her heart, "and I can't begin to tell you how many times they've set off that alarm on the door as they were trying to leave! Also, she keeps laying all her clothes out on the bed and saying that she's got to get to work!"

I sighed deeply. "I was concerned this would happen," I began. "I don't know what to do—"

"There's nothing you can do, honey," the nurse interrupted. "They're old, and they don't understand why they're here. We see it all the time."

Chris and I just exchanged glances and both shook our heads. I was about to say something else when down the hall a piercing, gravelly voice suddenly wailed out, "Alllllberrrrrrt!"

We all turned and saw a very little old lady scooting along in a wheelchair. Her expression was vacuous, but after a few seconds had passed with no response from Albert, whoever he was, she drew in a breath and screamed again, "Alllllberrrrrrt!"

The nurse walked over and bent down toward her face, trying to reassure her patient that everything was all right. She then positioned herself behind the chair and began to gently guide the lady back down the hall, presumably toward her room, looking at us over her shoulder, asking us to excuse her.

We followed them for some distance down the hall until we got to Grandma and Grandpa's room. As we came through their door, we again heard the unrelenting petition for "Allllllllberrrrrrt!"

Grandpa was sitting in one of the chairs provided by the nursing home, and Grandma was in her own rocker. My eye immediately caught sight of Grandma's clothes piled on her bed just like the nurse had said. After greetings had been exchanged, I foolishly asked Grandma why her clothes were not in the closet.

"Oh, we've got to go, Sweet," she said. "I can't stay in this room."

"Why not?" I asked—I honestly don't know what I was thinking.

"No, I can't stay in this room," she repeated.

Grandpa spoke up and told me they needed to be getting home.

My eyes met his; they weren't angry, just pleasant, clear-blue Grandpa eyes, like always.

"You need to stay here for a bit," Chris chimed in, followed quickly by, "Tell me, what'd you have for lunch?"

They started talking about food, and I was so thankful for Chris's quick thinking. I looked at Grandma and saw that she had her handbag resting in the chair by her leg with her forearm through the shoulder straps. As Chris and Grandpa talked, Grandma began to shift in the chair, struggling to get up. I stood beside her and helped her out of the chair.

"What do you need, Grandma?" I asked, puzzled.

Grandma got her bearings and began to stiffly walk around me, still clutching her purse. "I've got to be getting back to work," she declared firmly.

My mouth dropped open slightly, and Chris and I just looked at each other. Without another word, Grandma just tottered out into the hall and disappeared from sight.

"Well, she'll be back," Chris said with a slight chuckle. "I mean, where can she go?"

Shaking my head slightly, I turned my attention to the dresses on the bed. I gathered the hangers from the closet and began to put her clothes back where they needed to be.

After a few minutes, I looked up to see she was back. She stood outside the door for two or three seconds and then asked where the elevator was.

"Grandma, there's no elevator in this building. There's only one floor."

She looked at me with a dark, confused expression. After a few seconds, her face relaxed, and she took a step or two through the door. Then her gaze locked on to what I was doing. She came over to me, seized hold of the dress in my hand, and snatched it away from me with one quick jerk. I turned my head sharply to look directly into her face.

"I told you, I can't stay here!" she blurted out aggressively.

"Why not?" I demanded in a stunningly failed attempt to stay calm.

"Because this is Mr. Fred's room!"

"What? No, this is your room!"

"I'm a lady," she continued with agitation, "and I can't stay in Mr. Fred's room."

I looked quickly at Chris, hoping he could give me some help. He just looked puzzled and quietly asked, "Who's Mr. Fred?"

I mumbled that she was referring to a man she'd worked for many, many years earlier. I looked back at Grandma. Her face was in a knot, brows pushed together, lips slightly pursed, and her body tilted forward at her waist. My brain was nearly spinning in my head, trying to figure out how to respond to her, when all at once it crossed my mind to *not* contradict her. I pulled my chin up slightly and drew in a breath.

"All right, Grandma," was all I said.

She gave a slight nod of her head and dropped the dress back on the pile, then she shuffled her feet slightly to position herself in front of her rocker. She adjusted her dress and sat down as if nothing had happened.

I slowly slid up the side of her bed and sat down next to her chair. "How's your day been?" I ventured, friendly but cautious.

"Oh, fine, Sweet. Just a normal day," she answered pleasantly.

Oh, but the new normal was *anything* but normal.

As the days passed, we began to settle into a routine, awkward as it was. I was trying to get back to work, but every day was interrupted by various appointments I was having to make in order to deal with Meade business. And then there were the phone calls from the nursing home. Waverly was keeping me informed—informed about every escape attempt, every argument, every time a new therapist or their new doctor came by to see them. By the end of the week, it felt like I had surely been contacted by a representative of almost every conceivable field of medicine. I had talked with nurse practitioners, physical therapists, occupational therapists, RNs, and LPNs. The one that baffled me the most, however, was the speech therapist. I just couldn't imagine why either of my grandparents needed one.

I was finally introduced to their assigned speech therapist, Jennifer, as I was coming in for a visit one afternoon. When we talked, she began to explain why she was involved in my grandparents' care. It seemed that upon routine examination of Grandma's eating habits, Jennifer had discovered something which had the potential to be a serious problem.

"I believe she's aspirating when she eats," Jennifer explained. "When she goes to swallow her food, she starts coughing like she's about to choke."

I hadn't noticed anything particularly different about the way Grandma ate when we had shared meals during the last few weeks, but Jennifer explained it could have been going on for a while without anyone really noticing.

"Everyone experiences 'food going down the wrong way' from time to time. My concern is that in a person her age, the food she thinks is going to her stomach might really be heading down into her lungs," Jennifer said. "This can lead to all kinds of problems ranging from the development of pneumonia to possibly choking."

"Is there some way to help her not aspirate?" I asked. "I mean, what can we do?"

"Well, the first thing I want to do is send her out for a swallow study," she said. "They can take her by ambulance to one of the hospitals where they will essentially do an X-ray to watch her swallow and see where the barium goes."

"What happens if they confirm the food's going into her lungs?" I asked.

"At that point, we'd probably recommend she have a PEG tube put in," Jennifer answered. She went on to explain that PEG is short for "percutaneous endoscopic gastronomy," which is a medical procedure in which a tube is passed into the stomach through the abdominal wall.

"It would be a surgical procedure, then?" I asked her.

"Yes—if that's what the swallow study shows is necessary."

The thought of telling Grandma she might need surgery made me want to run screaming down the hall. She had experienced several surgeries during her lifetime—enough to make her tell me years ago that she would never let a doctor cut on her again.

"Let's just do the swallow study, and then we can decide what needs to be done from there," Jennifer said, sensing my hesitation. "We'll need your consent, and then I can get the test scheduled."

It was in that moment that I once again experienced the caregiver's dilemma. Knowing how strongly Grandma felt about having any type of surgery made me want to say "no" immediately. The flip side was I wanted to do everything I could to help her live as healthy and normal a life as possible. I knew I didn't like it whenever my food went down the wrong way, so I began trying to convince myself that maybe she'd be more comfortable with the PEG tube; but the way Jennifer had described it, the tube would always be there, sticking out from her abdomen. It would be hidden under her clothes, but noticeable to her even if no one else could see it. I didn't know if she'd be able to put up with it or not. More to the point, I wasn't sure if I could even explain to her why it was necessary.

After much mental debate, I did authorize the swallow study. My trepidation about her possibly needing surgery was outbid by the fear of something dire happening to her. I reasoned that if my refusal to allow treatment for a legitimate medical condition were to somehow cause her to suffer—or worse, if it contributed in any way to her death—I knew that would be more than I could stand. Besides, despite everything we had been through so far, I was just not ready to let go of her.

CHAPTER 16

THE HOSPITAL

The swallow study left absolutely no doubt: Grandma was aspirating almost every time something went into her mouth. Jennifer gave us the test results and said there was no question—Grandma needed a PEG tube.

"She has a much higher than normal chance of choking every time she eats or drinks anything," she said.

We sat down with Grandma and Grandpa, and Jennifer began explaining to them what was wrong and what she was going to do about it. I could see by the looks on their faces they weren't following what she was saying. I told Jennifer to just go ahead and set everything up; if the recent past was any indicator, I figured by the time the procedure was scheduled, they would have forgotten everything she'd said anyway. Even if they argued about it, we still had to go forward; the tube had to be put in for Grandma's safety.

Very early on Wednesday morning, my mother, Chris, and I converged on Waverly. Jennifer was already there, and she informed us that Grandma would be transported via ambulance to Shelby General Hospital where her PEG tube would be put in by a Dr. Zach Brantley.

"Have you said anything else to my grandparents about her going to the hospital?" I asked.

"Yes," Jennifer replied, chuckling softly. "She seemed fine with it, but Mr. Meade informed me that it really wasn't necessary."

I smiled slightly, but I felt my brows move together as I thought about how peculiar it was that Grandma should be "fine" with it. There just seemed to be so much about her mental situation that I didn't understand.

Jennifer returned to her office as Mom, Chris, and I walked toward my grandparents' room. All the way down the hall I was dreading having to face them; I didn't want to see Grandpa because I was so concerned he would argue the necessity of the PEG tube, and I was plagued by the feeling that if Grandma had been anywhere near her right mind and knew what I'd authorized for her, she'd be furious with me.

I worried unnecessarily during that season; the fact was that if she had been in her right mind to begin with, there would have been no need for me to make the decision for her. Even though intellectually I knew that was true, I never felt completely released from what Vivian had called "false guilt." My fear of making a mistake where they were concerned held me so tightly that it was almost debilitating. Circumstances were forcing me to learn that the answer to the question, *What do I do?* was not always going to be clear. It was a hard lesson for me; like so many people, I want to see the whole plan laid out. Walking by faith, depending on God's Spirit for direction—these things sounded great from a pulpit, but trying to live it out was scary . . . most of the time I felt like it was impossible. In my head, I knew God had brought us along this far without dropping us; getting that information from my head down to my heart was a *much* slower process. I was sluggish to comprehend He was worthy of my trust regarding not only my eternal salvation but also the matters of my earthly existence. So, in acknowledging His ability to completely take care of me, I had to commit to forward momentum with the Holy Spirit, however slow it might be.

When we arrived at their room, I saw Grandma lying back on her bed. Her face brightened as she made eye contact with me, and she struggled to sit up as she spoke out happily, "Well hello, Sweet!"

"And how are you doing today?" I asked as I approached her with a hug.

"Oh, I'm fair, I guess, but I sure am ready to go home!" She spoke with definite conviction.

Grandpa, sitting in Grandma's rocker beside her bed, had risen to his feet and was shaking hands with Chris when I turned around to hug him. As my chin rested on his shoulder, I glanced down at his bed and saw a small bundle of clothes all wrapped together in what looked like plastic wrap. Underneath the bundle were two of Grandma's photographs which I had placed on top of their wardrobe beside their little TV.

"Grandpa, what's this?" I asked.

He turned to see where I was pointing. "That's our clothes," he replied very matter-of-factly. "I've gotten them together so we can take them back home. Are you ready to take us home?"

I had to stonewall his question, frankly because I didn't know what to say to him. Instead I bent down toward the bundle, trying to figure out exactly what Grandpa had used to wrap the clothes in. Feeling confused, I shook my head slightly as I glanced back toward Chris. He shrugged his shoulders and began looking around the room for a plausible explanation. His eyes came to rest on the trash can beneath the sink.

"Oh," he said quietly, "it's the trash bag."

My eyes followed his glance, and I saw at once the can's customary opaque liner was missing. I shook my head as I looked back at the bundle of their clothes, failing to conceal the frustration I felt. I pursed my lips tightly together, then let out a long, slow sigh.

"Oh my gosh," my mother mumbled in disbelief. "We're going to have to rewash all those clothes."

I turned a stunned face back to Grandpa. He just stood there, looking at me like a child; his expression seemed to say, "Is there a problem?" I couldn't think of any way to address the fact that all their clothing had been crammed into a dirty trash bag. I decided to leave it alone for the moment, choosing instead to talk about what was going to happen with Grandma.

"Grandpa," I began, "Grandma's got to go out for a—" I broke off, not really sure how to explain it to him. I finally opted for the direct approach. "Well, she's got to have a feeding tube put into her stomach. I'm going to go with her, and I'll be with her every step of the way. Why don't you wait here, and when it's over, I'll get her brought back to you as quickly as I possibly can."

He looked puzzled as he glanced toward the floor, seemingly trying to find the right words. "She doesn't need that," he stated flatly.

I forged ahead. "The tube will help Grandma not choke on her food anymore," I said with confidence. "You know how she's always coughing when she eats? Now she won't have to do that. It's going to help her feel better because she'll actually be getting the food into her stomach instead of having it go down the wrong way."

Just then I heard a knock on the door. I turned around to see two uniformed EMTs with their stretcher in tow. Chris began talking to them as I turned toward Grandma.

"Grandma," I said, "these men are here to take you to the doctor, and I'm going with you. You don't need to worry about a thing; I'll be right there with you."

She smiled at me confidently and nodded her head slightly, but she never said anything. I moved aside so the EMTs could maneuver their stretcher into place. I remember being very impressed with their professionalism and their competent handling of Grandma as they moved her effortlessly from the bed to the stretcher. Once they got out of the room, I turned quickly to Grandpa.

"I've got to go with her," I said as I picked up my purse, "but I'll let you know how everything goes."

I hugged him around the neck and told him I loved him, then Mom, Chris, and I hurried down the hall to catch up with the stretcher. I saw Jennifer just as we were heading out the door.

"I'll call you later and tell you how she does so you can pass it on to my grandfather," I said. "Please take good care of him while she's gone!"

"Don't worry about anything here!" she called after me.

I stood outside and watched them put Grandma into the ambulance. The stretcher was propped up slightly so that she and I made eye contact before the back doors were closed. Her expression was fearful, as if she was unsure what was happening.

"Grandma," I called out to her, "I'm going to follow the ambulance in my car; I'll see you when we get there. Don't worry about anything, OK?"

"OK, Sweet," she answered with a weary smile.

The ambulance driver closed the door, and I felt strange, like I was sending her off alone into a dark and unknown place. She had become so like a child, naïve and unaware of the world going on around her. And I, like some kind of surrogate parent, felt compelled to protect her from . . . everything.

Our drive to Shelby General was uneventful, and after we parked we hurried to the entrance where Grandma was being taken in. We followed along behind the stretcher into a small room where she was to be prepped for surgery. Chris, who hadn't had any breakfast before we left home, decided to appease his growling stomach by searching for a vending machine. Shortly after he walked out, a nurse came in and started Grandma's IV, then two lab technicians came in to take her blood. Thus our foul hospital experience began.

"OK, Mrs. Meade," the first technician said, "give me your arm, sweetie, so I can get some blood."

She sounded way too eager at the prospect of using her needle. Grandma merely turned her head and looked at her, but neither spoke nor offered her arm. The technician looked over at me with a questioning expression.

"She has Alzheimer's," I explained.

"Oh," she said, looking back at Grandma. The technician heaved a deep sigh and raised her voice; I guess she thought if she talked loud enough it would cause Grandma to comply.

"Well, sweetie, I'm gonna have to have your arm 'cause I have to take some blood." She stretched Grandma's arm out and began searching for a vein to tap.

The second technician, standing ready with a rubber tourniquet and the needle, looked at me and asked, "Is she at home with you or in a nursing home?"

"She's in a nursing home with her husband. He's got a fairly advanced case of dementia as well, so they're in together."

"Which nursing home are they in?" she asked.

"Waverly."

The first technician looked up at me with a grim expression.

"Waverly!" she called out emphatically. "That's got to be the worst nursin' home in this city! I had a relative in there, and honey, she didn't do nothin' but waste away 'til she finally died. They just treat their patients awful! I remember saying I'd never put anybody I loved into *that* nursin' home!"

The second technician's eyes widened, and she just stared at her coworker like she wished she had a rubber glove to stuff into that babbling mouth. It was unbelievable the way she just rambled on and on about the evils of Waverly with no apparent regard for the way her scathing review was affecting my mom or me. When at last they left the room, I looked at my mother and said, "Make a note of that: no more relatives condemned to Waverly."

"She was really something," Mom said with disgust. "Somebody needs to tell her to shut her mouth!"

I moved nearer to Grandma's bed and pushed her hair back from her face. She looked up at me and smiled.

"I've been here before," she said, "but it's been years ago."

Mom and I glanced at each other. We both knew she had never been a patient at Shelby General, but neither one of us was going to argue the point with her.

Chris came back in after a few more minutes and shared part of a cinnamon roll with me. The morning wore on slowly, and just as we began to think they had forgotten us, two orderlies came in with a stretcher and said they were ready to transport Grandma to surgery.

"May I walk down with her?" I asked.

"Sure, that's no problem," one of them said.

So, the Meade parade went down together to a small surgical room where we finally met Dr. Brantley. He was a very pleasant man who thoroughly explained everything he was going to do and politely allowed me to ask him several questions. At last the time came for us to leave the doctor and his team to their work, so I walked over to where Grandma lay flat on her back, staring at the ceiling. I gently rubbed her forearm as I said, "Grandma, Dr. Brantley is going to take good care of you, OK? I'll be right here when you wake up; you're going to be fine. You know I love you."

She turned her head toward me and smiled slightly. She looked so helpless, my heart just nearly broke.

"And I love you, Doll," she said. She glanced around and saw Chris and my mother, then she cut her eyes back to me. "God be with you all," she said with a smile.

I squeezed her hand and then forced myself away from the table. Once I got out into the hall, I looked at Chris and my mother and said, "I think she believes she's dying!"

"But you know she's not dying," my mother said, fighting back her own tears.

"That's right," Chris agreed, "she's going to be fine."

"I know," I said, looking hard at the floor, "but it still shakes you up to think that *she* thinks she's dying!"

We stood around in the hall for a few minutes, not sure exactly where to go or what we could do to pass the time while Grandma was in surgery.

"I know exactly what we can do: let's find the cafeteria and see if they have anything worth eating!" Chris said with a grin.

My mom looked at him slightly sideways.

"Are you nuts? It's a hospital. What makes you think they'll have anything worth *actually* eating?"

They laughed together as they began trying to figure out which way the cafeteria was. All through lunch, Mom and Chris chatted lightly about different things, but my mind was so bogged down with thoughts about Grandma it seemed almost impossible for me to engage in normal conversation.

After we ate, we walked back over to the surgical room where we had left Grandma, only to find the door wide open. A lone nurse was standing in front of a counter, filling out some paperwork. She looked up as I stuck my head in the door.

"Excuse me," I said, "can you tell me where they've taken Mrs. Meade?"

"She's been sent to recovery," the nurse answered. "After she wakes up, they'll take her back to her room."

We decided we would return to Grandma's room and wait for them to bring her back. After about an hour, they wheeled her in. She was so groggy that I'm not certain if she even recognized me. I realized at once she was probably going to sleep through the remainder of the day, so after we made sure she was properly settled, we decided to leave.

When Chris and I got home, I called Jennifer and told her that apparently all had gone well. "I still haven't spoken with the doctor, but according to the nurses on her floor, there were no problems."

"That's great," Jennifer said. "I'll go speak to your grandfather right now and let him know she's all right."

After we hung up, I sat on the couch for a long time without moving. I thought about the day's events, and for the first time, I actually began considering how hard it might be to make Grandma understand that she wasn't to put food in her mouth anymore. I wondered if I would be able to make Grandpa understand that she was going to be fed through the tube in her stomach instead of eating by mouth—instead of doing what was *normal*.

Leah, Leah, I thought to myself. *What have you done to them?*

On Thursday morning, one day after Grandma's surgery, I walked back into my office for the first time in almost a month. I reasoned it was as good a time as any other to get back to work; Grandma was in the hospital with nurses to look after her, and Grandpa certainly wasn't going to try to run off without Grandma. Returning to work seemed strange because my job had been such a regular part of my precaregiver existence. Going back to the dull normality of the office actually made me feel like I'd just dreamed up all the chaotic events of the past month.

I started to sift through the work that had been piling up since my prolonged absence had begun, but despite my best efforts at concentration, my mind was overwhelmingly tied to my grandmother who was lying in a hospital room all alone, recovering from a surgery she probably didn't even remember having. I finally decided the only way I would get any work done was to put my mind at ease by calling the hospital to check on her.

"Nurses' station," a woman's voice snapped out.

I identified myself and told her what I wanted.

"Let me get her nurse," she said quickly, cutting off the last word as she clicked the *hold* button.

After a short wait, the phone was abruptly picked up, and another woman's voice came over the line.

"Mrs. Stanley?"

"Yes?"

"Mrs. Meade is highly agitated," the nurse blurted out, as if she had called me instead of my having called her. She then launched into a long dissertation about Grandma's uncooperative, combative behavior, and she concluded with the statement, "We need your permission to use soft restraints on her because if we don't, she's going to pull her IV out."

The irritation in her voice was unmistakable. My mind was working quickly to absorb everything she had said, but it was the words *soft restraints* that stung me like an angry hornet. That statement caused my thoughts to flash back to their first night in Memphis when we brought my grandparents into the ER. I recalled how the doctors there had been forced to use "soft restraints" on Grandpa. That action, though deplorable to me, had clearly been necessary under the circumstances. However, I was having more than a little trouble picturing Grandma, an eighty-eight-year-old woman who had undergone a surgical procedure not twenty-four hours earlier, aggressively fighting her nurse the way Grandpa had done in the ER. Foremost in my mind, though, was the recent memory of Audrey describing to me Waverly's restraint policy. She had stated quite clearly that sedating or restraining residents was never an option unless a patient was posing a threat to themselves or to someone else. Then again, if what the nurse had described was true, combative behavior could damage the PEG tube site or leave blood trickling out where the IV had been. I decided I should explore the matter further before agreeing to anything that this very aggressive nurse was requesting.

"Does that mean you're going to basically tie her down?" I asked as I vividly pictured what they had done to Grandpa.

"No," the nurse replied, "we have a set of mittens we use which will restrain the use of her fingers, but she'll be free to move her arms and legs."

What she described was clearly different than what I had seen used on Grandpa, but I still struggled with the decision. *How frightening*, I thought, *to be in a hospital and to have your hands confined in a pair of mittens. She wouldn't be able to pull her bed covers up or run her fingers through her hair, or even take care of an itch on her face. And what if she needed the nurse? How could she push the nurse call button if her fingers were wrapped in mittens?* I found myself involuntarily shaking my head, primarily because I felt like I was being pressured to do something that might not actually be necessary, so I probed further.

"Has she actually pulled her IV out?"

"Well—" I noted her slight hesitation, "she's pulled the tubing out once, although the needle itself stayed in. She's just really very agitated. She keeps asking for Ted. Is that her husband?"

I smiled at the mistake. "Yes," I answered, trying to not let my voice reveal the emotion Grandma's plea had provoked, "but it's Ed, not Ted."

"Oh well," the nurse callously responded, "whatever it is, she's calling for him something awful."

Her attitude struck me as being entirely out of place for a nurse. I got the distinct impression she really didn't care about my grandmother as a person. It sounded to me like she was only concerned with the fact that Mrs. Meade was being a bother, so I shifted gears in an effort to work toward a solution.

"Is she OK to be in that room by herself?"

"It would help us if someone was here with her," she replied bluntly. "One of us is having to be in her room almost constantly because of the way she's fussing. We just can't be in there all the time."

"I understand that, and I'm sorry she's not being cooperative," I said with thinly disguised frustration. "All I can tell you is that she has Alzheimer's, and she just doesn't understand what's going on."

"Oh," the nurse responded in a puzzled tone, "she has Alzheimer's?"

Her question left me absolutely speechless. This nurse, who had been assigned to take care of my grandmother for the day, *didn't know* she had Alzheimer's disease, even though it was noted in her Waverly chart information, which had been sent with her to the hospital. Also, just as a precaution, I had made it a point to verbally inform every staff member who was working with Grandma that she was an Alzheimer's patient. I cannot describe my aggravation regarding this apparent communication oversight between nursing shifts. What baffled me the most, though, was that this nurse, who ostensibly had professional medical training, had not been able to pick up on the overt symptoms displayed by Grandma and at least conclude she was suffering with *some* form of dementia.

"Yes," I responded irritably, "she has Alzheimer's, and besides letting you tie her up and me having to leave my office to come up there and sit with her, I don't know what else I can do to help you."

"Well, the sooner you can get here the better," she said firmly.

So that was it. I felt I had no choice but to go because that nurse, who gave every indication of being fed up with taking care of her patient, had issued a cold and unrelenting demand for me to get up there. No one else was available to help; Chris and my dad were both at work, and my mom had things she needed to tend to. With a bitter attitude, I began to gather my belongings to leave. One of my coworkers pulled me aside and said, "Remember, Leah, it's that nurse's job. Don't be afraid to make her do her job."

I nodded my head wearily at her as I left the office, but her words lingered in my mind as I drove to the hospital. I understood, at least to some degree, the nurse's frustration; nevertheless, it made me wonder what happened to patients who had no family to come and sit with them. Were they just left to themselves? Were they heavily sedated to reduce the amount of attention they would require?

I also began to wonder if there was other information noted in Grandma's chart that her nurse didn't know. Was she aware, for instance, that Grandma's new doctor at Waverly, Dr. Kern, had diagnosed her as a diabetic? Was she even aware that Grandma had had a PEG tube put in? In retrospect, I know that I was drawn to sit with Grandma at the hospital that day because I had absolutely no confidence she would be all right without me.

I drove my car almost mechanically toward Shelby General, and the closer I got the more strongly I resented having to leave my office. In a way, though, it seemed to go along with everything else I had discovered about being a caregiver. I was quickly learning that no one was as concerned about my grandparents as I was, and if I wanted them to receive the respect and top-notch care they deserved, it would mean I would have to personally oversee every detail. In the roughly four weeks during which I had served as my grandparents' caregiver, I had encountered many different medical professionals. The majority of them had been great, showing an exceptional level of professional care. Peppered throughout our experience, however, had been some real doozies. I was learning it was truly a game of chance; you didn't know what kind of doctor, nurse, or therapist you were going to wind up with. Many times over the course of my tenure as caregiver, I thanked God that my grandparents had the foresight to appoint their designated agent to act on their behalf. I couldn't imagine them being mentally incapacitated and winding up at the mercy of someone whose greatest interest was their own paycheck.

I pulled into the hospital driveway and realized almost every muscle in my body was tense. I walked at a slower than normal pace toward Grandma's room in an effort to settle the anger that had bubbled up during my half-hour commute. The last thing I wanted to do was show my irritation to Grandma. I stood outside her door for several seconds, trying to force my lips into a smile. Then I took a cleansing breath and walked into her room. She glanced over at me and smiled.

"Hi, Sweet," she said in a gravelly voice.

I leaned over and kissed her forehead. "And how is my grandma today?" I asked as I touched her cheek softly.

"I'm fair," she answered as she lifted one of her hands, "but I sure do wish I could get this glove off."

My eyes moved away from her face down toward her hands, and I could plainly see the "soft restraints." They were indeed different from what Grandpa had been subjected to in the ER. They were white and contained the fingers much like an oven mitt, but they were secured firmly around the wrists with a buckle and fastener. I tried to smile at her, but my face seemed frozen as the reality of her restraint went over me, and for a moment my breath stalled in my throat. My precious Grandma's hands were bound; those wonderful, gentle hands that had diapered me as a baby, brushed my hair when I was a little girl, and still reached out lovingly to me in my adulthood had been restrained by *my* authority. The muscles in my face tightened, and in my mind I cried out, *Oh, God! Why are you letting this happen?*

I couldn't respond to her right away; instead, I turned and put my purse down by the sink and walked around the bed to stare out the window. I watched the cars going along the busy street in front of the hospital, and for a moment I allowed my thoughts to roam. I wondered where all those cars were going. I watched people as they came and went in the hospital parking lot. I saw people chatting and laughing as they walked together; others were walking alone, quickly making their way to their destinations. Then, without warning, the focus of my eyes shifted, and I could see my own reflection in the glass. My face was pulled and heavy, appearing somewhat older than I had looked only a few weeks earlier. The situation in which I found myself appeared to be taking an actual toll on my physical appearance. Worry and anxiety are like poison to the human soul. They result not only in physical changes but also cause a permanent alteration to one's mental view of the world. The face I saw in the glass just stared back at me with a hopeless expression. I rolled my eyes up to the sky and muttered, "Oh, Jesus, please help me here."

I turned around to face Grandma once again, and the sight of what she was doing caused my jaw to drop just slightly. She had the wrist part of one of the mittens in her mouth, and she was biting at the buckle in an obvious attempt to loosen it. Her eyes met mine, and as they did, she pulled her arm away from her face and said, "Sweet, help me with this, will you?"

The pain of seeing my grandma that way burned an image into my mind that I don't think I'll ever be rid of. It went through my thoughts that everything in her life had dwindled down to that one moment. She looked like some kind of helpless animal. Her mind had deserted her, and I, her loved and *trusted* granddaughter, had given authorization for her to be restrained. I began to wonder where God was in all of it. Had He just abandoned us to that pathetic existence? I knew that couldn't be true, but at that moment it seemed neither one of us had even a shred of hope. I took a deep breath and walked boldly back to her bedside. I pressed her arm gently down on the bed, and she looked at me with the gaze of a child who had just been corrected.

"Don't worry about this, Grandma," I said with fake energy. "Tell me about your morning. What have you done today?" My own emotions were running so strong that I was not able to gently coddle her as might have seemed appropriate. I was gravely afraid of revealing to Grandma the deep pain I was feeling, and I knew that if I was anything other than "business as usual" with her, it would give way to a flood of tears, which I didn't want her to see. When I asked her what she'd been doing that morning, it was more of a conversational catch phrase as opposed to a serious inquiry. My hope was that it would put Grandma at ease because it was such a normal thing to say.

We spoke about ordinary things in an ordinary way, such as her room, her bed, and her hospital gown. Once those topics had been exhausted, my brain raced to come up with something new we could talk about. Several times throughout that morning, my selection of conversational tidbits seemed to run completely out, and an awkward silence, one like I had never before encountered with her, would settle over the room. During those lapses in conversation, she would resume biting at her mittens, the sight of which made me feel even more pressured to get her talking about something—anything. And as my mind worked feverishly, I was almost yelling at God for help.

As I writhed in mental agony about how to pass the time, I suddenly remembered how Grandma and Grandpa used to love to go on vacation. Through the years they had rambled all over the country, visiting every state in the union except for Alaska, Hawaii, and, thanks to a wrong turn, Rhode Island. Their road trips had long been a source of enjoyable conversation between us. All at once I was aware that God hadn't abandoned me, and the memory of their vacations was His profound grace for that moment.

"Grandma," I began with a renewed sense of hope, "did you ever visit the Smoky Mountains?" I knew full well she had been to the Smoky Mountains, and as I posed my question, I prayed that the memory of her travels had not dissipated.

"Oh, yes," she answered with a bright smile. That was all she needed. Off she went, telling me about that trip along with a dozen others. I prompted her with questions, and from time to time, I threw in a travel experience of my own. It was the closest thing to real conversation she and I had shared since the whole mess had started, and I soaked it up with the joy of a kid in a candy store. It made me feel like I was somehow cheating Alzheimer's because we were "acting normal," and at least for that moment, the grip of the disease was compromised.

Several times during our pleasant reminiscences, I would notice Grandma's eyes getting heavy, so I would discreetly get quiet and allow her to doze. As her breathing became deep and rhythmic, I would inadvertently begin watching the clock. The walls of that hospital room grew stifling after so many hours of sitting within them, and the boredom I experienced while Grandma napped became excruciating.

Shortly after the nursing shift changed, I began to make my plans to leave. I knew I needed to get home to cook dinner, and I still had a formidable stack of Meade papers I was working my way through. After making sure Grandma was comfortable and giving her a hug and a kiss, I stopped by the nurses' station to inform the evening shift that I would be at home if they needed me.

Friday was much like the day before, except that I didn't go in to work. I sat with Grandma during an uneventful day but still went home feeling worn out. I was continuously maintaining an up-beat, happy attitude and appearance for Grandma's sake, and I found that kind of mental exertion can leave you feeling almost like you've run a marathon. Before I left for the day, Dr. Brantley stopped by and said he wanted to keep Grandma a day or two more because her surgical site appeared to be developing an infection.

On Saturday, Chris and I had some errands of our own, so we didn't get to the hospital until later in the afternoon. I was overshadowed all day by a nagging worry about Grandma. *Was she fussing? Were they trying to be patient with her?* Those were still the early days of our marriage, and we didn't yet have even one cell phone between us, so there was no way they could contact me. I kept reminding myself that I still had responsibilities outside of my grandparents, so I would have to rely on the hospital staff to take care of Grandma in my absence.

As the day wore on, I began to convince myself that she was all right. She had been calm with me there on Thursday and Friday, so I continued reasoning with myself that she had settled down. I was almost ready to believe it. Then I walked into her room.

"What in the world?" I blurted out. The phrase fell short of expressing my true feelings as I stood in the door and attempted to process what I saw. Grandma was lying perpendicular to the bed, her legs entangled in the bed's safety rail. Her head was arched back and hanging down on the opposite side. She was flat on her back, flailing her arms wildly, her hands still encased in the restraining mittens.

"Oh, Grandma!" I cried out.

She rolled her head around completely upside down to look at me. "Please, help me!" she begged in an almost weepy voice.

I dropped my purse in the door as Chris and I rushed to her bed. I took her shoulders, and Chris got her legs, and together we maneuvered her properly back on to the bed.

"Are you all right?" I asked her.

She looked at me but didn't say anything. She struck me as being more "out of it" than usual. I looked over at Chris.

"Please stay with her," I said angrily. "I'll be back."

Grandma's room was at the end of the hall and therefore farthest from the nurses' station. That logistic fact was a distinct disadvantage for the nursing staff on duty that day because with every step I took, my rage grew. By the time I reached the nurses' station, I was ready to explode. So I did.

"I am Mrs. Meade's granddaughter, and I want to know *exactly* how long it's been since someone was in her room checking on her!" My voice thundered across the quiet nurses' station. Every head there turned to look at me. I didn't care. "I found her lying cross-ways on her bed, her feet all caught and tangled in the bed rail. Her head was hanging upside down off the other side. Clearly the position she was in didn't just happen in a few seconds! I want to know who's supposed to be taking care of her, because *they're not doing it!*"

One of the nurses jumped up. "Let me come with you to her room," she said. "I'm the nursing supervisor." She then turned to one of her co-workers and said, "Please, send Mrs. Meade's nurse to her room."

At least two other nurses accompanied the supervisor and me back to Grandma's room. Before it was all over, no less than five people were swarming around Grandma's bed, doting on her and, to all appearances, giving her the best care in the world. It flashed through my mind, *I wonder what the other patients are doing while their nurses are all in here.*

I turned to Chris and said quietly, "They're not fooling me. They don't care anything about her. They've been caught ignoring a patient, and they know it."

Chris nodded in agreement. "Yeah," he whispered back. "They act like they're running scared all right."

I turned back toward Grandma's bed and heard one of the nurses say, "I was just in here a few minutes ago, and she was fine."

Chris and I again cut our eyes toward each other. He knew, like I did, the position in which we found Grandma was not one she just slipped into over the course of "a few minutes." The nursing supervisor's eyes met mine, and I could see that she knew I wasn't buying it.

"When is Mrs. Meade's next PEG tube feeding?" she asked, looking away from me quickly.

"Oh, she's due for one right now," one of the aides replied.

I shot Chris another look. We were both wondering just how overdue her PEG tube feeding *actually* was. As I stood there at the foot of her bed, I watched all those nurses and aides making over Grandma, and it occurred to me what a hypocritical farce it all was. It was overdone, exaggerated. My impression was, as it had been all along, they didn't give a hoot about Grandma's well-being. I believe the dog and pony show was because they were concerned I might try to bring the hospital up on charges of neglect, so they were scrambling to put on this act of concern and superior care. I remember just shaking my head as I looked into Grandma's eyes, whipping myself down for not having stayed with her every moment. Time seemed to nearly stand still as the nurses and aides attentively checked her blood pressure, oxygen level, and pillow adjustment.

The overt pampering came to a screeching halt, though, when one of the aides pulled back her bed sheet, lifted her hospital gown, and reached to feel the pad between Grandma's legs to see if she had urinated on it. Grandma's response was quick and definite, one of fierce indignation; she jerked herself up and fairly yelled out, "Why don't you just *stop!*"

The aide withdrew immediately and looked at me. "She's not wet," she said sheepishly.

I looked back at Grandma's face and could tell that her rage had not yet subsided despite the aide's rapid retreat. A slight smile played around my lips as I turned to meet Chris's glance.

"Well!" he muttered. "She knew she didn't like that!"

I turned back to Grandma and patted her foot. "It's going to be all right, Grandma," I told her softly. I was still smiling slightly, primarily because her extreme reaction had made it clear that somewhere in her mind she still possessed a sense of propriety. To her mind, nobody had a right to be reaching between her legs like that. She was, after all, still a lady.

CHAPTER 17

FINANCIAL RESPONSIBILITIES

B y the first of the week, Dr. Brantley decided Grandma's PEG tube site was well enough for her to be transported back to Waverly. Chris and I had informed him that Grandma's stay at Shelby General had been one bad experience after another, culminating with the Saturday afternoon debacle. While he remained very professional with us, one of the night nurses told us he read the riot act to the nursing supervisor. He told her they were going to move his patient to a room right off the nurses' station, and if Mrs. Meade's family was unable to be present, then her door was to remain open so they could both see and hear what was happening in her room. We appreciated his fervor to correct the problems we had encountered, but even with those measures in place, Chris and I could not get Grandma out of there fast enough. We came in eagerly anticipating her exit without further incident; little did we expect that the hospital had one final act of incompetence to deal out.

Grandma was sitting up in her bed, and one of the nursing staff was standing beside her. I walked around to the other side of the bed and gave her a gentle hug. "You're looking a lot better today!" I said to her.

"Oh, yes, she's doing wonderful today," the nurse said with a big smile. "She just finished a great lunch—ate every bite of food on that tray!"

Chris and I both jerked up straight and shot her a look. Before I could even draw a breath to say a word, Chris was on it.

"She did *what*?!"

"Yeeess, she ate all of her lunch!" The nurse was beaming.

"Do you even know what she's been in the hospital for?" Chris aggressively pressed.

The nurse's face slowly lost the smile. All she said was, "Uh. . . ."

"She had a PEG tube put in," I said with undisguised aggravation. "She's not supposed to eat by mouth because she's at risk for choking! Who in the world ordered a tray of food *for a PEG tube patient*?"

The nurse stammered that she didn't know about the PEG tube. She looked at the floor, then at Grandma, but she wouldn't make eye contact with either Chris or me. Almost imperceptibly she began moving toward the door. My jaws tightened, and I closed my eyes, straining to keep calm. Chris came over to stand beside me, and before the nurse could get out of that room, he quietly but firmly said, "Since we first came here last Wednesday, we've encountered everything from rude staff to outright medical incompetence. It's time for you to gather whatever you people need to discharge her; Mrs. Meade is leaving here before anything else can happen."

"Yes, sir." The nurse's response was nearly inaudible. "I'll request an ambulance for transport. It may take a while."

"No," Chris said boldly, "we're not waiting for an ambulance. She's leaving with us. Immediately."

I didn't say a word, but I stood with Chris, looking the nurse straight in her eyes.

"OK," she said. "Yes, sir."

We knew it was safe for us to transport Grandma in our car because Dr. Brantley had said once she was discharged, an ambulance could be ordered or we could just drive her to Waverly ourselves; it was our choice. The PEG tube site was well bandaged, and the incision was now completely clear of infection.

Once we got Grandma safely back to the nursing home, we gave all her discharge papers to Jennifer and explained very factually all that had gone on while Grandma had been a patient at Shelby General.

"If either one of my grandparents ever needs to go to a hospital, there are other facilities in this city besides Shelby General," I told her. "I *will not* give consent for them to ever go to Shelby General again."

Jennifer was very supportive and said she would personally note that in their charts.

Grandpa was truly glad to see Grandma get back, although there was no overt display of emotion. As we got her settled in her bed, I watched Grandpa approach from her right side and bend over slightly at his waist as he touched her face so softly. He looked at her with a sweet mix of subtle joy, relief, and comfort as he said simply, "Hello, Sweet."

"He missed her so much," Jennifer said quietly. "He walked around the halls during the day with her purse on his arm; I kept telling him she'd be back soon. Then one afternoon I ran into him, and we talked about her together for a little bit. I could tell he was really missing her that day; he said to me, 'I just love her so much.'"

I appreciated Jennifer sharing that story with me because even though I knew he loved her, I couldn't recall a time when I'd ever heard him just say it out like that. Their time apart must have seemed like an eternity to him.

What was feeling like an eternity to me was dealing with the stacked-up Meade papers, bills, and overdue notices in my apartment. In addition to the load I had brought over from my grandparents' home, our own mailbox was being filled daily with envelopes from the various organizations my grandparents had been doing business with for years. Even after all the weeks that had passed since January 15, I was still working to corral all their financial business. Dealing with the forms required to transfer all the bills to me was taking time, and since the statements showing unpaid insurance, back property taxes, and overdue utility bills were all competing for my immediate attention, it didn't take long for me to realize the surface area of my desk was woefully inadequate to organize the load. At one point, I had amassed so many separate paper stacks on my living room floor, it resembled a huge board game.

Little by little, though, I began to make headway. I lost count of how many copies of the durable power of attorney papers I made during that period. I took one organization at a time, determining what they needed to get the Meade records current, then writing and mailing the necessary checks. Even though I was authorized to access funds from their account, it was at times awkward being a resident of Tennessee, writing checks from an Arkansas bank, especially since my name wasn't preprinted on their checks. I solved the problem by opening a new account for them at my own bank in Memphis. I transferred all their cash into the new account and ordered one box of inexpensive, plain blue checks. It seemed like quite a departure from the white checks with the pink border and the delicate rose in the upper left corner that Grandma had always used. The newly printed checks had my name along with both of my grandparents' names, although during the entire life of that new account, neither one of them signed even a single check.

As I wound my way along the paper trail, looking over the various things their Medicare supplemental insurance would and would not cover, I realized we had not yet applied for Medicaid. I had learned that Medicare and Medicaid were not the same thing. My grandparents already had Medicare, which is a federal health insurance program for people over sixty-five. Medicare, along with their supplemental insurance, paid for things like doctor's visits, hospital stays, and any procedures or medications they might need. Medicaid, however, was another federal health insurance system for those who required financial assistance—something my grandparents were definitely going to need in order to afford life in the nursing home. They had to specifically apply for Medicaid, and once they were accepted, a case worker would be assigned to oversee everything about their business.

I talked with Audrey at Waverly about the application process. I was so relieved to learn they would do the paperwork for me, but Audrey stressed that a big part of being accepted was proving medical necessity, definitively showing the Meades were not able to continue living on their own. I squirmed in my chair as I wondered what would happen if we failed to prove "medical necessity."

"We can send all the evaluations we've done since they first came here," Audrey said, "and if they don't accept them on the first try, we'll just apply again and work to make our case even stronger."

I couldn't imagine what would make a stronger case than the multiplicity of evaluations they had done on Grandma and Grandpa, but I knew I couldn't freak out over the "will they or won't they" question. I had to put it out of my mind for the moment, frankly because I knew there wasn't anything I could do about it. It was another one of those roads I had to travel with blind faith; God knew our situation. I began to pray His Word back to Him, looking particularly at Proverbs 3:5-6, which says, "Trust in the Lord with all your heart and lean not on your own understanding; in all your ways submit to Him, and He will make your paths straight."

I knew God had to go before us and give us His favor, and all my worrying wasn't going to amount to anything but stress for myself. I resolved to allow the Waverly team to do their thing, all the while thanking God in advance for taking care of the details over which I had no ultimate control in the first place.

"I think we already have most everything required by the State of Tennessee," Audrey said. "The only thing we're missing is copies of their driver's licenses."

"I probably need to get those and just keep them," I replied. "It's not like they're ever going to use them to drive again." I wondered how *that* conversation was going to go: *Hi, Grandma and Grandpa. Each of you needs to hand me your driver's license, please. No, I'm not going to give it back. . . .*

It turned out to be no trouble at all. Grandma was lying in her bed as I walked into her room with Audrey and told her I needed to see her driver's license.

"Is it in your purse?" I asked.

"Yes," she answered without suspicion. "It's in my wallet."

I reached for the purse, and while I was fishing for hers, Chris was telling Grandpa we needed to see his license as well. Without a word, he reached into his back pocket and took out his wallet. He handed Chris the license, then he looked at me.

"Just don't lose it," he said with a smile.

"I promise I won't," I said, smiling back at him. "They need to make copies of it for . . . insurance," I hesitated slightly, despising what I perceived as duplicity. I cut my eyes over to Chris, and he gave me a very slight reassuring nod.

Grandpa saw Grandma's license in my hand and leaned over to get a better look at it. He pursed his lips together as he regarded her picture. Then, just as cool as you please, he said, "That sure is a bad picture of your Grandma."

Chris and I looked at each other, and it was all we could do to keep from laughing out loud.

"Oh my," Chris mumbled, smiling as he turned away.

I took Grandpa's license from Chris's hand while unsuccessfully attempting to stifle a toothy grin of my own. I handed them both to Audrey who took them to the office to make copies. Chris and I were still trying to get our giggling under control as we settled in for a visit.

Everything in our conversation followed the path of the "new normal." Grandma talked about having to get back to work, and Grandpa asked when we were going to take them home. I had learned how to give him vague, unclear time frames like "soon" or "in a little while."

As we sat there, chatting easily about nothing in particular, Grandma suddenly looked over at Chris.

"Who is that?" she asked.

"That's Chris," I explained, caught a little off guard by her question. "You remember him. He's my husband."

Her whole face pushed into a frown; she appeared utterly shocked. "Your *husband!* You never told me you got married!"

"I did, Grandma. I promise, I did," I said with rising distress. "You and Grandpa weren't able to make the trip, so you didn't get to attend the wedding."

But she wasn't convinced. "I never knew you got married," she continued sadly. "You never told me. What am I going to give you for a wedding present?"

"Grandma, you already gave us your good china last May, right after our wedding; you told me that's what you wanted me to have for my wedding present from you. And I did tell you I was getting married. I promise, I did. We hated that you weren't able to be there. We missed you, but we understood."

"I'm sorry, Sweet," she said, settling back into her pillow. Her eyes looked sad as her expression grew cloudy, then the vacant look I had become so familiar with returned. For no apparent reason, she held her hands up to look at them, then allowed them to flop back to her side lifelessly.

Knowing she believed I had neglected to tell her about our engagement or even invite her to our wedding was crushing. They had first met Chris while we were still only dating, and I called to tell them about our engagement the day after it happened. My dad even offered to drive over there on our wedding day and bring them to Memphis for our evening ceremony, then drive them home the next day. They felt they couldn't be gone from home overnight, so they declined. Even so, we still ordered a corsage and boutonniere for them. After we got back from our honeymoon, Chris and I made a trip over to their house with my wedding dress, a tuxedo Chris had used for Concert Choir during high school, and a VCR to show them our wedding video. I put on the dress, Chris put on his tux, and we took pictures of the four of us just as if they'd been at the actual event. Later that afternoon, they had enthusiastically watched our wedding video. And now she had no memory of it.

As I sat shaking my head about it all, Audrey walked back in to return the licenses. She handed them to Chris, who leaned over to me and quietly asked what I wanted to do with them.

"I think it's too late; Grandpa's already seen them," I whispered back, taking Grandpa's license from Chris's hand. "We'll have to let him keep his for now."

Grandma turned her head and asked, "What's that in your hand?"

"It's Grandpa's driver's license," I said as I held it up for her to see.

She reached up and took it from my hand for a closer look. Chris and I were absolutely unable to hold back a good, hard belly-laugh as she raised her chin to look at it through her bifocals and pronounced, "That sure is a bad picture of your Grandpa!"

The State of Tennessee took its time in deciding to approve Medicaid for my grandparents. On the first attempt, they were both denied because their checking account had too much money. We knew that wouldn't be a problem for long because in addition to playing "catch up" with their taxes, utilities, and insurance, various medical bills had started showing up in our mailbox, and they represented every doctor who had so much as put a foot in my grandparents' door since January. All combined, they were steadily whittling away at the Meade funds. An additional expense was incurred when Waverly informed me I would have to pay them five-hundred-eighty dollars to hold Grandma's bed for the days she was away in the hospital. Audrey explained if we chose not to hold the bed, there was a very real possibility we could lose it, as new residents were being admitted during her absence.

I was also spending their money down on the maintenance of their Arkansas home. Remembering what Mack Proctor had said about their roof, I thought we should try to do something about it while there was still enough cash in the Meade account to cover it. Chris talked with his father, Frank, a semi-retired contractor, and asked him about putting on a new roof. The house was three bedrooms with one-and-a-half-baths and totaled roughly twelve hundred square feet. Frank purchased all the necessary materials and did the entire job for eleven hundred dollars.

There was one more thing I knew I had to do, and I calculated it would be the biggest expenditure yet. On the day they were admitted to Waverly, Audrey had reminded me I could spend down their money by updating their funeral arrangements. I scoured through the reams of paper I had brought from their home, and I did finally turn up an envelope with information about arrangements at a funeral home in Memphis. Chris and I made an appointment to meet with a funeral planner to see what was covered and what, if anything, had been left undone.

The good news was most of the big stuff was already covered, but I was encouraged to upgrade their caskets from the least expensive wooden box to the next-least expensive model. In addition, we learned they had not prepaid for a police escort, nor had they purchased the floral display commonly known as the family spray which would lie over the lids of their caskets. The police escort would be necessary because their burial plots were not near the funeral home, and I just knew how much Grandma loved flowers. I couldn't imagine seeing her in heaven one day and having to explain why I left the tops of their caskets bare.

The funeral planner totaled everything up, and I wrote two checks, one for Grandma and one for Grandpa, each in the amount of $3,401.

By the time we were ready to apply for Medicaid the second time, their resources had been significantly reduced. Waverly resubmitted their applications, and Grandma was finally accepted, but Grandpa was flatly denied. I nearly went into orbit.

"He was denied on the grounds of insufficient proof of medical necessity," Audrey said.

"What do they want?" I asked, completely vexed. "They've got all the information you guys had. What else is there?"

"Now we turn to the other physicians who attended them prior to their coming to Waverly," she said. "Who saw them? And what tests were performed? Do you have the names of those doctors?"

I immediately thought of Dr. Donnelly who had first diagnosed them in Walnut Ridge. I also remembered Dr. Weston in the ER when they had first come to Memphis and Dr. Carlton, the psychiatrist who had run tests on them once they had been admitted to the hospital.

"Those will be excellent," Audrey affirmed. "Contact them as soon as possible, and see if they will write letters detailing their observations of Mr. Meade."

I already had the brief letter Dr. Donnelly had written at their attorney's request, and Audrey said a copy of that would work, but to get statements from the others I was going to have to figure out how to contact them.

We found Dr. Carlton in the phone book almost immediately. I explained to his office staff what I needed, and they said they would get it sent to Waverly right away. We were never able to locate Dr. Weston, but Audrey said they were going to ask Dr. Kern, Grandpa's assigned physician through the nursing home, to also send his observations of Grandpa's mental condition. All of us who could see Grandpa face to face agreed he simply couldn't live on his own, but how could we get Medicaid officials to understand that? I found myself vacillating between knowing God could handle it but still wondering what we would do if He didn't.

The added material did make a difference. With Grandpa's third application, he was finally accepted on Medicaid. From that point on I had to write a monthly check to Waverly for what could really be considered their copay. We also had to include in that payment any money they received each month in their Social Security deposit which put them over the limit of two thousand dollars per person in their checking account. Because Waverly sent two separate statements, I developed a habit of writing two separate checks, one for Edward and one for Clara. At first it seemed labor intensive and almost wasteful to write more than one check, but when I realized we had to make an annual accounting to our Medicaid case worker for both of them, it turned out to be the most organized thing I could have done. I could easily show expenses for him apart from her, and vice versa.

Once they were finally established on Medicaid, I got really concerned about what we were going to do with their property. We could not simply keep one hundred twenty acres on ice, waiting for something to happen to my grandparents. Our Medicaid case worker told us it was going to have to become a source of income or it would have to be sold. Renting it out certainly seemed to be our best option. I resolved to give Mack Proctor a call to ask if he knew anyone who might be interested in renting my grandparents' house.

Spring of 1997 had shaped up to be a very difficult season; the heavy shroud of paperwork and decisions I faced during that period often left me feeling like I would suffocate. Trying to protect my grandparents' property from being sold and the money going into the coffers of a nursing home was just one of several things I was trying to manage. Another more immediate and troubling situation was the multitude of reports I was getting from Waverly about Grandma's PEG tube. Upon getting back to the nursing home and starting her liquid diet through the tube, Grandma made it clear she was entirely bothered by its presence. Nurses and aides frequently entered their room only to discover she was jerking at it and expressing irritation because she couldn't get rid of it. Occasionally they also found Grandpa pulling and tugging on it. Over and over, we all explained to them the tube was a necessity and they had to leave it alone, but one afternoon I finally got the call I had been dreading.

"Mrs. Stanley, I'm calling about Mrs. Meade's PEG tube. It seems Mr. Meade has pulled it out."

CHAPTER 18

SPRING

Grandma's second PEG tube experience was light years better than her first. Dr. Brantley sent her to a different hospital for the procedure, and while there she had no infections or sub-par care. She was able to return to Waverly much quicker than before, although I still had to write a check out of her account to hold her bed while she was gone.

Once she was settled back in the nursing home with Grandpa, Jennifer and I strategized how to keep them from messing with the tube again. She suggested gently wrapping Grandma's waist in what amounted to an over-sized Ace bandage.

"If we wrap it where it's not sticking out, she may be able to forget it's there," Jennifer concluded, "and if she forgets it, then he'll forget it."

I agreed it was worth a try. They would only have to see it at mealtimes, and then it would be under a nurse's supervision. The suggestion actually gave me a measure of peace; it was good to think there could be a way to avoid having to put a new PEG tube in every month or so.

As Jennifer implemented the new PEG tube wrap, Chris and I made yet another trip to my grandparents' house in Arkansas where my father-in-law was finishing their new roof. The morning air was still a bit cool, but the worst of winter was over, and hints of spring were everywhere. The two giant oaks had tiny buds just beginning to appear, and the grass bore a suggestion of green.

Grandpa always had a lot to do when the springtime finally came. There was grass seed to be sown, vegetables to be planted, and Grandma would peruse through a gardening magazine to see if there were any seeds or bulbs or a new plant she wanted to order. Every time I went over there, she would take me on a tour of her fabulous yard, pointing out all that was new and everything that had voluntarily grown up from the previous year.

She would start in the front yard, pointing out the unusual smoke trees. The bloom looked vaguely like a puff of red-brown smoke at the end of a branch, and it was so wispy and delicate I could never quite tell when I had touched it; there was an almost imperceptible sense of something feathery but somehow spongy at the same time. I had never seen the like of it anywhere else, so it became distinctly "Grandma" to me.

We would then walk to the front of the cabin where she had planted a sea of irises in every color imaginable. Every year the plants would come in thicker than the year before, and she would bend over and pry the leaves apart as she said, "I'm gonna have to thin these out, but I just don't know where I'm gonna put 'em."

Walking and talking together, we'd make our way to the back of the main house where she had a huge hydrangea bush, which the spring season loaded with big, fluffy, dark-blue blooms. Ambling on around to the side of the house, she would show me her rain lilies. The hearty stalks supported a delicate pink trumpet bloom not unlike an Easter lily, except smaller. She told me the west side of the house was the only place in her yard the rain lilies would grow.

As we came around the south corner to the front of the house, she would point out her rose bush.

"I just can't seem to get roses to grow," she would say as she nipped and picked at the fledgling bush. There were occasional blooms, but for the most part, it was decorative greenery under the bedroom window. She blamed the soil. "This ground is just too rocky," she lamented. "These roses never have done any good."

We would finish up on her front porch, peering into the white, slender flower box, which was thick with the lush, green, leafy plant peculiarly named Hen and Chicks. Grandpa, who would usually join us somewhere along the way, would have me look over the west fence into the pasture beyond and say, "If nothin' happens this spring, I'm gonna sow all that with new grass seed."

If nothin' happens this spring. . . .

In stark contrast to my warm memories, I found myself alone on the porch, staring down at that flower box. I realized the "something" Grandpa had always talked about *had* actually happened, and the result was there would be no spring flower tour that year.

I looked up to see my father-in-law climbing down his ladder from the roof. We met in the front yard and talked about the work he'd been doing, then he complimented my grandparents for having such a nice place and for maintaining it so well.

"Yes, it is a beautiful place," I said as I let my eyes wander across the yard, "but it's not the same without them here."

Frank looked up toward the cabin. "Hey, I wanted to ask you what you're planning to do with your grandfather's truck," he said.

I followed his gaze to Grandpa's silver pickup sitting in front of the cabin. It was funny, because after I had reported their vehicles as assets to our Medicaid case worker, I really hadn't thought any more about them. We had been told the cars could be sold and the money used toward their care, but I was not yet actively looking for buyers. Both the car and the truck were paid for, and I had cancelled the insurance on them since they weren't being driven; therefore, they were posing no financial drain.

"My old red truck is about to be on its last leg," Frank said. "Do you think we could buy your grandfather's truck?"

I told him I would be glad to sell that truck to him, and just a few days later we agreed on a purchase price of fifteen hundred dollars. I promptly reported the transaction to our Medicaid case worker; since I didn't want to go over the two thousand dollar per person limit and risk having them kicked out of Medicaid, I always maintained copious records and reported any changes in their checking account. For the following month, our case worker arranged for the nursing home statement to reflect a one-time overage in the amount of fifteen hundred dollars to be paid along with the normal monthly copay to Waverly. Several months later, I was able to sell their car, and I followed the exact same protocol.

After Frank and I discussed his purchase of the truck, Chris and I were getting ready to head back to Memphis. Before I left their house that day, I walked through each room to see if there was anything they could use at Waverly. I found it difficult to sort through the now jumbled belongings of my grandparents; most of the furniture pieces had been moved from their original positions, and a variety of smaller items had been strewn about willy-nilly. On a previous visit, we had discovered a break-in through the back door, and the culprit had started moving random items to the utility room just off the kitchen. Chris and I couldn't imagine what had kept them from emptying the entire house, but by that point it didn't even really matter; to me, the random mess was just another tell-tale sign that Grandma and Grandpa didn't live there anymore.

I made a quick sweep of the bedrooms and started back down the hall toward the living room when something caught my eye. Sitting on the bottom of a three-shelf hall table was the little white candy dish I remembered so well from my childhood. It had a solid white base and a short pedestal which supported the bowl, and around the outside and over the lid were delicate green leaves and clusters of purple grapes. Grandma used to keep gum and candy treats of all kinds in it. I found myself smiling as I looked at it. With almost childlike curiosity, I leaned over and lifted the lid—it was empty.

Figures, I thought to myself. *Just like the rest of this house—empty of what should rightfully be here.*

I replaced the lid and stood up, thinking I would just grab it the next time I came, but as I turned to walk away, I had the most overwhelming impression that if I wanted it, I needed to get it right then. The sense was so strong I actually turned and looked behind me—it was as if someone had said something out loud, but the hall was empty. I hesitated, trying to decide if my mind was playing tricks on me. Finally, with a surprising burst of energy, I bent down and grabbed the dish.

"All right, I'll get it now . . ." I mumbled.

I really hate having to admit it, but I just wasn't recognizing the voice of the Holy Spirit. At least I had the good sense to listen, even though I didn't realize it was Him. The little dish had no monetary value, but it certainly gave me a warm, "Grandma" feeling when I saw it. What I didn't know at the time was that if I had failed to grab it, I would have lost it forever.

We had been dealing with so much Meade stuff since January that I scarcely realized how much time had actually passed. I lifted my head out of the caregiver hole, which I felt like I was in most of the time, and discovered Karen and Jimmy's wedding was upon us. In 1996, Karen had served as maid of honor at our wedding; now, a year later, our roles were reversed. I'm still not sure how everything came together, but I had managed to throw her a bridal shower early that spring. Getting our apartment tidied up for the occasion was nothing short of a miracle. I am usually a very neat, organized person, but just a few days away from the shower I was stuffing Meade papers in every conceivable hiding place, and I squeezed a bridesmaid dress-fitting in between nursing home visits and caregiver planning meetings required by Waverly.

Along with Karen and Jimmy's wedding, May 1997 brought our own one-year anniversary; Chris suggested that we plan a short trip away to celebrate. He knew I loved the beach, so he recommended a few days in Destin, Florida. In addition to marking one year of marriage, he thought it was time for a break from the continuous caregiver responsibilities we had been shouldering for nearly five months. Since Karen and Jimmy were having a 4 o'clock ceremony, we decided we could leave right after they did, getting a little bit of the eight-hour drive under our belt.

I let Audrey know we would be out-of-pocket starting on Saturday, May 17, through the end of the week. "If something happens, please call Judy Sutton," I told her, giving her my parents' phone number.

"I'll make a note in their charts," she said, then added, "and I'm really glad to hear you're going to get away for a while. People don't realize what a toll it takes being someone else's caregiver. Taking breaks from time to time is essential."

I appreciated her encouragement because I was, in fact, feeling racked with guilt. It seemed frivolous for me to head to the coast when they were living life in a nursing home, but I was so spent from the physical and emotional experiences we'd had I nearly jumped for joy when Chris suggested the trip.

On the morning of the seventeenth, Chris and I were zipping suitcases shut and gathering what we needed for the wedding. With my dress on its hanger and my satin shoes under my arm, I was heading for the door when the telephone rang.

I didn't recognize the voice, but the woman identified herself as one of Grandma's distant relatives. I wasn't overly surprised since my phone line seemed to constantly buzz with kinfolks from the most remote parts of the family tree calling to get the story of "What happened to Clara and Edward?" and "How are they now?"; "Will they ever be able to go home again?" and without fail, they were all anxious to know, "Do they have a will?" But this lady's call was different; she wanted to file a complaint.

"I visited them yesterday," she said in a breathy voice, "and I was just appalled. Do you know they're having to share a bathroom with a *stranger*?"

I sank onto the arm of my couch completely stunned, thinking to myself, *That's your big complaint?* For a minute, I honestly didn't know what to say. I had been courteous to every family caller, politely deflecting even the most personal inquiries about their finances and disposition of their property, but *this* was just asinine.

"I'm very sorry that's bothered you," I began, "but they are just not able to live on their own anymore. My husband and I are not anywhere near qualified to provide them with the kind of professional care they need, and Waverly was the facility that had room to take a couple. It's clean, they're safe, and they're together, and that's the best I can do!"

I got off the phone and just let the bridesmaid dress crumple in a pile on the floor. I looked at Chris. "Why does it matter if they're sharing a bathroom with a stranger?" I rattled off.

"Don't let her get to you," Chris said. "It's like anything else in life: you're not going to please everybody. If they were receiving round-the-clock nursing care in their own home, I assure you there would be somebody lurking somewhere, complaining about something."

I knew he was right, but I was still battling my aggravation. Finally I picked up my dress from the floor and looked Chris straight in his eyes. "I've had enough," I said evenly. "As of right now, I'm officially off duty. On vacation. No more nursing home, no more griping about who's using which toilet! Let's go get these people married so we can escape!"

CHAPTER 19

CONTACT

O ur trip to Florida was wonderfully restful. Having several days without the immediate weight of concern about Grandma and Grandpa made me realize just how weary I had grown toward everything associated with "caregiving." I was also surprised to discover the extent to which I had come to dread the sound of a ringing telephone—it almost always meant the nursing home was reporting some kind of incident. On our trip, the phone in our hotel room never rang even once, and it was utterly freeing to know that if anything did go awry, Waverly would call my mother—not me.

As I spent time at the water's edge, I recalled how I got my love of the seaside from Grandma and Grandpa. They took me on my first trip to the Florida coast when I was about three years old. Grandma loved telling the story of how I reacted when I saw the ocean for the first time. She said I took a long, serious look at it and then said, "Whew! What a big bathtub!"

Evidently the size did overwhelm me because she said for a long time I wouldn't go near it. Grandma and Grandpa both tried everything they could think of to get me walking even a few inches into the waves, but to no avail. Finally Grandma noticed some low areas in the sand where the water had pooled. She took off her shoes and said to me, "Let's go get our feet wet."

The ploy worked. At first, she said I gingerly put my feet in the puddle, but after only a few minutes we were splashing and laughing together. With a twinkle in her eye and a smile playing on her lips, Grandma would then tell me the conclusion of the story:

"After a little while, when our feet got dry again, you came over and tapped me on the arm and said, 'Grandma, let's go get our feet wet!'"

Chris and I had several days of "getting our feet wet" as we walked on the beach and lounged in the sun. When it was time to leave, we packed up slowly, then covered the miles toward home at a leisurely pace.

Once we got back, I called Waverly to check in. I spoke with Jennifer to see how Grandma and Grandpa were doing, only to learn we had a whole new problem over the PEG tube.

"Since she had the tube put in, the kitchen no longer prepares a meal tray for Mrs. Meade," she said, "and this has upset Mr. Meade to no end. We have tried and tried to explain to him that she's not being starved or forgotten, that she's being fed through the tube, but he just doesn't understand why we don't bring her a tray along with his. So his solution is to feed her from his tray!"

"You're kidding," I said.

"We're trying to watch him," Jennifer continued, "and we stop him when we see him do it, but this is going to be a real problem because he thinks she's not getting any food. In actuality, he's the one not getting the proper nourishment because he's giving half his food to her."

Chris only smiled when I explained what was happening.

"He loves her," he said, "and he's willing to do without something to make sure she gets what he believes she's supposed to have. I guess that's the kind of love that keeps people married for sixty-five years!"

May rolled quietly and routinely into June. I was finally back to my normal work schedule, and my grandparents had settled into the nursing home life by developing a little routine of their own. They would decide it was time to leave, so they would push the front door open and cause the almost deafening alarm to sound throughout the facility. Various members of the staff had started taking turns going after them, gently leading them back by telling them all sorts of different things. Some told my grandparents it wasn't safe for them to just wander out; nurses and aides tried to reason with them about their condition, reminding Grandma of her PEG tube. Others tried to tell them they needed to wait for me to come and see them. They would come back inside, rest a short while, then start the whole process all over again. And I was informed . . . *every* time.

As exasperating as it was, the phone calls and episode reports actually achieved a quasi-normal status in my mind—*normal* being defined as what I was having to listen to over and over again—although it definitely lacked the peaceful comfort of our former lifestyle. I was emotionally adjusting to the new situation with my grandparents, but I never felt like I could say it was "right," only that "it's just the way things are."

Happily, there was one precaregiver norm that had remained unaffected by my new position. Almost from the day Chris and I had returned from our honeymoon, my parents had been inviting us over every Thursday night—for dinner, a free load of laundry, and a lot of laughing during great conversations.

On one such Thursday evening, I came home from work and sat down at Chris's desk to play Tetris on our computer, just chewing up a few minutes before I needed to leave for my parents' house. On that particular Thursday, Chris was involved in an activity with the youth group at church, so he had planned to just grab dinner on the run without coming home. As I sat there, mindlessly stacking the blocks on the screen, I suddenly found that I was mulling over a variety of possible ways to contact my two half-brothers, Tony and Duane. It had been five full months since everything had turned upside down with Grandma and Grandpa, and all at once I knew I couldn't wait any longer to get in touch with them.

The necessity of having to reach out to Tony and Duane was very intimidating to me. Since our respective births, I could count on one hand the number of times I'd had any kind of interaction with them, and there had never been any contact apart from Grandma and Grandpa. When I was a kid, I used to ask Grandma about them, how they were, and what kind of things they did. Her responses were rather vague, because she said they called only occasionally, and they came to see her and Grandpa even less. I always knew she wanted to be closer to her grandsons, but she didn't want to impose herself on them; rather, her desire was to have a relationship where everyone was mutually engaged. After experiencing such a profound rejection from Ray, she was extremely hesitant to put herself on the line and risk the emotional pain all over again, so she stood back and allowed Tony and Duane to approach her at their own pace. Grandpa, for much the same reason, stood back with her.

But now, as my grandparents' legally appointed caregiver, I knew the responsibility for contacting Tony and Duane was squarely on my shoulders. It may seem like it shouldn't have been that big a deal, but it was a *very* big deal to me. For one thing, I was truly ashamed of the fact that I had waited so long to inform them about the situation. The reason for my delay was basically two-fold: first, I had been instantly overwhelmed by the responsibility to get Grandma and Grandpa diagnosed and properly cared for, all the while playing catch-up with their long-overlooked finances, and second, I was scared nearly to death of the unknown. Dozens of questions swirled in my mind about Tony and Duane, two people who were essentially strangers to me: *How would they react? Would they think I had just stepped in and taken over so I could somehow get all the Meade money for myself? Would they get a lawyer of their own and attempt some legal maneuver to boot me out?*

My fear was rooted in the fact that all the information I had about them was secondhand at best. My grandparents had openly shared with me everything they knew about Tony, Duane, and their mother, Shirley. Grandma had always been polite about Ray's second wife, but I perpetually sensed an undercurrent of dislike and mistrust. She had told me many years before that Shirley only contacted them if she needed money. Grandma never gave her any, but apparently it never stopped Shirley from asking.

In addition to the scant information I had gleaned over the years, I also had my own recent observations. I was keenly aware that during the period from January to June, no one from Ray's family had called Grandma and Grandpa's Arkansas home phone; after I had paid their past-due phone bill, I had cancelled the service since no one was living in the house. If they had attempted to call, the "no longer in service" recording would have been a red flag that something had happened, and I reasoned they would have reached out for information, if not from me then certainly from Grandma's sister, Lena. Furthermore, Mack Proctor was keeping a watchful eye on everything at their house, and he continued to report that no one had come to visit the Meades since they had left. And notably, neither Tony, Duane, nor Shirley had been among the steady stream of concerned relatives who had been calling me since January. My only conclusion was they had no idea anything had happened.

I shut down my Tetris game and stared at the phone for a few seconds. *Where could I begin?* The last I knew from Grandma, they all three lived in Horn Lake, Mississippi. I pondered my options before I finally picked up the receiver and dialed the nationwide "Information" number.

For the next half hour or so, a very patient operator helped me search the Mississippi phone records for Tony and Duane. I started with Tony.

"His full name is Anthony Raymond Meade Jr."

"Nope," she answered definitively. "I see no Anthony Raymond Meade, Jr. or Sr."

Not locating "Sr." didn't surprise me, but I was puzzled by the lack of "Jr." "How about 'Tony Meade'?"

"Nope."

"Try just plain 'Anthony Raymond Meade' without the 'Jr.'"

"Nope," she said again. "Nothing."

Feeling frustrated, I switched gears. "How about his brother, Eric Duane Meade?"

I could hear her fingers clicking the keys in the background, but the result was the same.

"Nope."

We tried various combinations of their names, but failure after failure brought me to the conclusion the only word that operator knew was *nope*. I began to wonder if the sons had taken off for parts unknown like the father had. In utter exasperation, we both held the line while she continued to search everywhere from Olive Branch to Biloxi. I finally slid the phone's mouthpiece to my shoulder and started to pray—which is what I should have done before I dialed even a single digit.

Father, You know I need to get in touch with these guys, I said anxiously. *How can I do that if I can't find them? Help!*

I am so grateful that God's mercy reached out and caught me—again. Almost immediately I remembered Shirley's maiden name was "Bayless," and Grandma had told me that the last she knew, Shirley's mother lived in Horn Lake. I leaped on it.

"Do you see anyone by the name of 'Bayless' in Horn Lake?"

She paused briefly then said, "Yes!"

"Give me the number," I said eagerly.

At last! I finally had a number to try. I sat and stared at it for a long time, just breathing deeply and trying to figure out what I could say to the mother of the woman who had committed adultery with my biological father. It was certainly one of the most unsettling moments of my life.

I dialed slowly but deliberately. As the call connected and I heard the first ring, I could feel my breath coming in short bursts. I frantically reminded God that He had promised never to leave me, and I pleaded my case for His help.

"Hello?" an unfamiliar woman's voice answered.

"Hello, is this Mrs. Bayless?" I asked in a surprisingly steady voice.

"Yes," she answered.

"Mrs. Bayless, my name is Leah Stanley. I'm Edward and Clara Meade's granddaughter. I apologize for disturbing you, but I'm trying to reach one or both of your grandsons. I need to speak with Tony or Duane about the Meades."

Her response was polite enough, but she wasn't forthcoming with the information I needed.

"Has something happened to the Meades?" she asked.

"Yes, ma'am. It's a rather long story, but the short of it is they are both suffering with different forms of dementia. They had appointed me to serve as their caregiver and gave me legal power of attorney back in 1992. This spring, a series of events has left me with no other choice but to put them in a nursing home."

"Oh, I see," she said.

"I would like to speak with Tony or Duane, or if she's available, I'll be glad to talk with Shirley. It's just very important that I reach them and let them know about Grandma and Grandpa. Do you have a number where I can reach any of them?"

"Well, I have a number for Shirley, but I don't know that she'd want me giving it out," she said slowly.

I didn't know if it was mistrust of me or if Shirley was just fanatically private about her information. Either way, I offered my number to Mrs. Bayless and asked if she would give it to Shirley. It seemed to be the only choice I had.

"I'm actually headed out this evening," I told her, "so I'd like to give you another number in case she calls tonight and I'm not here."

I gave her my parents' number and told her I appreciated her time and help. When I hung up, I realized I was shaking all over. I couldn't believe how draining that simple, short call had been.

When I got to my parents' house, dinner was on the table, so we sat right down. I don't think I took two bites before their phone rang. The three of us froze and stared at each other as the sound of the ring hung heavily in the air.

"That's my call," I said after taking in a deep breath.

"God bless you," my mom said as I was reaching for the cordless phone. "He gives you wisdom about what to say."

"I need it," I said just before I answered.

On the other end of the line, I heard Shirley's voice for the first time in many years. The last time I had even seen her was in 1981 at the one hundredth birthday party for Grandma's father. Ray had been there too, sitting on a couch next to Shirley in a room at the back of the house where the party was being hosted. Neither of them spoke to me. I suppose I should have had enough backbone to approach Ray, but I was all of fourteen years old and in that awkward stage of being unsure whether I should talk to him or not. My adolescent shyness won out, so I remained in the front living room well away from them. Sixteen years later, I found myself on the phone with Shirley having a conversation that still felt awkward, but this time talking was not merely an option, it was a necessity.

"I really appreciate you calling me back," I told her. "We have a situation, and I didn't know exactly how to reach Tony or Duane."

"Well, that's fine," she said. "Now, tell me exactly what's happened."

I tried to briefly sum up the last five months; even a succinct overview took a fair amount of time. "It's been awfully hard to see," I said in conclusion. "Truly heartbreaking. My husband and I have been working day and night it seems, trying to get them and all their business taken care of since January;

and on that note, I want to apologize for having been so long about contacting all of you. It was so overwhelming when it all first happened, plus I had no idea how to reach Tony or Duane. Things have settled down somewhat so that I've finally been able to think what to do."

"Oh, I understand," Shirley responded. "It sounds like it was a lot."

The conversation was civil but remained very chilly, even though we were on the phone for a considerable length of time. I noted how up to that point, she hadn't offered so much as a location for either of her sons. I was considering how best to broach that subject when, out of nowhere, the call took a very unexpected turn, landing me in a surprisingly dark place.

"I want to tell you that I'm sorry about what happened to your mother all those years ago," she said.

I thought I was braced and ready for anything she could say, but I never saw that statement coming. My brain was racing to find the right response—I thought she was surely finished speaking her piece. But she wasn't.

"I promise you, I didn't know your daddy was married to her. If I had known, I never would have married him."

Breathe. Process. What was she saying?

"He never told me a thing about her," she continued. "I had no idea he had a wife and a child in Memphis."

Shirley's words evoked a long-forgotten memory of my mother's devastating experience when she met with Ray in late spring 1968 to sign the papers which dissolved their marriage. She, Grandma, and Grandpa had met Ray and a very pregnant Shirley at a gas station across the street from the home my grandparents were living in at the time. As Shirley was rhetorically urging me to believe she had no knowledge of Ray's first wife, I remember a thought cutting through my mind like a knife: *Well, you knew about her when he was getting legally divorced, so you obviously knew about her when you turned around and went through a second—legal—marriage ceremony before Tony was born!*

The memory burned like a TNT fuse—slow, smoldering, steady. I knew I couldn't possibly say it out loud, but what I really wanted to know was why she was telling me all this. Why now? What did she want *from me*?

All I could seem to do was hold that phone to my ear and look out my parents' front window, realizing I was completely stalled for a decent response. I had nothing positive to say, but thank God for the Holy Spirit! He entered into the dark place with me, effectively breaking my fall, even though I couldn't seem to utter any sort of cry for help. He led me back into the light with gentle ease, and His willingness to forgive me became my willingness to take my hands off her proverbial throat.

"You know, it's all water under the bridge," I heard myself answering her with polite confidence. "It's all in the past, and I think it's fine to leave it there."

"Well," she persisted, "I just wanted you to know."

I began to ponder what her life must have been like after Ray walked out on her, but after only a few seconds, she took the guesswork out of that too.

"He left me just like he left your mother," she said flatly. "Left me with those boys and bills. I even had the IRS calling me, trying to track him down. I told 'em I didn't know anything about where he was."

Her voice was completely devoid of all emotion. I remember thinking, *How is she not upset about what he did to her?* I figured maybe it had just been so long ago, she had actually been able to get over it, but as I continued to listen to her, I could see there was one very strong emotion present. She wasn't hurt and devastated; she was bitter.

"He was no good," she said in an even tone, "absolutely no good."

Feeling the need to steer away from any further emotional revelations, I gingerly began to shift the topic back toward Grandma and Grandpa by suggesting that she, Tony, and Duane might want to pay them a visit. Our conversation wound down as we made plans to meet at Waverly on Sunday afternoon.

"Duane'll come with me to see 'em, but Tony and his wife are living in North Carolina, so don't expect him," she said.

"Tony is married?" I asked.

"Oh yes, to a girl named Sheila," Shirley answered.

"Well, that's wonderful," I said. "I'm really happy for him."

I told Shirley she could give Tony and Duane my phone number, and they were welcome to call me any time. After I gave her the address for Waverly and the room number for Grandma and Grandpa, we hung up. I then sat on the edge of the bed for several minutes until my nervous energy subsided.

Saturday evening found Chris and me at home in our apartment, relaxed, cooking dinner, and enjoying our quiet night together. We had both expressed a degree of trepidation over our scheduled meeting with Shirley and Duane the next day, but after my conversation Thursday night, I felt like the element of the unknown had been somewhat diminished.

"Maybe they won't be disagreeable over all this," I speculated.

"They ought to be thrilled that it's you in the decision-making hot seat and not them," Chris said firmly. "It's entailed more than I ever imagined, and you've done a great job taking care of everything—and you've been honest with the money. Not every family has someone like that."

"Well, Tony and Duane don't really know me," I said. "They have no idea whether I'm honest or not."

"Well, the folks at Medicaid do," Chris answered, "and if you'd been trying to squirrel any of the money away for yourself, they'd have already stopped you."

I smiled at Chris and said, "So, I take care of Meade money with approval from Medicaid—and for more than a year now, I've been managing Stanley household finances too!"

He reached his arms around me for a loose hug as he smiled and said, "Don't tell my wife!"

The phone rang as I laughed and said, "She can't be as good with your money as I am!"

Chris reached over and answered the phone as I turned back to our simmering dinner.

"It's Mack Proctor," he said in a serious tone, "and he sounds upset."

"Hey, Mack, what's up?" I asked.

"We've got a situation over here," he began. "Earlier today, a big moving truck pulled up to your grandparents' place. I don't ever remember seeing any of those people before; I didn't know who they were."

"Oh, Mack," I began.

"I drove by, and Leah, they were taking things out of your grandparents' house. I didn't know who they were or what they called themselves doing there, so I called the sheriff. He and I went over and talked to them. One of the men said he was the grandson of Mr. and Mrs. Meade, and he said there was stuff in that house that belonged to them, so he and his mother were there to get it."

I shut my eyes as Mack delivered the final blow.

"Leah, they took everything. They have completely emptied that house."

CHAPTER 20

CONFRONTATION

For the first time since I became the legally appointed caregiver for my grandparents, I was truly furious over something associated with their business. It may have been pent-up anxiety over the whole situation, or maybe I was just releasing nervous energy which had built up during my call with Shirley—either way, the news Mack gave me about Duane and his mother taking every single item out of Grandma and Grandpa's house made me livid.

For one thing, I couldn't believe they'd actually done it. I had no idea how long it had been since either of them had last contacted Grandma and Grandpa, but the moment Shirley found out something had happened, the *first* action she and Duane took was to drive a moving truck over to their house and liberate the contents—lock, stock, and barrel. They went for the "stuff" before they could even go visit the people they were so ready to clean out.

Over the years, Grandma and I had talked on numerous occasions about how she and Grandpa wanted their furniture and possessions divided. In no uncertain terms, she said they wanted me to have the first choice of everything she and Grandpa owned.

"Tony and Duane can have their pick after you get what you want," Grandma told me. "The truth is they probably won't even care about anything we have, but I know some of this stuff has meaning for you like it does for us."

Apart from the toy box, the little white candy dish, a single plate hanging on the wall in their kitchen, and my favorite cereal bowl, I took for myself only six pieces of their furniture: an armoire and cedar chest which Grandma's parents had given her for her eighteenth birthday, along with their sideboard, china cabinet, and a tall stack of shelves designed to sit in a corner, which Grandma had always called a "whatnot." I had also taken Grandpa's cedar armoire from the cabin and a framed photograph depicting an aerial view of their property. I had taken Grandma's rocking chair and an assortment of pictures for them to have at Waverly, but their remaining living room furniture and all decorations, two beds, Grandma's dresser, vanity table, and bench, her quilt box and sewing machine, dishes and kitchen equipment, dining room table, and a hodgepodge of smaller pieces had remained in that house until Shirley and Duane had removed them.

Ironically, I actually did have all the pieces I wanted, but Shirley didn't know that. At no time during our phone call did we discuss the Meade furniture and other possessions, or what plans, if any, I had to divide them between us. Grandma told me she had not provided copies of the Meade wills or power of attorney documents to Tony or Duane, and she had never discussed the division of personal property with either of them. I found it presumptuous and arrogant that with complete autonomy they decided to take for themselves everything in that house which was not nailed down.

I stewed around angrily all evening long, but Chris finally made me laugh when he suggested I wait six months, then call Shirley and tell her that Grandma and Grandpa were suddenly better and would be going back home.

"Wonder if she and Duane would be able to produce everything they took," he said with a sly smile.

"I guess that depends on what they plan to do with it all," I answered, pondering the possibilities—*What would they do with it all? Pawn shop? Antique dealer? Yard sale?*

When it was finally time for bed, I felt tired, but my sleep that night was choppy at best. On Sunday morning, when Chris asked me how I had slept, all I could do was grunt.

"I dreamed," I said flatly. "All night long, I dreamed. I dreamed weird things like Grandma had died, and when I walked into the funeral home, I saw the mortician putting Grandma's body in her cedar chest."

The cedar chest was a lengthy, rectangular box with a lid attached by two hinges positioned on one of the long edges. Its similarity to a casket was undeniable, although I had never consciously imagined it in that way. It struck me as odd that I should have a dream which blended the vague, intangible element of my grandmother's death with the highly tangible element of her furniture. This particular dream had forced me to acknowledge two levels of loss: the impending loss of Grandma and Grandpa to death, and the current loss of my grandparents' remaining furniture to Shirley and Duane.

I believe the bizarre dreams I experienced as a caregiver were the result of unresolved stress; the dreams never made me feel better, but they did seem to express—in an unbridled way—a very palpable reaction to events that were beyond my control. I had concluded the only reason anyone other than my grandparents should be in possession of their worldly goods was if both of them had passed away. For anyone, including me, to have their things while they were still living seemed very wrong. Whether I was still angry about Shirley and Duane helping themselves to the household appointments—without at least running it by the girl who had durable power of attorney—or if my own conscience was trying to nail me to the wall for personally removing certain pieces from their house, my dream was at the very least strange; at most, it was painful.

I drug myself out of bed and showered mechanically, then I walked without emotion through the morning at church. I was experiencing a nagging anxiety over the meeting with Shirley and Duane, which left me with no appetite for lunch. I kept mulling over in my mind what I could say about the previous day's events; I figured it was bound to come up, especially in light of the fact that Mack had called the sheriff on them.

Before Chris and I left for Waverly, I had a brief phone call with my mother. She too was appalled by what they had done, but she was able to put it in perspective for me with a positive twist.

"You've already taken the pieces that are special to you," she said. "They've actually done you a huge favor by emptying that house. Now you don't have to worry about moving or storing any of that furniture. That's one less thing for you to have to deal with—it was a problem that's now off your plate!"

Chris and I entered the nursing home on Sunday afternoon with an attitude of just wanting to get this particular visit over and done with. When we walked into my grandparents' room, we saw Grandma in her rocker, Grandpa in one of the smaller Waverly chairs, and two people sitting on Grandpa's bed who could only be the all too familiar strangers, Shirley and Duane.

I probably wouldn't have recognized either one of them if I had encountered them on the street with no Meade context. From the few times I had seen Shirley, I recalled her hair had always been done up on top of her head, and I remembered it being medium brown in color. The woman before me had hair that was cut short and appeared more battleship gray with only hints of its former shade. My memory also pictured her rather short and thin, but the size of the woman sitting on the bed was hard to assess as she was wearing blue jeans and a loose-fitting long-sleeved shirt. But if I'd had any doubt about her identity when we came in, it was immediately dispelled once we made eye contact. Her eyes were the same cold, dark eyes I remembered from my childhood. They were steely, judging, mistrustful.

Duane was dressed in jeans with a short-sleeved T-shirt, but I could see the years had left him with a few extra pounds and thinning brown hair. I detected a suggestion of Ray in his features, but overwhelmingly he resembled his mother, down to the cold eyes and pallid skin tone.

I smiled at Grandma and gave her a hug like always while Grandpa got up to shake Chris's hand, then he came over to hug me. There was a strained politeness as Shirley, Duane, Chris, and I exchanged greetings. Chris and I sat down together on Grandma's bed, and Grandpa went back to the little chair. We chatted uncomfortably for several minutes before Grandma put her hand on my arm and leaned over to me.

"Who are they?" she asked, looking at them with a frown.

I forced a pleasant facial expression as I said, "This is Duane, your grandson, and his mother, Shirley."

She cut her eyes back over to them. "I don't know these people," she said bluntly.

Shirley and Duane just sat there not saying a word. I squirmed uneasily as I searched for a point of reference for her.

"He's Tony's brother," I said with a forced smile. "Your grandson."

"No," she said with a mistrustful stare, "I don't know them."

I looked at them, lowering my voice as I said, "This is how she's been."

Their faces remained stoic, completely void of emotion or expression. I moved quickly to change the subject.

"You mentioned that Tony is married," I ventured.

"Yeah, for a couple of years now," Shirley replied.

"And you said they live in North Carolina?"

"Yeah, but they're planning a trip down here soon to come see them," she tilted her head slightly toward Grandma.

The strain in the air was almost unbearable. The conversation moved forward with an edgy awareness that we were in opposing camps, but we were facing each other in a non-combative, social situation. I found that Shirley did most of the talking, even when Chris or I would directly ask Duane a question. He would give short, staccato replies, and Shirley would supplement his answers with her own observations. Awkward as it was, we were getting through it, but then I guess Shirley got comfortable, and rather arrogantly confident.

"We made a trip over to their house yesterday," she began boldly. "That neighbor of theirs, he called the sheriff on us. He said you told him to do it."

Adrenaline shot through my body. I knew there was nothing I could do but put my feet right up against the line she'd so belligerently drawn.

"Yes," I said steadily, "I told Mack just as we were leaving with Grandma and Grandpa in January to keep an eye on the house, and if he saw anything suspicious or anyone he didn't know that he should not approach them himself but call the sheriff and let him handle it."

"Well, that sheriff acted like he had sense. He left us alone after we told him who we were."

"I'm glad there was no trouble," I said as pleasantly as I could manage, "but, to be clear, I wasn't aware you were there until after you had already left. If I'd known you were going over there, I could have let Mack know."

"We got concerned," Shirley countered. "We got to thinkin' about all their furniture and stuff . . . didn't seem like a good idea to just leave it sittin' there."

"Well, I had no choice but to leave it all there with Mack looking after it," I responded in a polite but firm tone. "When this went down in January, my concern was not for their things. Grandma and Grandpa needed serious medical attention and help. *They* were the priority—not their things."

"So, you have power of attorney," she said, shifting the discussion away from Grandma and Grandpa. "I guess you're also the executor of the estate?"

My eyes met hers. What was she after? "Yes," I answered slowly without breaking eye contact.

"Well, then I guess that means you get the biggest share of the inheritance."

My brows pulled together slightly. I thought to myself, *You do realize they're not dead yet, don't you? And you're sitting here trying to carve up their property right in front of them?*

It was only by God's grace I was able to hold my tongue. I took a breath, harnessed my disbelief over Shirley's crass inquiry, and said aloud, "No. According to their wills drawn up by their attorney, the property is to be divided between Tony, Duane, and me into equal thirds. No one has a larger share than anyone else."

"Well," her eyebrows went up slightly as she tilted her head, glancing at the floor. "Usually the executor takes a fee, and that comes out of everybody else's share."

"No," I repeated with thinly veiled disgust, "I'm not interested in any executor's fee. I intend only to follow the terms specified by Grandma and Grandpa in their wills." My heart was beating so hard and fast I couldn't believe my jacket wasn't visibly moving to its rhythm. I could see that everything Grandma had ever told me about Shirley was not just in Grandma's imagination. Shirley's primary concern really was money. Just money.

"Well," Shirley muttered again, but nothing else followed.

I looked over at Grandma. She was just sitting and staring at nothing, completely oblivious to the clash taking place in front of her. I reached over and patted her leg. She looked up at me and smiled.

"You know, I was thinking," Shirley piped up again.

I turned my head to look her straight in her face.

"Maybe you could move them over to a nursing home closer to us in Horn Lake, you know, so we can help keep an eye on them."

Was she *serious?* The notion of moving them to Mississippi so they could be thirty minutes closer to *Shirley*—who hadn't so much as dialed their phone number for at least the last six months—was ridiculous. In addition, it was ludicrous to think she wanted them closer to herself, but farther away from me, the person who had the authority to make medical decisions for them. Sheer lunacy.

"No," I answered almost immediately. "They're here now and getting settled. I think here is just fine."

Our eyes met again as she pursed her lips, raised her eyebrows slightly, and gave a short nod.

"Well, I guess we better be getting back home," she said with no particular emotion.

We all stood up and exchanged reasonably polite farewells. Grandpa reached out and shook Duane's hand, but he didn't move toward Shirley. Grandma had stayed in her chair, but she looked up as they faced her to say goodbye.

"You take care of yourself," Shirley told her. The words suggested fondness, but the tone lacked sincerity. Grandma smiled slightly but didn't respond.

When they walked out, I found I was standing very stiff and straight-backed. My knees were locked, and I was staring at the empty doorway.

"Oh, God," I mumbled. "Thank you so much that that's over."

For the next few weeks, I lived in an anxious state of anticipation that the other shoe would drop. I don't even know what I was expecting to happen, but day after day all remained quiet. Every time I checked in at Waverly, I was told Grandma and Grandpa had had no visitors except for Chris and me, so little by little, my uneasy tensions began to subside. Then one day I got a call from one of the charge nurses, and all my vague concerns suddenly assumed a very definite shape.

"Mrs. Stanley, did you visit your grandparents this afternoon?"

"No, I haven't been in today. Are they OK?

"Yes, they're fine," she paused, "but I need to make you aware of something that happened a little while ago. Apparently, a young woman came to the nurses' station and requested to see Mr. and Mrs. Meade's charts. She told the nurse on duty that she was their granddaughter and insisted on seeing both charts at once."

I was floored. I am the only granddaughter they have. Who in the world would go into Waverly and identify herself as the Meades' granddaughter? And why?

Apparently, the nurse on duty paid no particular attention to the woman; most everybody on staff knew the Meades were being cared for by their granddaughter, although not all of them had met me face to face. The duty nurse just assumed it was me and pulled out both charts, allowing a total stranger complete access to the Meade records. Everything was looked at, including all tests and corresponding results, all doctors' notes, and all current medications. The charge nurse went on to explain that as the strange woman poured over the charts, she was taking copious notes; it was so unusual the nurse on duty finally asked her straight out, "Are you Leah?" At that point, the unknown woman answered, "No, I'm not," then closed the charts, thanked the nurse, and left.

Even though HIPAA (the Health Insurance Portability and Accountability Act) had been signed into law on August 21, 1996, it was so new that many people, including healthcare professionals, weren't very familiar with its privacy protections. I confess my own ignorance at the time regarding the scope of its provision; I only knew I was outraged at the notion of any medical professional handing over my grandparents' private medical information based solely on some woman announcing she was their granddaughter. I literally had no idea who this person was, so the next day, I went to Waverly and told the nursing supervisor I wanted a "Do Not Publish" label placed across the front of both Meade charts, thus ensuring that no degree of information would be given out to anyone but Chris or me.

As it turned out, I didn't have to wait too long to find out who the imposter was. My phone rang one evening shortly after I got home from work.

"Is this Leah?" a woman's voice asked.

"Yes," I answered.

"Leah, this is Sheila Meade. I'm Tony's wife."

"Well, hi, Sheila, it's good to meet you—even though it is just over the phone."

"It's good to talk to you too," she responded. "I wanted to let you know Tony and I were just in Memphis, and we got to go by and see your grandparents."

All at once I began putting the pieces together.

"The facility seems good, and they look like they are being well cared for," Sheila continued, "but I wanted to discuss some aspects of their care with you. Um, I noticed . . ." she hesitated, and I heard papers flipping. "I saw that Grandma had an upper GI done and they followed up with a PEG tube."

I was so caught off guard by her assertive tone, I felt like I was having to play "catch up" with the conversation. For her, Sir Francis Bacon was right: knowledge truly was power—*her* knowledge of everything that was in my grandparents' charts. In my stupor, all I could seem to attach to was the phrase, "upper GI." I had been told by one of the Waverly nurses that it wasn't a formal upper GI but rather a simple swallow study, so I repeated that information to Sheila.

"Well, that's an upper GI," she responded forcefully.

She clearly had the advantage for the moment; I felt like I'd been ambushed, and I found myself very much on the defensive.

"Do you work in the medical profession?" I asked, trying to establish the facts.

"I'm a nurse," she answered quickly.

I looked down and saw that my right hand had a death grip on the back of one of the dining table chairs. I released the chair, pulled my chin up, and took a deep breath.

"Well, what did you want to discuss about their care?" I posed my question calmly, but with growing determination that this total stranger wasn't going to dictate the terms of this "discussion."

"I noticed that Grandpa is on Haldol," she said. "Why is that? Haldol is an antipsychotic drug—it's bad stuff. Did you authorize this?"

Enough! I was done playing defense. I didn't know who this woman was, but she had so overplayed her hand with her aggressive, demanding-answers attitude; I decided it was time to slow the conversation down and establish who was actually in charge—and who actually had all the responsibility that went along with being *in charge*.

"Sheila, they were in very bad shape when their lawyer turned over the durable power of attorney documents to me, their designated caregiver, back in January." I spoke very deliberately because I meant to be heard and understood. "When we had to bring them to Memphis, Grandpa was extremely combative. Because of his cognition issues coupled with previously undetected aggression, the psychiatrist who first saw them recommended Haldol. Their doctor at the nursing home concurred with that decision.

Taking into account that these two different physicians, upon completing two separate exams, both felt Haldol was the best choice for Grandpa, I have not argued that decision."

My bold posturing worked. Sheila's response indicated she was backing down.

"I understand," she said. "It must have been awful."

"It was worse than you can imagine."

"Well, I'm sorry that everything has happened for them the way it has. They seem like really wonderful people."

"Yes, they certainly are that," I responded, "and I would do anything to stop this galloping advance of dementia. I would love nothing more than to have them well again so they could just go back to their Arkansas home and things could be the way they were before. As it is, I'm doing everything in my power to provide the best care possible for them."

Sheila and I continued to talk for some time. Things had gradually settled down to the point where I felt like she was finally understanding my position in the situation—and realizing that I wasn't the greedy, cold-hearted, power-hungry relative looking to get rid of the grandparents and take everything for myself. When the conversation seemed to be drawing to a close, I even felt that a fledgling friendship was being established. Then, very unexpectedly, I began to hear someone yelling angrily in the background on her end. Sheila hesitated slightly, then explained what was happening.

"Tony is very upset," she said.

"Well, I understand that. What's happened to our grandparents is horrible."

"It's not just that. He's angry about Grandpa being on Haldol, and Grandma on Prozac," she said.

"Let me talk to him, Sheila," I said boldly.

"Oh no! You *do not* want to talk to him when he's like this."

"Please let me explain the situation to him," I pressed.

"Oh, no, no. If you talk to him now, you'll never want to talk to him again. Let me explain things to him. Right now, he's too angry; he doesn't understand everything that's happened. He'll settle down, but you absolutely do not want to talk to him right now."

"Sheila, please, please explain to Tony that *none* of this has been taken lightly by me or any member of my family. I cannot begin to tell you what we've been through over here. I have had to make some ugly decisions, and it's hurt me to my core. I've racked my brain to remember things that Grandma said they wanted, and I've gone to great lengths to avoid things I knew they didn't want. But in everything, no matter what else was going on, I've always put them first—talking to doctors and other professionals, trying to do what's absolutely the best thing *for them*."

"I believe you have," Sheila said with a quiet confidence. "And you have done a good job in a really tough situation. I'll talk to Tony. You'll be able to talk with him later. It'll be fine, just not now."

I hung up the phone slowly, closed my eyes, and breathed out a long sigh. Chris got up from the couch where he'd been sitting since the call started.

"Well?" he said expectantly.

"I believe we have détente."

The days of summer became more relaxed as the events of June receded into the past. My grandparents' acceptance of life in the nursing home was better, though nowhere near fully achieved. Grandpa still asked where his car was, and they both continued to sound the alarm in the facility with their repetitive attempts to "go home," but at least now all family members had been appropriately notified about the situation, and for the first time in nearly two years, all the Meade bills were paid in full and up to date.

I had only one major task left to perform and that was to find a tenant to rent the Meade property. It turned out the Proctors were able to help us yet again. Mack's wife, Betty Jo, had an adult son from a previous marriage, and he was looking for a place where he and his wife could settle down with their two children. Betty Jo told me they would be glad to rent the Meade place even though they knew there was no hot running water in the house, so we asked Bruce Hollis to draw up a twelve-month rental contract. In it, we specified they were agreeing to rent the property "as is," and if anything broke, they were free to fix it at their own expense, but the Meade money would not be used to repair anything. At the rate of only one hundred dollars per month, they eagerly accepted our terms.

In July 1997, Chris and I, along with my parents, made one more trip to my grandparents' home to meet our new tenants, sign the lease, and give them their new house keys. We drove up to an empty shell—literally. While the yard was thick and lush, the flowers were blooming with wild abandon, and the two huge oak trees were sporting their rich, green leaves, I found the house completely stripped of character, personality, and life. I stood in the empty living room in a type of shock. There was no furniture, no pictures, nothing. The Meades were gone, and now their things were gone too.

"Well, Shirley and Duane flat took everything," my mother observed as she peeked her head into the vacuous formal living room.

"That they did," I said quietly.

"You don't realize how much stuff is here until it's all gone," Chris said as he came back in from the utility room off the kitchen.

"And the good news is," my dad said as he put his arm around my shoulders, "you don't have to worry about *any* of it!"

I smiled slightly, and as I acknowledged he was right, we heard a car pulling up to the house. Betty Jo's son and daughter-in-law had arrived.

After the brief introductions, we chatted about the house and the wonderful people who had most recently lived there. We also told them how much we appreciated all the help Mack had given us during the trying events of the last six months. They were very friendly people who seemed genuinely thrilled to be renting the house.

Once the task of signing the rental papers was done, we took our leave, and as we backed out of the carport, I recall watching the young parents and their two small boys disappear around the western corner of the house heading toward the garden, exploring their new digs.

At last, I thought, *the place is going to be a home again.*

CHAPTER 21

LOST AND FOUND

For the remainder of 1997 all the way through August 1998, the rent checks came in our mail at the first of every month; no payment was ever missed or even late. And each month, I duly deposited the one hundred dollars into the Meade checking account. The monthly statements from Waverly were amended to recoup the exact amount of the rent in our copay to the nursing home; at no time did the Meade rental property ever turn a profit.

It was also during the summer of 1998 that the State of Tennessee performed the first annual review of my grandparents' case to determine if they still qualified to have Medicaid foot the bill for them to live at Waverly. Along with the proof of continued medical necessity, I provided a copy of the Meade property's rental agreement. Our caseworker had explained to me that as long as the property was making any amount of money which could be used toward their care, it wouldn't have to be sold. By the end of summer, I had been notified that Grandma and Grandpa would be allowed to remain on Medicaid for another year, but I subsequently learned that Betty Jo's son had decided to move his family out and not renew their rental contract with us.

Hardly missing a beat, Betty Jo was once again able to steer me to a prospective tenant, a single woman with no children. She was not as reliable in paying her rent, and after just a few months, she called to tell me the well had run completely dry; there was no water, hot or cold, coming into the house. I reasoned that if I was already having trouble getting the rent money out of her, it would be utterly futile to expect her to pay to live in a house with no water at all. I let her out of the contract and pondered what I could do to keep the house protected.

Several weeks passed as day after day my grandparents' house remained vacant. I felt like I was at the end of my "landlord" rope. As time went by with no paying tenant, I felt a growing concern we might lose everything my grandparents had spent years of their lives building and developing. Chris and I realized if we could just get the well and the water heater fixed, we could much more easily find a prospective renter; the trouble was, we didn't have anywhere near the kind of money it would take to straighten it all out. The water heater alone might have been financially manageable, but digging a new well would cost thousands of dollars. I struggled as I prayed through it; I would start to approach the Lord, but then my own thoughts would rush in and assert dominance by screaming, *There's no way anyone's ever going to rent that house again!* The only solution *I could see* involved money we didn't have. I was, yet again, walking in my own flesh and failing to exercise the faith to believe that what God had already said in His Word was true:

> *Now to Him Who is able to do immeasurably more than all we ask or imagine . . . to Him be glory . . . (Ephesians 3:20-21)*

> *Jesus looked at them and said, "With man this is impossible, but not with God; all things are possible with God." (Mark 10:27)*

I have come to appreciate the way God deals with His people. Sometimes it's with the softness of an impression; other times He takes the chin of His frantic child in His strong, gentle hand and He calmly says, "Trust Me."

One afternoon, as my workday was drawing to a close, I received a phone call on my direct office line from a man who identified himself as Jason Cope. He explained that he had heard my grandparents' house was for rent, and he wanted to know how much we were charging.

"Yes," I told him eagerly, "the property is for rent, but I feel I need to inform you the house has no running water."

"Well, ma'am, if it's all right with you, then it's all right with me," he replied with a definite southern drawl.

I could not believe what I was hearing. Clearly he had misunderstood what I'd said.

"It's not a problem for me," I replied, then reiterated, "but are you sure you don't mind living in a house where the only water you'll have is whatever you bring in yourself?"

"Ma'am, we'd be thrilled to live in that house, water or no," he responded.

I briefly outlined the terms of the rental agreement, then clarified for a third time that if he didn't mind the lack of water, I'd be glad for him to rent my grandparents' house. I explained I would immediately have their lawyer draw up a new contract, and after he signed it, I would provide him with a key and he could move in as soon as he was ready.

"I can't tell you how much I appreciate it, ma'am," he replied with genuine sincerity.

After we hung up, I thought about how he sounded so content with his new living arrangement, but I was left wondering how he was going to wash his hands or brush his teeth. Or flush the toilet.

I never did find out how he got the phone number of my direct office line, but honestly, I didn't even care. The relief that washed over me was indescribable. I remember asking God, *Who are You? And why are You so good to us?* Thanks to the gracious God who prompted Jason Cope's call, the next Medicaid review would show only a reasonable gap between two tenants, which would cause no flap. The property was once again protected from premature sale, which meant that my grandparents would still have an inheritance to give to their grandchildren.

When I got home that night, I told Chris what had happened. Neither of us could quite wrap our heads around the fact that out of the blue, a total stranger called and said he wanted to rent that house—*without* the basic necessity of running water.

"That's God's provision," Chris said with conviction. "That's God directing our steps just like we asked Him to—just like He said He would."

After the first year of Grandma and Grandpa living in the nursing home, I had come to realize that I got to see them far more often than when they were living in Arkansas more than two hours away from me. Chris and I would pop in to visit during evenings and weekends and on every holiday the calendar could offer. Every few weeks Chris would go pick Grandpa up and take him to the barber shop, and they played checkers regularly, although as time went along, it became apparent Grandpa's game was losing its edge. I would file fingernails and clip toenails, first hers, then his, while Grandma and I would talk about whatever topic she happened to introduce.

During one of the required care-plan meetings with the nursing home staff, it was brought to my attention that Grandpa wandered around during the daytime hours looking bored and drinking coffee—a *lot* of coffee, and apparently all the caffeine was making him cranky with the staff.

"Well," I responded, "he has nothing to do, and the coffee is readily available throughout the facility. But, truth be told, he is a man of the outdoors.

He had a garden at home, and he kept cows, and he took his dog on long, frequent walks. He doesn't have any of that here; I don't know what to tell you."

One of the social workers in the meeting said she had an idea, but she would need the director's approval before we could do anything.

"What if we gave him some space in the courtyard where he could plant a few vegetables? He could water them and tend to them daily, and it might make this place a little more like home for him."

Chris and I both affirmed what a great thing that could be for him, and once we got approval from the director, Grandpa and I were provided with seeds and a few gardening tools. For me, it resurrected vague memories of the little girl who used to help her Grandpa by handing him some specific tool he needed. He and I spent an entire afternoon together in Waverly's courtyard, moving some of the landscaped flowers, then tilling up a whole section of dirt where we were going to plant seeds for tomatoes and green beans. As the hot sun inched its way across a vibrant blue sky, I would give him first the trowel, then the three-pronged claw as he loosened the dirt, and then we placed the seeds in their new home. Every time I came to visit, he and I would walk out to the courtyard and observe the progress of our tiny crop. By the time fall was underway, we had a few tomatoes, but the green beans had grown like they were on steroids. One evening Chris and I left Waverly, carrying a bag brimming over with the chubby pods that were ready to be snapped and cooked.

I chuckled and told Chris, "We should turn Grandpa and his green thumb loose at a farmer's market—he might not need Medicaid's money anymore if we did!"

The fall days began to get shorter and cooler as the year marched resolutely toward the holidays. Life for all of us had settled down and remained largely unchanged; sometimes Grandma and Grandpa would have an unexpected visit from Grandma's sister, and very sporadically one or two of Grandpa's younger siblings would run by to see them. My parents and my maternal grandmother would each occasionally stop in, but since June 1997, neither Shirley, Tony, nor Duane had been in to visit. Tony's absence I could understand, since he lived in North Carolina; visiting for him meant having to drive several hours one way and required an overnight stay before he could return home. Shirley and Duane were little more than a half hour away but never made the drive—no one on staff at Waverly ever saw them; their non-appearance left me simultaneously baffled and relieved.

One nice thing had emerged from my encounter with that particular branch of the Meade family tree: Sheila and I had developed quite a nice friendship over the phone as one of us would call the other one, either to inform or catch up on how Grandma and Grandpa were doing. Essentially, there was nothing new to report, but the conversations allowed us to get to know one another, and I appreciated having that opportunity. Tony and I had had a few brief but pleasant occasions to chat, although my contact with them up to that point was mainly through Sheila.

On the evening of October 12, 1998, Sheila called me with a very serious tone in her voice. I could immediately tell something was wrong.

"You know I told you a while back that ever since Tony and I got married, I've been doing a lot of research, trying to find your father?" she began.

I always hated it when anyone referred to Ray as "*my* father," but as I could sense the urgency in Sheila's tone, I decided to let it slide.

"Well, I think I've found something," her voice fell quiet as she hesitated. "The trouble is, I'm not a hundred percent sure."

"Tell me what you think you've got," I said with a growing sense of anticipation.

"I found out about a body that was recently discovered at a truck stop in Alabama," she said. "A white male in his late 50s or early 60s. Everything I saw—race, age, gender, occupation—suggested it could be Ray, so I called the authorities in Alabama and told them I wanted more information on the body found at the truck stop."

"What did they say?" I asked anxiously.

"They said they couldn't tell me anything unless I could prove I was actually a family member of the missing person I'm looking for," she said with aggravation. "It sounds like it really could be him, but there's no way for us to know since they won't release any information without proof of relationship."

"What kind of proof do they want?" I pressed.

"The lady said any official documents that we actually have in our possession. They can be tax documents, a driver's license—even one that's expired—a birth certificate or passport—"

A birth certificate. I remembered among the reams of paper I had sifted and sorted through in the early days of taking care of Meade business, I had run across Ray's birth certificate. My first inclination had been to throw it away, but I decided instead to keep it with their personal papers—just why I kept it I couldn't have told you at the time, but God's funny that way. . . .

"Sheila, I have Ray's birth certificate," I said. "Give me a fax number, and I'll have a copy of it in your hands tomorrow morning."

The next day, I faxed the document to Sheila, and then Chris and I waited for news either way. Her call came late that evening.

"It's him," she said simply.

Chris was almost holding his breath as he stared at me with unblinking eyes, waiting for the answer. I sat down on the opposite end of the couch and looked at him, repeating Sheila's words back to her.

"It is him." I breathed in slowly through my nose, then let out a long sigh as I said, "Are you sure?"

"Yes," she said with conviction, "and thank God you had that birth certificate. That one document unlocked it all . . . and it's *bizarre*."

Sheila said she was given the official facts regarding the death of Anthony Raymond Meade, fifty-eight, so identified by the driver's license found on the body. He was in the cab of his rig, and he had been dead for several hours prior to discovery. There were no indications of foul play; the presumed cause of death was heart attack, though no autopsy was performed. His body was riddled with open sores, which the medical examiner attributed to undiagnosed and/or untreated diabetes.

"The rest of the story I got from—get this—*his next of kin*," she said with an edge of disbelief in her tone.

"What?" I blurted out. "And just who, exactly, was his next of kin?"

"*His wife*, a woman named Beverly."

"You've got to be kidding," was all I could say.

"Oh no!" Sheila responded. "I'm not kidding. And it gets better. Apparently, he and Beverly have been married since 1993. They live in Macon, Georgia. Well, Beverly lives in Macon; Ray's just buried there now."

"Hiding in plain sight . . . and using his own name," I mused. "It doesn't make any sense. Shirley said the IRS kept calling her, wanting to know where he was. I wonder why they couldn't find him if he was still using his own name."

"He may have altered his social security number," Sheila speculated, "or he may have given false addresses, spelled his name differently, who knows?"

Sheila said she asked for a contact number for Beverly before she got off the phone with the officials in Alabama. She had just spoken to Beverly before she called me.

"I bet the third Mrs. Meade was surprised to learn about Ray's *other* family," I said sarcastically.

"Well, not exactly," Sheila said with hesitation. "She knew he had a son, Ray, Jr., from a previous marriage. Ray had told her that Jr. was a fighter pilot with the rank of lieutenant colonel in the Air Force and that he was stationed in Afghanistan! I guess that's how he got away with never introducing his son to his new wife."

"You're probably right," I said, then added with disgust, "I guess some things never change: my mother always said when it came to telling lies, Ray was second to none. What did he say about Duane—that he was the U.S. ambassador to India?"

"No," Sheila paused briefly. "Beverly said Ray had told her that Jr. was his only child; neither you nor Duane were ever mentioned at all."

"Oh, my," was all I could utter. I considered the cascade of Ray's lies to Beverly, as well as the glaring omissions from his lineage. Leaving me out went along with everything he'd ever done where I was concerned; for years I had suspected I was the unwanted product of his first marriage, *and* I was female. But why omit Duane—a son and a full brother to Tony? This, Ray's latest rejection of me, may have cracked open an emotional scab in *my* heart, but I could not imagine how it would make Duane feel to learn that his father acknowledged his older brother while leaving him out completely. How much pain and damage was it possible for one man to cause?

"There was something else," Sheila added. "He told Beverly that both of his parents were dead."

That was the kill shot. Stinging, hot tears poured out of my eyes so spontaneously I was utterly incapable of stopping them. That statement was, without a doubt, one of the hardest things I've ever had to hear. My heart absolutely broke for my grandparents.

"He said they were dead." I slowly repeated her words after struggling for a few seconds to compose my voice. "Unbelievable."

As Sheila's information began to settle in my brain, I realized Ray's duplicity regarding his parents shouldn't have surprised me. A couple of weeks after he had walked away from his Mississippi home in 1985, he actually did call Grandma from somewhere in the Carolinas, asking her to wire him two hundred dollars. She sent him the money and got a receipt showing he had received it. After that, she never heard from him again, so I guess from that moment on, his parents were, for all intents and purposes, dead *to him*— but only after he put one last financial squeeze on them.

Just like countless times before, I found myself struggling with the notion that someone could just up and leave the way Ray had done—not once, but twice. I wondered if he had another "wife" waiting in the wings in 1985 like he did in 1968; I thought it was weird that a man who apparently didn't want an actual marriage sure did seem to enjoy going through the motions of having a wedding. Beverly was his third wife—*that we knew of.* All at once I began to contemplate the time frame between Ray's disappearance in 1985 and his marriage to Beverly in 1993. That left eight years completely unaccounted for. I asked Sheila if Beverly had mentioned anything about him prior to their marriage.

"Not a word," Sheila answered. "The only other thing I can tell you is that she said he's buried in a Veterans cemetery."

We hung up after she said she would let me know if she found out anything further. I leaned back into the couch cushions and let the cordless phone fall into my lap. For a couple of minutes I just cried openly; I couldn't seem to stop it, and I didn't understand why I was even doing it.

"This makes no sense," I told Chris as I wiped my eyes. "Why on earth would I be crying for Ray? I never even knew the man!"

"I think that's exactly it," Chris said quietly. "I think as long as he was missing, but still perceived as being 'alive,' you knew the opportunity existed for some kind of acknowledgement from him. Now that he's officially deceased, that opportunity is gone."

As soon as he said it, I knew he was right. All opportunities for me to experience any level of reconciliation with Ray completely vanished once he died; it was the first time I can ever remember realizing just how final death is. What truly left me reeling, though, was pondering the blow his death would be to his parents. What was I supposed to tell Grandma and Grandpa?

"If I tell them Ray has been found and that he's dead, they'll be devastated for as long as they remember it. And if I don't tell them what I know, I'll feel like I'm cheating them out of something they have a genuine right to know," I sighed and shook my head.

"I don't know that you need to tell them," Chris said pensively, almost to himself. "There's no funeral for them to go to, and, like you said, they won't remember it."

The next day, when I walked into Waverly, I ran straight into Grandma and Grandpa who were standing in the lobby. In light of the new information I had locked up in my head, just the sight of them caused a heavy grief to settle on me. They smiled when they saw me, and Grandpa, who reached me first, gave me a gentle "Grandpa" hug. I pulled my arms around his shoulders and just embraced him, lovingly, but somehow different than usual, and my eyes blurred with tears. I found I was extending consolation to him for a loss he didn't even know he had. He pulled back and looked at me, regarding my pained expression.

"Oh, Grandpa," I choked slightly, unsure how to finish what I'd started without telling him what I absolutely did not want to say. "Grandpa, I—love you."

CHAPTER 22

GONE FISHIN'

January 15, 1999, marked the two-year anniversary of my tenure as a caregiver. So much had happened since that date in 1997; I felt so changed from the care-free newlywed I had been when I received that first phone call from Mack Proctor. Chris and I had endured the firestorm of decisions, medical diagnoses, legal documentation, and quirky relatives perched on the outer edges of obscure family tree branches.

Through it all, both Grandma and Grandpa had consistently remembered me, but as time went by, I could discern they knew little else. Grandpa continued to ask me about his car, but the frequency with which he made the inquiries had become less and less; they both intermittently talked of going home, but neither one of them ever made any exact reference to a specific location. They never mentioned Duke or Grandpa's cows, Grandma's flowers, or the house itself, and, without realizing it, I had come to accept all those omissions as "normal."

I continued to receive calls from Waverly on a regular basis—but usually no more than one or two times a month. Either they were trying to wander off again or Grandpa was being combative with someone on staff—a reality which had become more and more frequent the longer he lived in the nursing home.

On Wednesday, January 27, 1999, I received a call from one of the nursing supervisors, but it was entirely different from any other call I'd ever received from them. I was being asked to authorize *Grandpa's* transfer to the emergency room because he was exhibiting what they thought were early symptoms of pneumonia; I immediately gave my permission. I called Chris to let him know what was up, then I grabbed my purse and headed out. I remember thinking how odd it was for Grandpa to be the one I was rushing to the ER to see. As far back as I could remember, Grandpa had been the picture of health. It was a major paradigm shift for me to imagine him having any physical sickness symptoms at all.

I arrived at the ER at Winchester Hospital ahead of Grandpa, so I was there when they brought him in on the stretcher. He was sitting up and looked like he felt perfectly fine. We were chatting lightly about nothing in particular when the doctor came in.

"Well, Mr. Meade," the doctor asked, standing at the foot of the stretcher, looking over the chart, "what seems to be going on with you today?"

Grandpa looked at him pleasantly and said, "Well, nothin' much really."

The doctor looked at me and smiled slightly. I lowered my voice and said, "He's a dementia patient."

"I see," he replied. "I noticed his chart said he lives in a nursing home."

He walked around to Grandpa's right side and began checking him over. "They said they think you might have pneumonia," he continued, pulling out his stethoscope. He asked Grandpa to lean forward and began listening to various places up and down his back.

"Well, I don't hear much to raise any red flags," the doctor announced as he adjusted Grandpa's blanket, "but all the same, I think we'll run a few tests just to make sure we're not missing anything."

"That's fine with me," I told him. "I'd rather make sure he's all right before we try to send him back to Waverly."

Once again, I found myself authorizing medical testing, signing ER admission papers, providing a copy of Grandpa's durable power of attorney document, and pulling his Medicare and supplemental insurance cards out of my purse. After the paperwork was completed, the waiting game started.

Between the orderlies popping in and out, taking him to the various scans and X-rays ordered by his doctor, Grandpa and I had a perfectly delightful day of casual conversation. Even though sitting in the ER wasn't where either one of us wanted to be, the familiar feel of only Grandpa and me talking together was pleasant. My body may have remained confined in that room, seated in the chair beside the stretcher, but in my mind I was walking in the woods with him again, being amazed by the fact that he knew what every single tree was just by looking at the leaves or the bark. I recalled the comfortable sense of talking with him about things like how cows twist their feet slightly as they walk and why he chose cypress as the siding for his house. Our conversations were neither intellectual nor complex, but they were wonderfully precious—and all too brief.

In my mind's eye, I could see us walking together down the well-worn path that took us behind his vegetable garden. I could picture the sight of swaying branches, which would compel us to listen as the wind would play gently in the tops of the trees. The previous year's leaves would cushion our steps as the trail wound down a slight hill and curved back toward the west. At the bottom of the hill we would pass by the pond Grandpa had dug out, and I recalled times when we'd chuckle at the sight of one of his cows standing knee-deep in the water, swishing its tale slowly but deliberately from side to side as it turned to glance at us with absolutely no enthusiasm.

A slight smile played at the corner of my mouth as I clearly pictured Grandpa in his faded navy cotton-blend work pants and shirt, complete with a cap and dirty, well-used boots. I was remembering a lifestyle that was long gone and sorely missed as I regarded him sitting up on the stretcher. He was anchored to that gurney only by his advanced years and weakening body, certainly not by his own will, and I found myself wishing I could take his hand and lift him out of that bed to go stack some firewood or to help him relieve the peach tree whose branches were so heavy with fruit they were pulled to the ground in a dramatic flourish. As I sat reminiscing, he looked over at me and smiled.

"Sweet, I sure am glad you're here with me today," he said pleasantly.

"Well, I sure am glad to be with you—even though I wish you didn't have to be here," I responded.

He smiled and nodded.

As the afternoon began to fade toward evening, the doctor came back in and announced there was a slight infection, but he thought Grandpa was well enough to go back to Waverly.

"I can see why they sent him," the doctor told me, "but at this point there's not much reason for him to stay in the hospital. He can take meds at the nursing home as well as here."

I thanked the doctor, then he turned and shook Grandpa's hand.

"It's been nice to meet you, Mr. Meade," he said.

While we were waiting for the ambulance, which had been ordered to transport Grandpa back to Waverly, Chris popped his head in the door.

"Surprise!" he said with a smile.

"I didn't expect to see you here," I said as Chris came around and stood on the other side of Grandpa's stretcher.

"Well, I hadn't heard from you, so I came by to get the scoop. How's everything?"

I told him what the doctor had said, and he looked at Grandpa with a smile.

"Good—you won't have to be away from Grandma tonight!"

"No, I guess I won't," Grandpa said, smiling back at him.

The three of us continued to chat casually until the ambulance medic came in and asked Grandpa if he was ready to go. I leaned over and hugged him.

"I love my grandpa!"

"And I love my Leah too," he said, just like always, as he hugged me back.

I looked him briefly straight in the face, and as our eyes met he said, "I sure am glad you were here with me today, Sweet."

I noted the fact that he had already said that to me earlier, but I wrote it off as the dementia talking. I smiled and answered as if it was the first time I'd heard it.

"Well, I sure am glad I was here with you too! I wouldn't have been anywhere else."

Chris and I walked out behind the stretcher and saw the medics slide it into the back of the ambulance. I nodded my head briefly, having seen him safely in and ready to ride back to the nursing home.

"Come on," I said to Chris, "I didn't have any lunch—I'm ready to eat just about anything!"

He asked where I had parked, and I pointed toward the lot behind the hospital.

"Good, that's where I am," he said. "Let's drop a car off at the apartment and go grab some quick dinner."

"Good idea," I said as I started walking away from the ambulance.

I had gone two, maybe three steps when I felt a sudden urge to see Grandpa's face again, to actually make eye contact with him before they closed the doors. I took another step and turned slightly at my waist back toward my right. I saw Grandpa sitting up on the stretcher just like before. Nothing amiss. Our eyes met, and I smiled as I waved my hand to him. He smiled, raised his arm, and waved back. Then the door closed.

It was around midafternoon on Tuesday, almost a week after my day in the ER with Grandpa, and I was busily working on a variety of communications projects that had fallen into my lap. It was unseasonably warm for February, with temperatures climbing into the midfifties; I wasn't even having to use my portable heater underneath my desk. My focus was interrupted when my phone rang sharply. I reached for the receiver automatically, without even looking at the caller I.D.

"Mrs. Stanley?" a woman's voice asked.

I sat up straight and looked at the phone. It was Waverly. "Yes," I answered quickly.

The woman identified herself as the nursing supervisor, and without further ado, she began explaining to me that Grandpa's condition seemed to be getting much worse.

"It appears he's having difficulty breathing," she said, "so we are asking you to authorize our sending him back to the ER."

I didn't even hesitate. "Of course," I told her. "Do whatever you think is necessary." I was so tied up with work, trying to meet deadlines established by various media outlets, that I asked the nurse how long it would be before an ambulance could arrive at Waverly and get him transported.

"Dr. Kern instructed us to call for the ambulance as soon as you gave permission," she said, "so I'm about to make the call to Presbyterian Hospital. I'm not sure how long it will take for them to get here."

The thought of Grandpa going back to the ER at Presbyterian stirred up awful flashbacks to the night I first brought Grandma and Grandpa to Memphis. Images of Grandma fighting the sedative and Grandpa in restraints—ugh.

"All right," I mumbled, more to myself than to the nurse. "Will the staff at the ER contact me when he arrives?"

"I can ask them to," she said.

I hung up the phone and doubled down on my efforts. If Grandpa was doing worse, it was conceivable I might have to miss a few days of work, so I wanted to wrap everything up as best I could.

I worked steadily for another hour or so, then my phone rang again. The ER nurse called to tell me Grandpa had arrived and they were going to have the doctor see him as soon as possible. I thanked her, then began to wrap up the loose ends of my projects. I glanced out of my office window and I could see the sun setting over the tall, well-established trees of Midtown. For a few seconds I let myself slow down. I took a minute and mulled over the fact that Grandpa was back in the ER, and the Waverly staff seemed to think his condition had grown worse.

He's as strong as an ox, I reasoned to myself, *and he's never been sick a day in his life. This is probably just precaution on the part of the nursing home. He'll be fine. . . .*

I turned off my computer and called Chris to tell him I'd need to make a trip to the hospital that evening.

"No problem," he said. "Come home first, and we'll go in one car."

I also called my mom.

"Let us meet you at your apartment," she said. "Dad and I will go with you too."

As I put away the last of my file folders and tidied up my desk, my phone rang again.

"Mrs. Stanley?" It was a man's voice this time.

"Yes, this is Leah Stanley," I answered.

"Mrs. Stanley, I'm Dr. Kemp calling from the ER."

"Oh, yes," I acknowledged, somewhat stunned that an actual doctor had called instead of another nurse.

"Mrs. Stanley, we've got your father over here, Mr. Edward Meade," he said. "I understand you have power of attorney for him?"

"Oh, actually he's my grandfather," I stammered, "but yes, I do have durable power of attorney for him."

"Oh, sorry about that," he said. "I just wanted to touch base with you about his condition. I've looked at the chart, and I see the nursing home sent him out for some tests a few days ago?"

I explained about our day in the ER the previous week and how the doctor there said Grandpa didn't seem that bad, so he was sent back to the nursing home with medication.

"I've only learned today that the staff at Waverly felt like he needed to be seen again," I concluded.

"Well, he's having significant difficulty breathing, so much so that I'm actually going to put him on oxygen."

"I'm getting ready to leave my office right now," I said as I stood up. "Do you need me to come up there right away?"

"Well, maybe not this minute," he replied, "but sometime this evening would probably be good."

"My husband and I were already planning to get up there as soon as we both get off work," I told him.

"Sure, I think that'll be fine," he paused, then went on. "Oh, and one more thing, Mrs. Stanley, I just want to be sure I understand correctly: you don't want a Harvey Team, right?"

That one question brought the full weight of the situation down on me. A "Harvey Team" is brought in whenever a patient's heart stops beating or if they stop breathing. To say "no Harvey Team" means you are going to allow the patient to pass away with no intervention or attempt at resuscitation. It means you are authorizing the medical professionals to stand down and allow the situation to run its natural course. For a few seconds I absolutely froze as the implication of Dr. Kemp's question sank in; a heavy silence hung on the line between the doctor and me.

"No," I finally managed to mumble, but my hesitation clearly revealed how shockingly unprepared I was for that question. My voice was barely audible as I repeated, "No Harvey Team."

I hung up the phone, staring hard at the receiver. I pushed it back slightly from the edge of the desk, away from me. For several seconds I simply didn't move at all. Everything was still. The outer office was quiet; most of my coworkers had already left. I looked out of my window and saw the sun had gone completely down without my realizing it. My eyes slowly wandered without purpose around my office, finally coming to rest on my wall calendar. I love the impressionists, so I had a calendar with the work of the impressionist masters: Monet, Degas, Renoir. I had only turned the February page up the day before, and it displayed a work I was unfamiliar with. Done mostly in greens, the image portrayed a large house comfortably visible between two beautiful, well-proportioned oak trees, and there was a lovely lake in the foreground. I was captured by the feel of the picture: soft, gentle, at ease, nothing wrong anywhere. As my eyes studied the details, I heard a voice in my head very clearly say, *A quiet, peaceful place . . . by a lake.*

I looked around my office, half expecting to see someone there. But I was alone. I looked at the picture once more, pondering the phrase that had passed through my mind. Then I grabbed my purse, turned off the light, and closed the door behind me.

My parents, Chris, and I walked at a steady pace down the long, tiled hallway which connected the parking garage with the main building of the hospital. No one spoke. For my part, I was lost in thought, trying to figure out how I was going to explain to Grandpa that he had to stay in the hospital until he was better. I knew he wouldn't like being away from Grandma, and I hoped he would be cooperative.

We got off the elevator and started for his room. The halls were quiet; I didn't even see very many staff members moving around. About halfway down the hall, we found Grandpa's room on the left. I rapped with my knuckle two or three times then pushed the door open.

I gasped and stopped in my tracks at the sight that met my eyes. The room was lit solely by the wall fixture above the head of his bed, flooding the ceiling with a stark, white light. Grandpa was lying on his back with his arms at his sides, and an oxygen mask completely covered both his nose and mouth. His entire body jerked and shivered as the oxygen was forced in, then exhaled. His eyes were closed. I don't know what I had expected to see, but the reality—the seriousness—of the situation was almost unbearable.

"Oh, no, no, no, Grandpa, no, no . . ." I muttered involuntarily as I stood in the door. We all stood there, frozen, trying to comprehend how bad the situation really was. My breath came in short, halting puffs. I took another step or two toward the bed, then I turned abruptly and walked back out into the hall. I leaned against the wall outside the door, trying to get my bearings. I looked up to see Chris, Mom, and Dad had all come out with me. No one said a word.

I'm not sure how long I stood there, but I began to realize my face, my hands, and the top of my shirt were soaked with tears. My mother was crying too, and Dad and Chris both had very grim expressions.

I saw a young man dressed in scrubs walking down the hall, so I wiped my eyes with the back of my hand as I said, "Excuse me," and took a step toward him.

"Yes, ma'am?" He stopped.

"I'm Mr. Meade's granddaughter, and I'm his caregiver. Can you tell me the latest information you have on his condition?"

"Yeah, he's Dr. Kemp's patient who came in earlier today," he said. "He's got pneumonia, a pretty bad case of it by the look of things."

"Yes, I spoke with Dr. Kemp earlier," I said, still trying to regain my composure. "We were just in his room. He looks . . . he looks . . . bad."

The nurse nodded at me, then he went into the room to check for himself. When he came back into the hall, I blurted out, "The doctor verified that we don't want a Harvey Team. I know what a Harvey Team is, but why was the doctor asking about it? Does it mean what I think it means? Does Dr. Kemp think this is it?" I stopped rambling as suddenly as I had started.

"Honestly, when they're his age, you never can tell," he said gently. "These old fellows, they can surprise you. They look like they're going to die one minute, and the next thing you know they've rebounded. There's just no way to know for sure. But what I do know is that you need to talk to him. Let him know you're here."

"But he's unconscious," I said slowly. "How will he know?"

"He'll know," the nurse said calmly, "and you'll know."

I looked at Chris and my parents. My mother was still crying as Chris said, "You need to."

My dad agreed. "When you're ready," he said, rubbing my back.

I nodded slightly and wiped my eyes again. I breathed in deeply, then slowly walked back into Grandpa's room. The sight of that gentle, kind man, laboring so intensely for every breath, was heart wrenching. I took slow, hesitant steps as I approached his bed with my husband on one side and my mom on the other, while my dad moved in behind me like a rear guard. I stopped just inches from Grandpa's left side, listening to the sounds of medical progress. A monitor registered heart rate and blood pressure while the oxygen pumped nonstop with controlled bursts regulating the flow of air. Grandpa continued to shake with the ebb and flow of a deeply disturbed breathing pattern, and I found that I too was shaking as I sobbed in grief. *What could I possibly say to him now that would matter?*

We had always talked so openly, so freely, and I just couldn't believe that our conversations were about to be over. Inside my head, my frenzied thoughts raced through the halls of my memory for everything "Grandpa." In a matter of just a few seconds, I was trying to hold on to a lifetime.

Please, Grandpa, let's talk some more, just a little longer. Tell me, why do the cows like to eat hay? Let's go for a walk in your woods, Grandpa. Show me your newest calf. How many belts does it take to make a gasoline engine run? Does pine or oak make better firewood? Let's share one more watermelon from your garden, Grandpa. Can I help you snap the beans? Peel the peaches? Split the logs? Grandpa, you made me laugh when you found a hole in your sock and told me you had dropped it and it broke. Grandpa, let's have coffee and play checkers.

I looked at his blank, unconscious face, and finally I spoke aloud, summing up the meaning of all my thoughts in one phrase.

"I love my grandpa. . . ."

And for the first time in my life, he gave no response.

The phone rang at 5:25 a.m. on Wednesday, February 3, 1999. I came to immediately and jerked the phone from its cradle.

"Mrs. Stanley?" a calm woman's voice said.

"Yes, yes, this is Mrs. Stanley," I answered as my breath came short and shallow.

"Mrs. Stanley, I'm calling from the hospital."

"Yes. . . ."

"I'm sorry to have to tell you that Mr. Meade has expired."

Shortly before noon, Chris and I were sitting in the office at the funeral home, signing the papers for Grandpa's final arrangements. They had time open for a service on the morning of Thursday, February 4, and we agreed to take it. The only thing left to do was to provide them with a suit for Grandpa to wear.

As it turned out, I already had a coat, shirt, and tie, but I never found any dress pants among his clothes, so Chris and I said we would make a quick shopping trip to buy some khaki pants and socks. I asked if he needed shoes.

"No, ma'am," the funeral director replied. "We bury them wearing every garment except shoes."

Chris picked out a nice pair of dress pants which matched the jacket perfectly, and after the clothes were dropped off at the funeral home, I had the unpleasant task of notifying the family. I called Grandpa's sister, Pearl, asking if she would notify the Meade side of the family, then I called Lena. When I told her Grandpa had passed away, she misunderstood and thought I'd said "Grandma."

"Well, bless her heart," she responded.

"No, it was Grandpa," I repeated. "Edward."

She seemed genuinely shocked. "I can't believe he went before her," she said. "He seemed so much stronger than she does."

Tony had a similar reaction. "*Grandpa?*" He exclaimed in utter disbelief.

"I know," I told him. "I never guessed it would go down like this."

I gave him the schedule for the visitation and the service, and he said he'd be there. He also agreed to notify Shirley and Duane, but he said Sheila would be unable to make the trip because she couldn't get off work.

Thursday morning dawned sunny and clear, but still not as cool as a normal February day in Memphis. Chris and I arrived at the funeral home at 8:30 a.m. followed shortly by my parents. The funeral director invited us into the chapel for a private viewing before other people began to arrive.

The four of us entered the chapel, and the instant my eyes landed on the casket at the far end of the room, I was so glad I had decided not to try to tell Grandma what had happened—for much the same reason I hadn't told either of them about Ray's death. I had decided if Grandma was told that Grandpa had died, it would do nothing but upset her for the brief time she understood it. I felt very awkward about not telling her that her own husband had passed away, but by then I had come to understand she'd never remember it; her cognition had declined to the point that having even a basic conversation with her was very difficult. Going forward, the most profound thing that did worry me about her was being able to explain Grandpa's prolonged absence.

I approached the casket slowly, and the minute I reached Grandpa's right side, hot tears began to fall spontaneously. His suit looked nice, and the flowers were beautiful, but everything was so very still. I discovered there is no still like "dead" still. Was it only the night before last I had seen him laboring so pitifully for every breath? I found myself staring at his face in disbelief. Grandpa was gone, but just like the night in the hospital, I found I wanted to talk to him; then, realizing our time for talk was over, I experienced the devastating emptiness of grief. Even his life of eighty-six years somehow didn't seem like it had been quite long enough to compensate for the intense break in relationship brought on by his death. He was gone, and in this case, there truly was no way to un-ring that particular bell.

People began to arrive and express their condolences, and as I stood beside Grandpa's casket, I was pleasantly surprised to find that I was able to talk to them without going all to pieces. When Reverend Benjamin Tucker arrived, he asked me to briefly review the eulogy notes with him. Grandpa had no pastor in Memphis, so when he passed away, I called our church to see if there was a minister who might be available to do his funeral. Benjamin returned my call almost immediately, saying he'd be glad to handle everything for us. I gave Benjamin a full page of information about Grandpa's life and family. I had conspicuously omitted any reference to Ray, and I briefly explained to Benjamin just why we wanted to keep it that way. He was kind and discreet, assuring me he would say nothing.

Tony arrived when the visitation was about halfway through, and he hugged me with a gentle politeness. As I continued to greet various people, I noticed Chris and Tony were chatting together very pleasantly. I began to watch for Shirley and Duane, feeling a nervous rush every time I thought I saw them come in, but it always turned out to be someone else. When it was time for the service to start, they were nowhere to be seen. I couldn't believe it.

As we were about to get seated, Jimmy and Karen approached Chris and me.

"Do you have enough pall bearers?" Jimmy asked.

We had gone over potential pall bearers the night before. Chris told me he wanted to serve, and since we'd arrived at the funeral home, he had asked Tony and two of Grandma's nephews.

"We'll be fine if you and Hugh will help," Chris told him.

Hugh was my friend Julie's husband of five years. I had known Julie since the first grade—she was one of my canoeing buddies along with Lisa and Karen, having spent a fair amount of time in Arkansas with Grandma, Grandpa, and me. Hugh and Jimmy both readily agreed to serve, so with the six pall bearers in place, we sat down, and the service began.

Benjamin did a phenomenal job of talking about Grandpa as if he'd known him, and in a clear, uncomplicated way, he presented the gospel—something we'd specifically asked him to do. When the service concluded, the motorcade began the slow, inevitable drive toward the cemetery where Grandma and Grandpa had chosen their final resting place together. I remember that upon turning into the driveway of the cemetery, I noticed one of the motorcade policemen stood at attention with his hat off, placed respectfully over his heart. Just the sight of it brought me to tears.

We followed the hearse around the winding thread of a road which brought us to Grandpa's gravesite. As the pall bearers lifted the casket and positioned themselves to walk toward the canopy, I took my place behind them, in line with Grandpa; it was monumentally important for me to walk with him one last time. Mom walked beside me on my right, and my dad was on my left.

Chris and I took our seats on the front row under the canopy, and Tony sat on Chris's right. Benjamin quietly and gently made his final statements about Grandpa, reading the poignant words of Paul to the Thessalonians:

> *Brothers and sisters, we do not want you to be uninformed about those who sleep in death, so that you do not grieve like the rest of mankind, who have no hope. For we believe that Jesus died and rose again, and so we believe that God will bring with Jesus those who have fallen asleep in him. According to the Lord's Word, we tell you that we who are still alive, who are left until the coming of the Lord, will certainly not precede those who have fallen asleep. For the Lord himself will come down from heaven, with a loud command, with the voice of the archangel and with the trumpet call of God, and the dead in Christ will rise first. After that, we who are still alive and are left will be caught up together with them in the clouds to meet the Lord in the air. And so we will be with the Lord forever. Therefore encourage one another with these words. (1 Thessalonians 4:13-18)*

When Benjamin concluded the graveside service, I sat with my head down and tears just pouring out of my eyes. All at once, a single rose had made its way into my hand, and the funeral director was in front of me, saying something—I honestly have no idea what. He straightened up and backed away from me, and I remember standing up and walking to the casket which was positioned for burial. I sobbed hard as I gently placed the rose on top of the closed lid, clearly separated from the family flower spray. Before I knew what had happened, Tony had come up beside me and embraced me tightly, sobbing as hard as I was. For a long time we stood, weeping, embracing, grieving together.

I couldn't believe how much it had all hurt. From the moment I became his caregiver, to bringing him to Memphis, coming oh-so-slowly to grips with the fact that he too was afflicted with dementia, to signing the paper to put him into a nursing home, to seeing him unconscious and straining for every breath, to the moment I saw the backhoe approaching as Karen, Jimmy, Julie,

Hugh, Lisa, Tony, Chris, and I stood talking after everyone else had left—it was then that I knew it was finally time for me to leave Grandpa's tired, aged body for its final disposition. And Jesus, infinitely good and gloriously patient, graciously allowed me to realize it was OK for me to leave the cemetery; after all, Grandpa wasn't there either.

Chris and I came into Grandma's room the next day. She was lying in her bed, but her face brightened when she made eye contact with me.

"Well, hello, Sweet," she said.

I sat beside her on the edge of the bed, took her hand and asked her how she was doing. She told me she was fair, but tired. She glanced over at Grandpa's empty bed, and I felt the tears beginning to brew. Then she looked at me and said with a puzzled expression, "I don't know where Grandpa's gone to."

I drew in a long breath. What could I say? All at once, she looked me straight in the face and said, "I guess he's gone fishin'."

I told her that was exactly right—because he was with Jesus in a quiet, peaceful place . . . by a lake.

CHAPTER 23

HELLO, SWEET

The weird dreams began almost immediately after Grandpa's death. I would dream of seeing him in a variety of contexts, but the bizarre thing was he never spoke. Sometimes I would dream he was standing right in front of me, and I would call his name, but he would only turn and walk away, not saying a word.

With his passing, a number of things began to change. Waverly immediately revised the way they billed us, now sending only the one statement for Grandma. There was a noticeable decrease in the amount of mail in my box; forms and bills that I had been receiving in Grandpa's name began to dwindle down until at last there were none at all. As I went through the list of organizations that had to be notified of Grandpa's death—Social Security, Medicaid, his supplemental medical insurance, his lawyer—I discovered they all wanted the same thing: a certified copy of the death certificate. The funeral home had advised me to order several copies of the document for just that reason.

Another significant change we had to endure was that Grandma had been assigned the first in a series of new roommates, all of whom were widowed ladies. Despite the hustle and bustle which accompanied moving a new tenant into her room, she never seemed to notice the stranger's presence or Grandpa's absence. She never once asked about Grandpa—which was a great relief for me to not have to explain it all to her, but a source of grief at the same time because it reinforced her lack of cognition to understand her own loss. But while she didn't seem to realize Grandpa was gone, I sure did. I don't think I ever got used to seeing a total stranger on Grandpa's side of their room.

By the time March had rolled around, things seemed to be falling back into a pattern which could be marginally referred to as normal. Funny thing about life, though, is things don't tend to *stay* what we perceive as normal.

One Tuesday morning, I got up and was getting ready for work. All at once I felt a slight wave of nausea. Eventually it passed, and I was able to drive on to my office. I stopped by to tell my boss I was there and briefly filled her in on what had happened. I assumed the cause was related to something I had eaten, and I assured her I was fine to be at work. As I turned to walk out of her office, she stopped me and suggested there might be something else going on. She adamantly told me to go have it checked out at once, not even allowing me to go into my own office to see what the day's workload looked like. I did as she asked, and it turned out she was right. Food had nothing to do with it; Chris and I were going to be parents.

I remember the year 1999 being one that was chock-full of milestones. In addition to losing Grandpa in early February, Chris and I had put money down to start building our first house on Valentine's Day, and less than a month later, we found out we were expecting our first child. I continued to work full time as my pregnancy advanced and as our new house was being built; I also stayed on track in providing care for Grandma. When I told her I was pregnant, she got very upset, saying once more she didn't even know I was married. Time and time again, during those nine months I had to go through the motions of explaining to her that yes, she did know I was married, then watch her fret for a moment or two until she finally relaxed and settled back down because she'd forgotten the subject of our discussion.

Even though the spring and summer months of 1999 had an air of excitement with our first home and our first child both being "under construction," my sleep continued to be plagued by the strange dreams about Grandpa. Sometimes they even took on a nightmarish feel. One of the most vivid and disturbing I can remember featured me outside at night, wearing a long, white cotton nightgown, digging with my bare hands in the dirt. No one was with me, but in the dream I had somehow been given to understand that a baby had been left out there in the dark, covered over with loose soil. Even in my sleep I felt compelled—driven—to rescue and protect the helpless infant. I was digging frantically until I suddenly realized I had uncovered Grandpa, lying there in his burial suit with his eyes closed. It seemed that during my waking hours, I was providing actual, tangible care for Grandma, but at night, in my sleep, I was still trying to take care of Grandpa too.

As summer began its invariable transition into fall, I began to really see how my conversations with Grandma were becoming very strained because her cognition was so degraded. I remember sitting one evening on the edge of her bed, listening to her tell me bits and pieces about things from old days that were long gone—mere fragments that were left over as her mind seemed to be on its final descent into permanent slumber. She had turned ninety-one on the fifth of August, and with every day that passed, it seemed there was less and less of the Grandma I remembered.

"I just put Raymond to bed," she said, pointing to her roommate's mattress.

I smiled at her and said, "Well, I'm glad you were able to do that." I held her hand, gently running my thumb across the backs of her fingers. "Speaking of bed time, it's almost mine!" I said as I prepared to stand up. "I guess Chris and I need to be getting home."

I paused, looking straight into her eyes. "I love my grandma," I said with conviction.

She squeezed my hand and smiled; her eyes brightened in a familiar, comfortable way. "Goodnight, Sweet. And you know I love you too."

I leaned over and kissed her forehead.

As Chris and I walked out, I pressed my lips together and shook my head slowly. "She's getting weaker and weaker; I hate seeing her like this. She's not living—she's existing at best." I paused and looked at Chris. "I wonder if it's a terrible thing for me to ask Jesus to just let her go home?"

For thirty-one hours I labored, and at 12:10 p.m. on Saturday, October 9, 1999, our son, Andrew Allen Stanley, was born. Drew, as he came to be called, was a very strong, healthy baby, but being the new and inexperienced parent I was, the thought of taking him into Waverly was fraught with concern. I had been going in and out of that nursing home for nearly three years without a single thought of what germs might be floating through the air, but the prospect of my newborn breathing in there sent a chill up my spine. By mid-November, though, I began to have a sense of urgency about taking Drew to see her. I knew she'd never remember it, and Drew certainly wouldn't know as he was not yet seven weeks old, but I knew I'd always remember.

So on Thanksgiving Day, November 25, 1999, Chris and I finally took Drew to see Grandma. She was lying in her bed like always, and she smiled brightly as I came in and gently set Drew on the bed beside her. She went on and on about what a beautiful baby he was, and she held out her finger which he immediately took and squeezed.

"He's strong," she said with a smile.

We didn't stay too long, but I'm so glad we went; I'll treasure the memory forever.

A mere four days later, Monday, November 29, I received a call from Waverly. The nursing supervisor told me Grandma had had a very bad fall, forcefully hitting the back of her head against the floor. They were asking for permission to send her out to the ER because they wanted her head X-rayed immediately. Chris and I met at the hospital and went to her ER room together. When I walked in, her eyes caught sight of me, and her face brightened into a slight smile. The nurse noticed the change in her expression.

"Who is that?" she asked Grandma.

"That's my granddaughter," Grandma answered immediately, "and I couldn't love her any more if she was my own daughter!"

The nurse looked at me and smiled. "Well, she's been fuzzy about a lot of things, but she's clear enough as to who you are!"

I stood at the foot of the bed and rubbed Grandma's feet and ankles under the warm, white, stretchy-knit blanket. "That's been a real blessing throughout this whole Alzheimer's ordeal," I told the nurse. "She's consistently recognized me."

The nurse turned Grandma's head toward her right shoulder for a closer examination of the area which had hit the floor. She ended up having to shave a small patch of hair around the wound site in order to clean it properly. She said the doctor had ordered a couple of tests that would show if there were any injuries resulting from the fall.

And so we slowly passed another lengthy day in the ER; Grandma's cognition was so poor we spent most of the time sitting in silence. Sometimes silence is comfortable and idyllic, but not that day. Silence had never really been part of our paradigm; as far back as I could remember Grandma and I always had things to talk about. Now, on that cool November day, Grandma's lack of conversation was, in its own way, as heartbreaking as when I had watched my normally active, healthy Grandpa struggle for every breath.

When I was finally able to speak with the doctor, he said there was no fracture or concussion, so his plan was to send her back to Waverly with pain meds if she needed them. Chris and I knew we needed to go because we still had to pick Drew up from my mother's house, so once the ambulance was ordered to take Grandma back to the nursing home, we decided to go ahead and leave. I felt somewhat like I was abandoning her, remembering how I had stayed with Grandpa until he was safely in the ambulance; but in truth, after she had initially made eye contact with me when we first entered the room, I'm not sure she was really aware of our presence. She spent most of the day turning her head from one side to the other while her eyes remained, for the most part, closed.

Earlier in the afternoon, I had recalled how one of the nurses at Waverly made the comment that sometimes when a patient lingers on and on, it can help if they hear a loved one tell them it's all right for them to let go of this life. It had sounded crazy to me when she first said it, but as I regarded Grandma's pitiful state, I gave it considerable thought, pondering the implications of my saying it and her hearing it. I experienced an emotional ambivalence which left me confused and unsettled. As we were about to leave, I found I was still deeply entrenched in my quest for understanding as to whether it was the right thing to do or not. I leaned down to hug Grandma and told her I loved her. A pair of weary eyes gazed back at me.

"And I love you, Doll," she said in a tired, gravelly voice.

I smiled slightly, and all at once I had peace to lean over and put my cheek against hers. "It's OK, Grandma," I said directly in her ear with a voice that was barely audible. "It's OK for you to go be with Jesus. . . ."

But I knew in my heart that, selfishly, I still wasn't quite ready to let her go.

For the next eleven days, Chris and I were living in a swirl of sleepless nights as Drew suffered with colic. I was also adjusting to being back at work after maternity leave had ended. In truth, I just wanted to stay at home with my son, but we hadn't yet examined the financial possibility of my quitting work. During those eleven days, often with Drew cradled snugly in my arms, I was on the phone with Waverly, listening to them describe to me how Grandma just seemed to be going down, down, down. I was sleep deprived and grief-stricken, pathetically trapped somewhere between begging God to just let her go home to be with Him and at the same time sadly pondering how much I would miss her when she was gone. I was intensely grieved as I regarded her present condition: alive, but seemingly without purpose, confused, and having neither the energy nor the inclination to spend her days doing anything other than lying in a bed, waiting for her life to draw to its inevitable end.

I recalled how I had hated putting Grandma and Grandpa in the nursing home in the first place. Now I found myself realizing I would actually miss the trips to Waverly, having learned the reward for going there was being able to see them. I would consider the reality of Grandma "going home," realizing what a truly great thing it would be for her to shake off that old, tired, weak body and be able to stand with new youth and vigor, strong and energized in the presence of Jesus. Paul gave voice to the notion that being with Jesus was much preferred over staying in this difficult, challenging life when he wrote to the Corinthians:

> *We are confident, I say, and would prefer to be away from the body and at home with the Lord. (2 Corinthians 5:8)*

But the psalmist also makes us aware that God has a specific time allotted for each of us:

> *. . . all the days ordained for me were written in your book before one of them came to be. (Psalm 139:16)*

I felt pulled from one side to the other: did I need to pray for her to go be with the Lord or pray for her to get better so she could live out the full span of her life? What if her full span had been reached, and this was actually the appointed end? How could I know which was right? It seemed my ability to judge the situation was completely compromised by the wide range of my emotions, and the "right thing to pray" got lost in the utter confusion.

It finally all came down to the evening of Friday, December 10, 1999. I had settled down on the couch, having just eaten dinner. I was changing Drew into his pajamas, playing with his hands and feet, when the phone rang. It was the nursing supervisor at Waverly.

"Mrs. Stanley, it's about Mrs. Meade," she began. "She's just not doing well at all. Her breathing is very shallow, and we are deeply concerned. I would like your permission to have her sent to the ER."

I told them to send her at once, then I scooped up my little boy and snuggled him close, cradling his head in the crook of my elbow. I sat back on the couch, stroking his cheek gently while my brain worked frantically, trying to figure out how I was going to sit in an ER all night when I had a two-month-old at home who needed his mom. Chris assured me he would take care of Drew, and he told me it was no problem for me to go be with Grandma. I wrestled around trying to decide where I was needed most. My considerations were interrupted by the phone ringing again. It was Dr. Kern's nurse practitioner.

"Mrs. Stanley," she began gently, "I'm sorry the nursing supervisor bothered you with this. Please forgive me, but I need to be clinically direct with you. Mrs. Meade does not need to be moved. It will be best for her to stay right where she is."

"Well, all right, if that's what you think is best," I responded, somewhat confused. "It sounded so serious when the nurse called earlier, telling me Grandma's breathing is shallow—"

"Yes ma'am, it is," the nurse interrupted, then paused slightly before continuing, "but there's nothing the ER can do. Frankly, Mrs. Stanley, Mrs. Meade's situation is very likely critical. That's why the nursing home wants to move her, because, to be blunt, they'd rather not have a death in the facility if they can help it."

"Oh," I whispered. I looked down at Drew who was reaching his small hand up to my chin, and all I could do was repeat, "Oh."

"Dr. Kern has ordered oxygen for her, and we've made her as comfortable as we can. She's asleep right now."

Oxygen. I immediately recalled the image of what Grandpa had endured when they gave him oxygen. The clear plastic tubing. Over the ear, under the nose, and up over the other ear. Strained breathing. It made me shiver.

"I'm very sorry, Mrs. Stanley," the nurse said quietly.

"I understand," I said, forcing myself to remain composed. "Please do what is best for her."

Chris looked at me when I hung up. My eyebrows pulled together as, one after the other, slow, hot tears dripped onto Drew's blanket.

"What do I do?" I asked him. "Do I go to Waverly and sit with a woman who's asleep? Who may never wake up? And what about my baby? I need to be here, I'm his mom. . . ."

Chris sighed heavily. "I don't know what to tell you, but I support you in whatever you decide," he said quietly. "I can take care of Drew if you want to go."

I thought of the oxygen again, and it was in that moment—after nearly three years of doing so many things that had seemed unthinkable: facing the Alzheimer's diagnosis, uprooting them from their home, soft restraints, nursing home admission, contacting relatives, and having to bury Grandpa— that I finally blinked.

"I can't go," I said with a catch in my throat. "I just can't see her . . . on oxygen. I just can't. There's nothing I can do for her, and I just can't bear to see her like I saw Grandpa. I'm so sorry."

At 2:30 a.m. my home was dark and cool and quiet. Drew was sleeping finally, while Chris and I were lightly slumbering, hoping that the cries of

colic were over for the night. Into that quiet—though not very restful—atmosphere, the telephone rang with the call I had known was coming.

"Mrs. Stanley?"

"Yes," I replied calmly.

"I'm calling from Waverly. . . ."

"Yes." It wasn't a question, more of a statement—a resignation.

"I need to tell you that Mrs. Meade has breathed her last."

Chris had sat up as soon as he heard the phone. When I laid the receiver down on the nightstand to go get the information for the funeral home, he told me, "I'm so sorry."

I turned to look at him, smiling slightly, but with wet eyes. "I'm not."

He nodded. He understood.

I knew what he meant, and yes, I was certainly grieved because the time for Grandma and me together in this life was over, but how could I possibly be sorry—she was in her right mind for the first time in years . . . and she'd just seen Jesus.

Drew and I were up doing the feeding routine around 5 a.m. I had been awake since Waverly had called, and the need for sleep was catching up to me. I propped myself up on the cushions of my couch as Drew snuggled with his head resting on my shoulder. My head slowly tilted back as sleep came. And with sleep came another dream.

I found myself sitting on a tall stool without a back support. In front of me was a large piece of lattice, and although everything where I sat was dark, what I could see through the lattice was vivid, bright, beautiful, intensely blue sky, vibrant green bushes on thick, spongy grass, and fully bloomed flowers in unimaginable brilliance. As I continued to look, I saw Grandma walking into this lovely garden. I could see her face clearly. All at once, approaching from my right, I saw Grandpa walking toward her, and for the first time since his death, I heard his voice. He was talking to her, and even though I could not understand a word he said, I could hear the voice—unmistakably his—and I knew exactly what he was saying to her:

"Hello, Sweet."

CHAPTER 24

RELEASE

M onday, December 13, 1999, dawned rainy and cold, a very fitting weather forecast for the day's events. I stood looking down at Grandma with her hands folded across her middle—glazed, frozen, colorless, dead hands. I remembered my conversation about "dead hands" with Vivian Holmes from almost three years earlier, and the recollection brought a fresh wave of grief. I shut my eyes, breathing deeply, inhaling the fragrance of live flowers spread across the top of the casket, and I sought to compose myself for the funeral that was upon me.

Grandma's visitation was identical to the one for Grandpa eleven months earlier. The mourners were almost exactly the same—except that my mother-in-law, Sarah, had stayed home to take care of Drew. Chris was once more gathering the pall bearers, and I again found myself standing beside my half-brother Tony, this time pondering the death of the last person who linked us. Neither Shirley nor Duane ever darkened the door of the funeral home—not in February for Grandpa, and not in December for Grandma.

We were very blessed to learn that Reverend Benjamin Tucker was available to officiate at Grandma's service. He had done such an amazing job when he spoke at Grandpa's funeral; he was the only one who came to mind after I learned of Grandma's death. I handed him the three-page eulogy that I had put together, and he started reviewing it during the last few minutes of the visitation.

As everyone was getting seated, I began to move toward the section reserved for the immediate family. I could tell the service was about to begin; but despite the shortage of time, I found myself walking back to Grandma's side. I stood alone, silently regarding the empty shell, which was all that remained on this earth of the wonderful woman I had known simply as "Grandma." I reached into my pocket and pulled out, of all things, an old refrigerator magnet. It had once been a white rectangle with a lacy border, but both had yellowed with age. In soft, blue letters it bore the inscription, "*Grandma—meaning 'Love.'*" I had given it to her an untold number of years before, and on one of my multiple trips back to their house during the first half of 1997, I had removed it from their fridge and kept it in a drawer in my desk. Before leaving the house for her funeral, I had reached in the drawer and slipped it into my pocket. I'm not even sure I had a plan to do anything with it, but somehow I wanted it with me. Now, as I stared down into that lonely box, I knew what I wanted to do. I read and reread the words until they were completely obscured by tears, then slowly I lowered it until it came to rest just above her hands. A silly refrigerator magnet—but it said in three words more than any tome could ever have communicated.

The service began with the music of *Precious Memories* and *What a Friend We Have in Jesus*; I remember feeling almost numb at times, then the reality of the moment would wash over me, and I would again experience the anguish of loss. I recall that as Benjamin spoke, he made another wonderfully clear presentation of the gospel, just like he had done at Grandpa's funeral. As he was concluding Grandma's service, my attention was captured by his final remarks.

"For many years, Leah and her Grandma wrote letters to each other when they couldn't be together. Leah has written one final letter for her Grandma—only a temporary 'goodbye'—and I'd like to share it with you. She writes,

Grandma,

I remember how I couldn't wait to come see you and how I always hated to say "goodbye." We'd hug each other tight and say over and over how much we loved each other. How I rejoice that you're with Jesus now, and how I thank you that you made sure I knew Him before you left. I love you so very much and will never forget you, my grandma.

Goodbye.

246

As Benjamin began to pray, the funeral director approached me quietly to say that a cool, pelting rain had started to fall, and the cemetery was likely going to be muddy. He asked if I wanted to conclude everything at the funeral home, or if I wanted to proceed with the scheduled graveside service. I momentarily considered the choices, but in my heart I knew what I had to do, even if no one else went with me.

"I have to see her to the very end," I said quietly.

I looked at Chris and he nodded.

"Please let people know they don't have to accompany us," I told the director, "but I *have* to go."

He smiled pleasantly and moved over to stand beside the now-closed casket where he announced there would be a graveside service, but because of the rain, the family would understand if anyone wasn't able to attend. He then instructed the pall bearers to come forward to place the casket in the hearse.

For the second time in less than a year, we made the slow, plodding journey to the cemetery, and just as I had done with Grandpa, I took one final walk with Grandma to her last stop under the canopy. As the raindrops came down gently, Benjamin again reminded us that the grave does not mark the end of life for the believer in Jesus; he looked at me directly, assuring me that since we both knew Jesus, I would see Grandma again. After he prayed, he came over and shook my hand warmly.

As I stood up and turned around, I was surprised by the number of people who had accompanied us to the cemetery despite the rain. Several family members and friends began to come around us under the canopy with hugs and condolences, but as the crowd thinned, and I walked out into the blowing mist, I looked up and saw Karen standing directly in front of me.

"I wanted to tell you I'm sorry," she said. "It was the weekend, and for some reason it didn't occur to me I could order flowers until this morning. By the time I called, it was too late. I didn't get to send any flowers for her."

Karen looked devastated, but I smiled back at her, remembering the dream I'd had right after Grandma had gone. "Don't worry about it," I said, putting my hand on her forearm. "I believe that where she is now, she's got more flowers than she's ever had in her life!"

Chris and I left the cemetery and sat down for a quick lunch, then we drove to Waverly to see if there were any Meade belongings I needed to retrieve. When I walked in and saw Grandma's empty bed, it was like a fresh shock—another deeply painful realization that she was, in fact, gone. All that remained was the plastic tubing from the oxygen they'd given her Friday night.

It was loosely coiled on Grandma's rocking chair, and just the sight of it made me draw back. I had no trouble imagining a physician standing beside Grandma's bed, pronouncing her death while a nurse turned off the flow of oxygen and removed the tubing, casually casting it aside in the chair where it had remained undisturbed. I looked at Chris, and I could see he was thinking the same thing. The plastic tubing paired with the empty bed brought my feelings of emotional perforation to a head; I felt like something huge had been torn away from me, and I stood there, trying in vain to calculate how to repair the damage.

I quickly determined the only thing I wanted to take with me was a large, framed picture that I had purchased for their room. It was a beautiful mountain landscape and quoted at the bottom was Psalm 119:18 (KJV): "*Open Thou mine eyes that I may behold wonderous things out of thy law*"; both Grandma and Grandpa had always loved the mountains, and Psalm 119 had been one of Grandma's very favorite passages.

There were very few personal items remaining in their room, and no pictures at all; I had removed those of Grandma's parents, as well as the photo of me in my wedding dress, because Grandpa would "pack" them up for the never-to-be-realized trip back to their Arkansas home.

I looked through the wardrobe at the various dresses Grandma had worn, some of which were hers and some of which were not. Even with her name written in the collar of every garment, Waverly never could keep the laundry straight. I wound up telling Audrey to just keep all the clothes as well as Grandma's rocking chair, thinking another resident in the facility might be able to use them. And so, with only one large picture in tow, Chris and I unceremoniously drove away from Waverly for the last time. I rode past all the familiar neighborhood landmarks without perceiving any of them because warm tears were spontaneously falling from my eyes, making a wet trail down to my chin.

"Well," I told Chris, "I cried when we had to bring them here, so I guess it's no more than right that I should cry when we leave for the last time." I sighed heavily, then smiled slightly as a new thought occurred to me. "But you know, they've been released from this place, and Grandpa just got his greatest wish: they both finally made it home."

With Grandma's passing, I knew that I had also been released from my legal role as her appointed agent with durable power of attorney. It was now time for me to serve my grandparents one last time as the executrix of Grandma's last will and testament. I called Bruce Hollis's office and informed Phyllis of Grandma's death, telling her that the only thing I knew for certain was the Arkansas property had to be sold. I asked her if she could explain to me all the legal proceedings that had to be completed before we could put the property on the market.

She informed me that Grandma's will would have to go through probate, a legal process that entails proving in court that a deceased person's will is valid, as well as identifying and appraising the value of all owned property, making full payment of any outstanding debts or taxes, and finally distributing the property as directed by the will. She said the process would take several months and could begin as soon as they received a certified copy of Grandma's death certificate.

I could see that my early struggle to straighten out the mess that Grandma's lack of cognition had caused was about to pay off; when Grandma died, there were no outstanding taxes or debts, so it would simply be a matter of having the will "approved" by the circuit court judge, putting the property on the market, then dividing the proceeds into thirds.

I told Phyllis I would send her the death certificate immediately, then I would contact my half-brothers to let them know what to expect.

On Sunday evening, I sat down on the couch and dialed Tony's number. I told him what Phyllis had said, and I let him know I would keep him apprised as the situation progressed. He said he would take care of contacting Duane and keep him informed, an offer of help that I gladly accepted.

The year 2000 passed quickly; before I even knew it, autumn had arrived, and the probate process was complete. We were finally able to list the property for sale with a realtor who had been recommended by my grandparents' lawyer. We had offered to let Jason purchase the property, but he had declined, citing financial reasons. We also spoke to our realtor about Mack Proctor who had once expressed interest in buying the Meade property. We had lost touch with the Proctor family after our second tenant was let out of her lease due to the dry well. We were grieved to learn that Mack had passed away several months earlier, and our realtor said he had no knowledge of where Betty Jo was presently living.

As the weather turned cooler and the leaves were beginning to fall from the trees, Chris and I made our last run over that familiar, rough-hewn gravel road to my grandparents' former home. As we drove up, I could see nothing major had changed since the last time I had been there more than three years earlier. The driveway wound around toward the house like always, and the two huge oak trees were stately and tall, standing just as they had done for an untold number of years.

Even though Grandma had been gone for nearly a year, and Grandpa almost two years, I felt their absence in Arkansas more keenly than I did anywhere else. Everywhere I looked, there were memories of my grandparents, but all my eyes could perceive was vacuous, empty space boldly announcing, "they're not here anymore." I did smile slightly when I saw how tightly packed the remaining iris leaves had grown in front of the cabin, remembering how Grandma had wanted to thin them out. I thought about how beautiful the blooms must have been during their summer peak. The seasons, much like life itself, had seen a variety of changes, and those multicolored blooms had crested and fallen as the changes had occurred. My only solace came as I thought about Grandma's heavenly garden where her flowers undoubtedly bloomed at the height of perfection, being perpetually in season.

"I'd like to take one last walk," I said to Chris, and I started for the metal gate behind the house.

I lifted the latch and walked into the abandoned pasture. There were still remnants of hay pressed into the mud, sticking out among the random mixture of grass and weeds—memories of a time long gone. We walked down to the tree line, then turned left to head west along the winding path that went down by Grandpa's pond and out into the large, open field where his cows used to pass so many of their lazy summer days. I stood and looked around, remembering the sight of Grandpa and his dog, standing with his face in the sun, pointing out all the things he was planning to do.

"He sure did love it here," I commented.

"He loved the outdoors," Chris answered, "and this was a perfect place for him to enjoy his retirement."

I took one long, last look around. "I think I'm ready to go," I said quietly. "I'm not sure what I'm waiting for. I guess I know I'm never coming back, so I want to take it all in one last time."

The property was sold before Thanksgiving, and we closed almost exactly one year to the day after Grandma's death. The inheritance had been divided three ways as directed by Grandma's will, and Bruce's office had dispatched the three portions without delay. With my grandparents peacefully at rest, their property sold, and the inheritance disbursed, my task as their "caregiver" had come to an end. I sat down to call Tony one more time, just to make sure they had received everything in good order. Once the business portion of our call was done, Tony and I had a wonderful, friendly, long-overdue conversation about our memories of Grandma and Grandpa . . . and their son.

"Do you remember being over there in the summer time," Tony asked with a chuckle, "when it was a thousand degrees inside the house, and you were trying to sleep with only the window open for air?"

My face broke into a spontaneous grin. "Oh, do I!" I answered. "You would be fanning yourself like crazy, but you couldn't go to sleep and keep the air moving."

"Yeah," he said, then he added, "I remember laying on that bed spread-eagled, feeling like I was going to melt, and they would be in that room across the hall, snoring happily like it was seventy degrees! I never understood how they did that."

"I guess they were just used to it," I said. "They were good country folks who grew up without air conditioning."

"They grew up very different from us, that's for sure," Tony said with a sigh, "and you and I grew up very different from each other too."

I considered his statement; he had clearly opened the door, so for one brief moment, I decided to let my guard down and go there.

"What was he like, Tony?"

"Who? You mean Daddy?"

"Yeah," I said carefully. "What was life with him like?"

Tony paused, but only briefly. "Unsettled."

I found that description was not entirely unexpected.

"Truth is, he was never there much," Tony continued. "He was on the road a lot. And he made pretty good money, but we never lived like he made good money. I mean, we never saw any of it."

"Well, I ask because I never knew him at all," I said flatly. "I think I can count on one hand the actual number of personal encounters I ever had with him."

"You know," Tony said in a pensive tone, "he was a good father—*when* he was there. He just never was there much."

"That's the way my mom described him: absent more than he was home."

"That's about the size of it," Tony responded. "But you know, sometimes I would go with him on his over-the-road trips, and it was great. In fact, that's the last memory I have of him—on the morning he left, he was asking me to go with him. I was asleep on the couch in the living room; it was real early, I don't even think the sun was up yet. He woke me up and told me he was getting ready to head out, and he wanted me to come with him. I rolled over and told him I didn't want to go. I remember turning to look at him as he was standing in the front door. He looked at me with a big smile on his face and said again, 'I sure wish you'd come with me.' I just pulled the blanket up and went back to sleep like it was nothing." He paused slightly. "But that was it. He never came back."

"I'm so sorry," I said slowly, "and you never heard another word from him at all?"

"Nope."

"I know that was hard to swallow," I waded in a little deeper. "I know the emotional pain I've dealt with, and I never even had any kind of relationship with him. I honestly can't imagine what you went through."

"Yeah," he responded gruffly, "it kinda stunk. I always wondered what would've happened if I had gone with him. Would he have come back?"

"Maybe," I answered quickly, "but he might have just disappeared at another time. Remember, he'd done it before."

"Yeah, you're probably right."

"I know this sounds like a self-centered thing to ask, but I am curious. Did he ever talk about me at all?"

"Never," Tony said without any hesitation. Then, with a slight chuckle, he added, "You and me, we both got a raw deal."

"From Ray, yes," I said, "but not with Grandma and Grandpa. Did you ever know two people who loved their grandchildren more than they did?"

"No, you've got me there," he answered in a lighter tone. "They were special."

"I remember the Christmas break you and I spent together up at their place. It was 1980. Remember running around in the cold with the sparklers on New Year's Eve?"

"Yeah," Tony said with a laugh, "and do you remember that their house wasn't finished yet, but Grandpa took us in there and lit the place up with kerosene lanterns?"

"I do remember that," I said smiling. "And I remember everything over there was always an adventure—from snapping beans to splitting wood, feeding cows and planting flowers!"

"Oh, man, he sure loved those cows, and she was crazy about her flowers," Tony said.

"And they loved each other so much," I said, "and now I thank God they have all of eternity to be together."

EPILOGUE

It was understood from the beginning where this story was ultimately headed. The inevitable end was for me to take that final walk with Grandma and Grandpa to their graves, but the events we encountered along the road we traveled made the journey a strange amalgamation of joy, fear, and heartache.

While Grandma and Grandpa went to be with Jesus, Chris and I remained here to walk the path of marriage and family, personal and professional growth, and, hopefully, to mature as believers in Christ. It is our greatest desire to grow daily in His grace and live in a way that will point people to Jesus, ultimately giving all glory to Him.

As painful as my grandparents' funerals were for me, Tony's presence at both events marked a turning point in our relationship, which allowed us to resume our separate lives as friends. What had started with the mutual tears and cathartic embrace beside Grandpa's casket eventually led to the very open, pleasant conversation we enjoyed after our inheritance had been disbursed. I have often wondered if Tony's initial anger toward me was the result of insinuations made by his mother when she first contacted him about my care of Grandma and Grandpa. I can only imagine the kinds of things Shirley might have said to him in the beginning, so I am very grateful for the opportunity we had to talk together so candidly, and, in a bizarre way, it seems to have filled an empty place left in my life by the person with whom Tony and I share paternal DNA.

As for Shirley and Duane, since our meeting at Waverly in June 1997, I have never heard from either of them again. Tony's wife, Sheila, told me in a phone conversation during the fall of 2000 that Duane had called Tony, demanding to know where his share of the money was, but Duane never contacted me directly. Tony told him to be patient because probating the will and finding a buyer for the property would not be a quick business. From his silence, I concluded Duane was satisfied when his portion of the inheritance was paid out to him.

As we wrapped up the final details of handling business for my grandparents, Chris and I found that I was able to do something I'd wanted to do since Drew was born: quit my job and stay home with my son as a full-time mom. Our family picture was complete when, in June 2002, we were blessed to welcome our daughter Faith into our home. Although Drew and Grandma's lives did briefly overlap, neither he nor Faith ever had the privilege of really knowing my grandma or grandpa personally, but they've certainly heard the funny stories and the wonderful colloquial expressions used by my down-to-earth, delightfully country, and altogether amazing grandparents. Through the years, there have been moments when I've spied either Drew or Faith looking at my grandparents' portrait, and they'll ask me questions about Edward and Clara Meade.

"Those are your great-grandparents," I say with a smile. "Come and let me tell you all about them."

CPSIA information can be obtained
at www.ICGtesting.com
Printed in the USA
BVHW071540141218
535506BV00003B/3/P